TROUBLEMAKERS

On the March for Civil Rights
From Selma to Black Power

Also by Gary G. Yerkey

Still Time to Live
A Biography of Jack Belden

Dying for the News
Honoring Tom Treanor and the Other Reporters
Killed Covering World War II

He's Coming to Start Riots
On the Road to Black Power
With 'The Reverend' Willie Ricks

South to Selma
'Outside Agitators' and the Civil Rights March
that Changed America

A Pilot's Pilot
Gen. Caleb V. Haynes and the
Rise of American Air Power 1917-1944

A Fever in My Blood
The American Life and Tragic Death of Darrell Berrigan

TROUBLEMAKERS

On the March for Civil Rights
From Selma to Black Power

Gary G. Yerkey

Contents

PREFACE

It was as close to Martin Luther King Jr.—and to history in the making—as I would ever get, that bright Sunday morning in Selma, Alabama, fifty-six years ago.

At the start of the Selma-to-Montgomery voting rights march—perhaps the most celebrated civil rights march in U.S. history—King told us that we would be writing "a new chapter in the history books of our nation."

"Walk together, children," he said. "Don't you get weary, and it will lead us to the Promised Land. And Alabama will be a new Alabama, and America will be a new America."

It was heady stuff, to be sure, his voice rising as he said that we would be serving a cause greater than ourselves, which to me at least was something of a new idea.

Now, more than a half-century later, I am still at a loss to explain what drew me to Selma in the spring of 1965. I would like to say it was the cause being pursued—nothing more, nothing less. Mentors like Rev. Jerry Thompson, then-chaplain at Ripon College, where I was a student, played a pivotal role. Others did as well. It could have been something in the 1960s air. Or maybe it was just the prospect of escaping the lingering Wisconsin winter for the warmer Deep South.

The historian Dan T. Carter, former president of the Southern Historical Association, has said that the Selma-to-Montgomery march was the "nova" of the civil rights movement—"a brilliant climax, which brought to a close the nonviolent struggle that reshaped the South."

John Lewis, the civil rights activist, told me before he died last year that the Selma-to-Montgomery march, which began on Sunday, March 21, 1965, and ended five days later at the Alabama state Capitol in Montgomery, was a turning point not only for the South but for the entire country.

"The Selma-to-Montgomery march had a profound impact on the psyche of all Americans," Lewis said, adding that white students from the North like us had played a crucial role in ensuring its success. "It was like Gandhi's march to the sea. It transformed American politics."

But Lewis also said that the march—along with the campaign of nonviolent civil disobedience in and around Selma that preceded it—was the "last act" of the civil rights movement as he knew it.

"Something was born in Selma during the course of that year," he said. "But something died there, too. The road of nonviolence had essentially run out. . . . After that, we [as a movement] just came apart."

Throughout his life, Lewis would continue to urge anyone who would listen to make "good trouble"—*nonviolent* trouble—in the struggle to attain racial and economic justice for all Americans.

"Get in good trouble, necessary trouble," he said, "and help redeem the soul of America."

After Selma, the radical black activist Stokely Carmichael, who would soon replace Lewis as chairman of the Student Nonviolent Coordinating Committee (SNCC), began to cast doubt on the efficacy of nonviolence as strategy for the movement.

A year after Selma, in the course of another civil rights demonstration—the so-called March Against Fear from Memphis, Tennessee, to Jackson, Mississippi—Carmichael marked a major turning point in the movement when, at a rally in Greenwood, Mississippi, he repeatedly employed the phrase "Black Power" to stir up the crowd.

At the start of the march, in June 1966, Carmichael had threatened to forcefully confront an overly aggressive law enforcement officer who had shoved him. Other march leaders, like King aide Andrew Young, advised him against it. "What was he going to do?" Young asked. "Beat up an armed state trooper single-handedly?"

But Carmichael would have none of it, saying he was done with nonviolence. "To hell with nonviolence," he said. "If someone shoves me, I'm going to shove him back."

Later, Carmichael said that King—with his strategy of nonviolent civil disobedience—was employing "moral force" as a means of achieving justice. But what Carmichael and his followers were doing, he said, was "building a force to take power." His fellow SNCC activist, James Forman, added that they were "shedding the mantle of nonviolence as a tactic."

This book tells the story—through the dual lens of the Selma-to-Montgomery voting rights march of 1965 and the March Against Fear the following year—of the strategic shift in the civil rights struggle of the 1960s from mobilizing mass demonstrations of nonviolent civil disobedience, championed by Martin Luther King Jr. and others, to engaging in a more confrontational approach designed to enable African Americans, as Carmichael put it, "to take power" and to create "powerfully organized communities capable of sustaining political struggle."

Chapter 1: The Telegram

Those of us from the North who ventured South in the mid-1960s to join the civil rights movement were called "outside agitators"—a catchy phase that was meant to dishonor us but that also accurately portrayed what we were up to. Yes, we were agitators. Agitators for justice. And, yes, we were not from Selma.

"You are here to cause trouble," Dallas County Sheriff Jim Clark told us when we arrived in Selma in the spring of 1965. And we agreed. "You don't live here," he said. "You are [outside] agitators, and that's the lowest form of humanity."

James Farmer, executive secretary of the Congress of Racial Equality (CORE), disagreed, saying that we were not outsiders "because we're Americans." But it was Martin Luther King Jr. who put it best. "Injustice anywhere is a threat to justice everywhere," he wrote in his "Letter from Birmingham Jail" in April 1963. "Anyone who lives inside the United States can never be considered an outsider anywhere within its bounds."

The 1960s were turbulent years—to be sure. President John F. Kennedy was assassinated. Four young black girls were killed in a Ku Klux Klan bombing at the Sixteenth Street Baptist Church in Birmingham, Alabama. Three civil rights workers in their early twenties—Michael Schwerner, Andrew Goodman, and James Chaney—were murdered by the KKK in Mississippi. A white Unitarian minister from Boston, James Reeb, was beaten to death by four Klansmen outside a restaurant in Selma less than two weeks before we arrived. And the homes and churches of African Americans throughout the South were being attacked and burned on a daily basis.

The South was thought to be so dangerous that a joke circulating among civil rights workers told of a would-be activist from the North kneeling and praying to God, "Please, Lord, send me a sign that you'll go with me to Mississippi." After a long pause, a deep voice answered, "OK. But I'll only go as far as Memphis."

But it was also a hopeful time. After the Selma-to-Montgomery march, President Johnson signed into law (on August 6, 1965) the landmark Voting Rights Act of 1965, which forbade once and for all the discriminatory voter registration policies and practices that had disenfranchised millions of African Americans. It is widely believed that the president and the Congress would not have acted so quickly—or perhaps not at all—had it not been for Selma.

For me, the trip to Selma effectively began on March 7, 1965, when, unknown to me or to others at Ripon College at the time, Andrew Young picked up the phone in Selma and called King in Atlanta to say that something horrible had just happened.

Young told King that John Lewis of the Student Nonviolent Coordinating Committee and Hosea Williams, an aide to King in the Southern Christian Leadership Conference (SCLC), had been leading about six hundred protesters across Selma's Edmund Pettus Bridge in what was supposed to have been the first leg of a voting rights march to Montgomery, 54 miles away, when they were beaten badly by Alabama state troopers and sheriff's deputies hurling tear gas canisters and wielding billy clubs.

Dozens had been injured in the melee, including Lewis, who had suffered a fractured skull. "I'm going to die here," Lewis later recalled, saying that his head was bleeding badly and exploding with pain.

Several women, including 53-year-old Amelia Boynton, also lay bloody on the pavement at the foot of the bridge. "As I stepped aside from a trooper's club," she remembered, "I felt a blow on my arm . . . Another blow by a trooper, as I was gasping for breath, knocked me to the ground and there I lay, unconscious. . . ."

King, of course, was horrified by the news. He briefly questioned the wisdom of continuing to pursue his strategy of nonviolent protests. But in the end he decided that the planned march from Selma to Montgomery would go ahead, despite fears that further violence would follow. It was too important to be abandoned now, he said.

That evening, as Lewis, Boynton and dozens of others were being treated for their injuries, images of what had transpired at the foot of the Edmund Pettus Bridge earlier that day were being broadcast on national television by ABC News, which had broken into its Sunday night telecast—the television premiere of Stanley Kramer's *Judgment at Nuremberg*—to air the shocking footage from Selma.

Forty-eight million viewers watched in horror as they saw their fellow Americans being attacked by Alabama law enforcement officials. At one point, the voice of Sheriff Jim

Clark could be heard yelling, "Get those goddamned niggers!"

Lewis said later: "Women and children being attacked by men on horseback. It was impossible to believe."

But the local newspaper—the *Selma Times-Journal*—played down the the news, saying that the protesters had not dispersed when ordered to do so and were "routed" by the authorities. Several marchers, according to the paper, were "knocked down or fell during the scramble with officers." A brief outbreak of "missile throwing by Negroes," it said, was countered by law officers who drove them back to Brown Chapel A.M.E. Church. This, it said, was followed by a quick "mop-up operation" that cleared the streets of the city, noting that thirty minutes after the "encounter" with the state troopers, "a Negro would not be seen walking the streets."

The "mop-up operation" had been merciless. More than a hundred state troopers and sheriff's deputies had chased the marchers over the high-arching steel bridge and for a mile or so back to downtown Selma, attacking with a vengeance those who were left behind. White posses beat people in front of Brown Chapel and the police hurled teargas to disperse the crowd.

Among those who saw the attacks and offered assistance to the wounded was Rev. John B. Morris, cofounder of the Episcopal Society for Cultural and Racial Unity (ESCRU). Earlier in the day, he had been on the same flight from Atlanta to Montgomery with Andrew Young, and they had shared a ride to Selma.

It was not the first time that Morris, who was white, had been involved in the civil rights struggle. The 35-year-old Episcopal priest had been active since the 1950s and had organized a "Prayer Pilgrimage" in 1961, in which 15 black and white clergy were arrested and jailed in Jackson, Mississippi, after attempting to eat at a segregated lunch counter. He had also participated in countless other civil rights protests, and under his leadership, ESCRU had organized groups of clergy from around the country to participate in the so-called March on Washington in August of 1963, where King had delivered his "I Have a Dream" speech.

Now, in March 1965, Morris was at the epicenter of the movement in Selma, where, after aiding injured protesters from the Edmund Pettus Bridge confrontation, he was among those who spoke with King in Atlanta by telephone to discuss how the movement should respond to the "Bloody Sunday" attack.

Morris and Young convinced King to issue a call to prominent religious leaders in the North who were known to be sympathetic to the civil rights cause to come to Selma and join a voting rights march to the Alabama state capitol in Montgomery. In this way, Morris said, the United States "representatively through its clergy, could bear some of the burden Selma residents had suffered [on Bloody Sunday]."

Within hours, several hundred telegrams signed by King were sent from SCLC headquarters on Auburn Avenue in Atlanta to every religious leader whose address the organization's program director, Randolph T. Blackwell, could find.

"In the vicious maltreatment of defenseless citizens of Selma," the telegram read, "where old women and young children were gassed and clubbed at random, we have witnessed an eruption of the disease of racism which seeks to destroy all America. No American is without responsibility. . . . I call therefore, on clergy of all faiths to join me in Selma for a ministers march to Montgomery. . . ."

For his part, Morris spent hours on the phone urging his fellow clergymen to come to Selma, and the National Council of Churches' Commission on Religion and Race in New York City issued an appeal of its own, asking pastors and lay leaders from around the country to respond to King's call to action.

Over the next few days, thousands of clergy and other activists from around the country began to descend on Selma to show their solidarity with the movement, including more than five hundred Episcopalians. Eventually, about 10 percent of all the Episcopal clergy in the country including then-Presiding Bishop John E. Hines, would join the entourage—over the strong objections of the bishop of the Alabama diocese, Charles C. J. Carpenter, who called the Selma protest "a foolish business and sad waste of time." He urged his fellow Episcopalians to go home. But they did not.

Students at colleges and universities throughout the North were also moved to act.

A 23-year-old student at Chicago Theological Seminary named Jesse L. Jackson, for instance, jumped onto a table in the school cafeteria on Monday, March 8, and shouted, "Pack your bags." Soon, he and about twenty other students and five professors—most of them white—were piling into several cars and heading south, caravan-style, to Selma some 750 miles away.

Also on the move were 11 students from the Episcopal Theological School in Cambridge, Massachusetts, including Jonathan Myrick Daniels, whose twenty-sixth birthday was just two weeks away. He and the other leaders of the student government—after learning, also on March 8, of King's call to come to Selma—had endorsed their participation in the initiative, and $600 was raised to finance their trip.

That evening, at Boston's Logan Field, the ETS students boarded a flight to Atlanta, arriving exhausted but in good spirits in the middle of the night. Anxious and fearful, they spent the rest of the night at SCLC headquarters. Those who were able to sleep at all found comfort in sofas or chairs or on the floor, some in King's office.

The next day, the group boarded a bus for the five-hour ride to Selma, buoyed by the sights and sounds of movement veterans singing protest songs. But soon their mood turned serious, when the driver of the bus refused to take them beyond Birmingham, saying that he feared an attack by white segregationists. A new driver was dispatched, and the bus continued on to Selma.

By then, King had also arrived in Selma, telling an audience of about a thousand at Brown Chapel late on March 8 that the suffering caused by the beatings and the bloodshed at the Edmund Pettus Bridge the previous day had not been in vain.

"We must let them know that if they beat one Negro they are going to beat a hundred," he said, "and if they beat a hundred, then they are going to have to beat a thousand."

Following his speech, which ended at around 10:30 p.m., King met with several of his aides, including Young and Hosea Williams, at the home of Selma's only black dentist, Dr. Sullivan Jackson, to discuss what to do next. Their decision—taken in the early morning hours of March 9—was to proceed with the march to Montgomery later that day, despite an earlier threat by U.S. District Judge Frank M. Johnson Jr. to prohibit the march pending a hearing on the matter.

Daniels and his fellow seminarians, meanwhile, were escorted from Brown Chapel A.M.E. Church to the George Washington Carver housing project across the street, where they were given a place to sleep.

The next morning, Daniels awoke to find buses, taxis, and rental cars disgorging newcomers to the African American neighborhood surrounding Brown Chapel. An estimated 800 people had arrived from 22 states, and the number of demonstrators who were gathering to participate in the expected march over the Edmund Pettus Bridge had grown to between 2,000 and 2,500—more than half of them white, including some 450 clergy who had heard King's nationwide appeal to join him in Selma.

Included among the clergy was James Reeb, the Unitarian minister from Boston, who like millions of his countrymen had seen the footage on television the evening of March 7—"Bloody Sunday"—showing black demonstrators being clubbed and teargassed by white law enforcement officials.

"I want to go to Selma," Reeb told his wife, Marie, the next day after receiving a call from the regional office of the Unitarian Universalist Association, whose head office had just received a telegram from King seeking volunteers for the trip to Selma. But his wife was opposed.

"I don't want you to go," she told her husband, pointing to the obvious danger involved. "There are others to go. You belong here." But Reeb insisted. "No," he replied. "I belong there. It's the kind of fight I believe in. I want to be part of it."

That evening, after saying good-bye to his four children, the 38-year-old minister left for the airport to cath an 11 p.m. charter flight to Atlanta—the same plane that Jonathan Daniels and his fellow seminarians were on. "I'll be back soon," Reeb told his wife, who dropped him off at the entrance to the airport terminal. "Take care," she responded. "We will be waiting for you."

Like Daniels, Reeb arrived in Selma around midmorning on Tuesday, March 9. He left his suitcase at Brown Chapel and joined the others—black and white clergymen, SNCC workers, SCLC staff members, and local black townspeople—who were gathering to march later in the day.

Shortly after noon, King emerged from Brown Chapel to address the crowd.

"I say to you this afternoon," he said, "that I would rather die on the highways of Alabama than make a butchery of my conscience." At 2:17 p.m., according to FBI observers, he stepped off, leading the protesters toward the bridge and ignoring an order to desist issued by a U.S. marshal on behalf of Judge Johnson.

But just over the bridge, on U.S. Highway 80 leading to Montgomery, the demonstrators were met by a contingent of state troopers—this time numbering about 500—who ordered them to halt. Sensing the possibility of another violent confrontation and not wanting to alienate the federal authorities, particularly since he had not yet received assurances from President Johnson that federal troops would be dispatched to protect the demonstrators, King instructed the marchers to return to Brown Chapel.

Inside the church, King defended his decision to abandon the march. But some SNCC organizers said they had lost faith in his leadership, telling the marchers they should have challenged the state troopers on the other side of the Edmund Pettus Bridge and not turned back.

"Why was there violence on Sunday and none on Tuesday?" SNCC Executive Director James Forman asked the crowd from the pulpit of Brown Chapel. "You know the answer. They don't beat white people. It's Negroes they beat and kill."

One African American resident of Selma responded by saying that, yes, Forman was right but that the reason "they didn't beat us today [was] because the world was here with us. That's what we want. Don't let these white people feel that we don't appreciate their coming."

That evening, while most of the Episcopal seminarians, except Daniels, were making their way to the airport to return to Boston, Reeb and several other Unitarians headed out for dinner. The place they chose, on the advice of Diane Nash at SCLC headquarters just around the corner from Brown Chapel, was Walker's Cafe, known by locals as Eddie's and frequented exclusively by blacks.

At around 7:30 p.m., after they had finished eating, Reeb's dinner companions—Orloff Miller, also from Boston, and Clark Olsen, from Berkeley, California—stepped outside while Reeb phoned his wife back in Boston to tell her he was staying in Selma another day.

Then, the three ministers started walking in the dark back to Brown Chapel—Olsen on the inside, Miller in the middle, and Reeb closest to the curb. They had only taken a step or two, however, when they noticed four white men across the street coming toward them. "Hey, niggers," one said. "Hey, you niggers." Reeb and Miller did not look back, but Olsen did just as one of the men was raising a large club or pipe and striking Reeb hard and squarely on the left temple, causing him to stagger and fall to the pavement.

It was over in less than a minute, and the attackers fled into the night after also having beaten Miller and Olsen. "Now you know what it is like to be a real nigger," one of them was heard to say.

Soon, Reeb's speech became incoherent, and he complained of a severe headache. Back at the SCLC office, an ambulance was called, which took him to Burwell Infirmary, where Dr. William Dinkins—one of only two black physicians in the Selma area—knew at once that there was something seriously wrong. Soon, Reeb fell into a coma and was transferred to University Hospital in Birmingham for the care he required.

The next day the hospital released a statement saying that Reeb's condition was "extremely critical and the prognosis is poor." It said he had sustained multiple skull fractures, and a large blood clot had formed on the left side of the brain.

Later that day hundreds of local people and clergy from around the country, including Jonathan Daniels, set off from Brown Chapel to march several blocks to the Dallas County Courthouse to protest the assault on Reeb. After only a couple of blocks, however, the marchers were stopped by Selma's public safety director, Wilson Baker, and Mayor Joe T. Smitherman, who told them they were banning all marches.

"We are going to stop any demonstrations," Baker told the protesters. "It is too risky under the present circumstances."

This, in turn, led to a standoff on Sylvan Street in front of Brown Chapel between the demonstrators and law enforcement officials that would last for several days—even as Baker was announcing that three of the four men charged in the assault on Reeb had been arrested.

On Thursday, March 11, at around 7:30 p.m., with the three men and a fourth now under arrest but already released from jail, Baker showed up at a vigil being held on Sylvan Street to break the news that Reeb had died. He pledged to rearrest the men on murder charges, which he did—only to see them released again later in the week.

Newspapers across the country took note of Reeb's death in their Friday editions, as well as of the growing outrage among the nation's clergy at the events in Selma.

Mass demonstrations in support of the Selma protestors were held in cities across the country, including Washington, D.C., where a group of national religious leaders organized protests in front of the White House in an effort to persuade President Johnson to send troops to Selma to protect the marchers.

On Friday morning, according to the Right Reverend Paul Moore Jr., the Episcopal suffragan bishop of Washington, D.C., President Johnson acceded to "pressure and the importunities of some of his staff" and agreed to meet with him and about a dozen other leaders of the protests.

"We tried to convey the frustration of the civil rights people and of black America at the apparent lack of sympathy on the part of the White House," Moore wrote, "and to build a case for federal troops to protect the Selma march."

Moore said that the president had told them that, when the pressure was on him, "I feel like a mule in a hailstorm. I put my head down, hunch up, and let it rain." He said he was deeply sympathetic to the plight of the "Negras."

The next day, after meeting Alabama Gov. George C. Wallace—and as more than a thousand civil rights protesters demonstrated outside the White House—Johnson told reporters that the events of "Bloody Sunday" in Selma "cannot and will not be repeated." He said that the protests in Selma were against a "deep and very unjust flaw in American democracy itself."

"Ninety-five years ago our Constitution was amended to require that no American can be denied the right to vote because of race or color," Johnson said. "Almost a century later, many Americans are kept from voting simply because they are Negroes."

He said that, therefore, he would be sending legislation to Congress that became known as the Voting Rights Act of 1965. But he did not commit to calling up the National Guard or to sending troops to Alabama, saying only that he was ready to do so if he concluded they were necessary.

"What happened in Selma was an American tragedy," he said. "The blows that were received, the blood that was shed, the life of the good man [Reeb] that was lost, must strengthen the determination of each of us to bring full and equal and exact justice to all of our people."

The standoff between demonstrators and the police on Sylvan Street outside of Brown Chapel in Selma, meanwhile, continued. On Sunday, March 14, the developments in Selma received widespread coverage in newspapers nationwide, and vigils and marches supporting the protesters were held in major cities including New York, Philadelphia, Boston, Cincinnati, Louisville, Toledo, Milwaukee, Los Angeles, and St. Louis, as well as some smaller cities and towns.

A front-page letter signed by Mayor Smitherman and Dallas County Sheriff Jim Clark also appeared in the *Selma Times-Journal* on Sunday asking the people of Selma— "both white and Negro"—to give them their support and prayers as they continued to deal with what they said had become a serious situation.

"For reasons known only to themselves," the two men wrote, "outside racial agitators have chosen to make Selma what they call a 'focal point' in their national drive to raise money, gain political power and to pressure the president of the United States and the Congress of the United States into enacting new and stronger civil rights laws."

Mass demonstrations, meanwhile, continued outside the White House on Monday, while inside the executive mansion a team of speechwriters that had worked through the night revised and tweaked a draft of an address focusing on civil rights that President Johnson was scheduled to deliver at a joint session of Congress that night.

In Selma, plans were being made for a memorial service for James Reeb that afternoon. Dignitaries gathered to pay tribute to him, including presiding Bishop Hines of the Episcopal Church; Walter Reuther, president of the United Auto Workers; and Greek Orthodox Archbishop Iakovos.

The service—presided over by Martin Luther King Jr., who had arrived in Selma from a weekend of speeches in Chicago—was held at Brown Chapel, which was filled with many prominent clergy from around the nation.

King told the audience that Reeb's crime was that he "dared to live his faith." He also spoke dismissively of indifferent religious leaders who "kept silent behind the safety of stained glass windows," and he criticized the federal government for its "timidity" in dealing with the crisis in Selma.

After the service, which Coretta Scott King called "perhaps the greatest and most inspiring ecumenical service ever held," some 3,500 people, including King, marched to the courthouse for a brief ceremony honoring Reeb and other civil rights martyrs.

That evening, President Johnson went before Congress to say in a nationally televised address that what was happening in Selma was part of a larger movement "which reaches into every section and state of America. It is the effort of American Negroes to secure for themselves the full blessings of American life."

"Their cause must be our cause, too," Johnson said. "Because it is not just Negroes, but really all of us, who must overcome the crippling legacy of bigotry and injustice. And we shall overcome!"

Watching the speech on television at the home of local Selma black dentist, Dr. Sullivan Jackson, were several leaders of the civil rights movement, including King and John Lewis, who was still recovering from the beating he had received at the hands of Alabama state troopers on "Bloody Sunday" a week earlier.

"Along with seventy million other Americans who watched the broadcast that evening," Lewis later recalled, "we listened to Lyndon Johnson make what many others and I consider not only his finest speech of his career, but probably the strongest speech any American president has ever made on the subject of civil rights. . . . His were the words of a statesman and more; they were the words of a poet."

Lewis said that King must have agreed, noting that he had wiped away a tear when Johnson said, "We shall over-come!"

The next day, U.S. District Judge Frank M. Johnson Jr. ruled that the Selma-to-Montgomery march could proceed, arguing on the basis of an elaborate plan for the fifty-four-mile march written by James M. Nabrit III and his colleagues at the NAACP Legal Defense and Educational Fund that the right to petition the government for the redress of griev-ances extends to "large groups," and that these rights may be exercised by marching, "even along public highways."

Johnson's ruling thus cleared the way for the march to begin again—this time under the protection of federal troops on March 21.

Chapter 2: 'Good-Natured Louts'

As a young college student listening to President Johnson's speech, I was reminded how shocked and angered I had been when I first learned of what was happening in and around Selma earlier in the month.

I remember thinking it would be irresponsible of us, even a thousand miles away at Ripon College, a small, liberal arts college in central Wisconsin, not to do something. But what?

Traveling to Selma seemed to be unrealistic. We had no money. We had classes to attend and papers to write. And the message being sent by local Alabama law enforcement officials to northerners like us was not encouraging. "You'll march over my dead body," Dallas County Sheriff Jim Clark said one day. I remember taking him seriously and thinking that I was too young to die.

I had decided to attend Ripon College because it was relatively close to home, which was Crystal Lake, Illinois, about 120 miles to the south, yet far enough away to discourage inquiring parents from visiting campus too frequently.

The city of Ripon and the college campus were also a lot like Crystal Lake: white, mainly Christian, and without any obvious complications.

My best friends in high school were Mike, Lee, Kevin, and Dick. Lee told us one day he wanted to be a millionaire by the time he was thirty. We thought that was a great idea. With Lee in charge, we were on our way—headed for success and doing all the right things to get there. We didn't study much, we played sports and drank beer and smoked cigarettes when we could get away with it, and we went to church on Sunday. While Rosa Parks was fighting for a seat on the bus, we were preparing to run the company that *owned* that bus.

At Ripon, my friends were Jack, David, Bob and a disheveled and brainy guy named Dick Grimsrud, who never said he wanted to be a millionaire—or at least that I can remember. He thought the world had problems, beginning with Selma, and he wanted to fix them. I also thought that was a great idea.

Over time, I would also cross paths with—and admire for a lifetime—the college chaplain, Herman Jerome "Jerry" Thompson, who had clearly missed the millionaire train. Like Dick, he was interested in other things.

Born in Baldwin, Wisconsin, in 1923, Thompson graduated valedictorian of his Cameron (Wisconsin) High School class in 1941. He attended St. Olaf College in Northfield, Minnesota, before transferring to the University of Wisconsin where he excelled at baseball and football and graduated summa cum laude. He went on to coach a string of successful football and track teams at high schools and colleges across the Midwest.

But in his late thirties—with a wife and four children—he decided to pursue a divinity degree, which he obtained in 1961 from Luther Theological Seminary in St. Paul, Minnesota. The next year, as an ordained Lutheran minister, he established the department of religion at Ripon College, where he served as professor of religion until he retired in 1985. He was also commissioner of the Midwest Collegiate Athletic Conference and chairman of the Fond du Lac County (Wisconsin) Democratic Party. And in his later years, as a tennis fanatic, he was ranked first in Wisconsin, second in the Midwest, and nineteenth in the nation among 65-year-olds and above.

The president of the college, Fred O. Pinkham, had set as a priority pushing through a much-needed face-lift of the campus. During his time in office (1955–1965), he oversaw the construction of new dormitories, a state-of-the-art science building and several other facilities, which led to a near-doubling in student enrollment, to 822, and an increase in the school's operating budget from $814,000 to $2.2 million.

"Bricks and mortars, endowments and facilities do not alone give meaning to Ripon," he said, "but they are the things that make Ripon possible."

But the student body, for its part, remained largely unchanged—concerned about the things that had preoccupied students since the school's founding 100-plus years earlier.

George F. Kennan, the American diplomat, political scientist, and historian, whose father attended the school, visited the campus in February 1965 (a month before we left for Selma), and he later called our student faces "open, pleasant ones, but with curiously little written on them at all."

Kennan was best known as the author of the "Long Telegram" and the subsequent article "The Sources of Soviet Conduct," which set out the strategic vision that would define U.S. policy toward the Soviet Union until its collapse in 1991.

Now, in early 1965 and a week shy of his sixty-first birthday, he was met at the train station in Columbus, Wisconsin, by members of the Ripon College History Department. From there, he was driven 40 or 50 miles to Ripon "over wide straight roads, past frozen, snow-covered fields and prosperous dairy farms with beautiful red barns and less beautiful houses done in the dirty yellow brick of the region. . . . My companions were solemn, correct, and amiable, but a bit intimidated, I suspected, and guarded."

His impressions of the students at Ripon were mixed. The "girls," he said, were more mature than the "men" and superior to them, too, "socially and in style: more cosmopolitan, less provincial, more part of the age, in general more like modern women in Vienna or Milan or wherever else you like than the men of similar age in those places."

He said that Ripon's female students took a larger view than the men did of the "competitive sphere in which they considered their lives to evolve—the reflection of an awareness, perhaps, of the relative uniformity in women's problems everywhere."

The Ripon men, however, were "good-natured louts, immersed in their world of records and athletics and fraternities and summer jobs, mildly curious about the great wide world beyond, but less closely keyed to it than the women." It is the woman who is "truly international," he observed.

Kennan said that he learned after visiting the school that his appearance had been extremely controversial. His invitation, he said, had come from the History Department, which was chaired by John F. Glaser, and not from the college, which meant that President Pinkham was nowhere to be seen during Kennan's visit to the campus.

"I [was] too liberal, if not worse," Kennan wrote, noting the conservative "political atmosphere" of that part of Wisconsin, which he called Republican "Senator [Joseph] McCarthy's state."

By all accounts, Kennan, who was born in Milwaukee, was a Midwesterner at heart (even though he would leave the region in 1921, at seventeen years old, to attend Princeton University and never to return to live). His enduring fondness for and understanding of the Midwest was clear in his writings throughout his life.

Recalling his visit to Ripon in 1965, for instance, he captured the uniqueness of the region in his 1989 memoir *Sketches from a Life*, in which described Wisconsin's "strange, still flatness" as being "like no other flatness, subdued and yet exciting, as though filled with deep unspoken implications. . . . I knew I was close to home."

Kennan said that in the Midwest a bank of clouds appearing on the horizon could create the illusion of a range of low mountains. "What, one wondered, would life and people have been like had there been such a mountain range there?" he asked. "Life, presumably, would have been more varied, more violent, more interesting; but the massive inert power of the midwestern tradition, with all its virtues and all its weaknesses, sufficient to constitute the spiritual heart of a nation, would not have survived."

He recalled that the face of Ripon was overwhelmingly that of a small New England town, with its wide streets lined with tall trees, spacious lawns, and quiet, well-worn wooden houses. But the houses, he said, were uninspiring, noting that "like so many other Victorians," the builders had prided themselves on the quality of their workmanship and material rather than on creating a thing of beauty.

The old sandstone buildings that dominated the Ripon College campus, moreover, which were "already in existence when my father came to the place ninety-five years ago," were "severe and without architectural ambition, presiding stubbornly, self-assertively, without apology or compromise, over their changed and changing environment."

On the evening of February 11, 1965, as a blizzard blew across the farm fields of central Wisconsin, Kennan delivered a lecture to several hundred students and faculty in the school's "bare-boned gymnasium, with its shiny floors, its overhanging basketball boards, and its faint smell of sweaty tennis shoes." Not surprisingly, given his years as a diplomat, he spoke about international affairs and, in particular, the tendency of the United States to make "moral crusades" out of its foreign involvements.

"It is simply not in character for such a country as ours," he told the audience of several hundred, "to try . . . to produce great changes in the lives of other people, to bring economic development and prosperity to everyone, and to assure to everyone complete peace and security under law."

As Kennan spoke, the voting rights campaign that had been launched in Selma by Martin Luther King Jr. at the beginning of the year was now in full swing. On February 1, King was arrested and imprisoned after leading a mass-protest march down Sylvan Street, which focused national attention on his campaign. A front-page article in *The New York Times* the next day appeared under the headline, "Dr. King and 770 Others Seized in Alabama Protest."

As the month wore on, the protests continued—and accelerated—in Selma, the county seat of Dallas County, and in other cities including nearby Marion, the county seat of Perry County.

A seven-page "special report" prepared by the SNCC office in Atlanta, dated February 4, said that plans were also being made to expand SNCC's operations to other "Black Belt" counties in Alabama. It said that African Americans made up 57 percent of the Dallas County population, yet only 0.9 percent were registered to vote. Adjoining Wilcox County was 78 percent African American, but none of them had been registered. Similar statistics could be found throughout the state.

On February 18, the King-led protests in Selma and surrounding towns came to a head when Alabama state troopers joined local police in Marion to break up an evening march. In the ensuing melee, a 26-year-old pulpwood worker and deacon at St. James Baptist Church named Jimmie Lee Jackson was shot twice in the stomach by one state trooper. He died eight days later in a Selma hospital, which prompted a call by one of King's top advisers and strategists, James Bevel, to organize a march from Selma to Montgomery to petition Governor Wallace to ensure the right of African Americans to vote.

"Be prepared to walk to Montgomery!" Bevel told a mass meeting at Brown Chapel in Selma on February 26. "Be prepared to sleep on the highway!" A few days later, King approved the idea, saying that the march would begin on Sunday, March 7—a day that would be later known as "Bloody Sunday."

It was against this backdrop that some of us at Ripon College were beginning to look south to what was happening in Selma a thousand miles away. Some students thought it had nothing to do with them; others thought it did.

Dick Grimsrud and I, along with several other students, discussed the issue and decided to approach Chaplain Thompson, who we knew would be sympathetic to initiating some sort of Ripon-sponsored show of support for the civil rights protests in Alabama.

Thompson had already been active in the civil rights movement by fostering, for example, cooperation between Ripon students and their African American counterparts in the South. In the spring of 1964, he coordinated an exchange program with Tougaloo College, an historically black school of about nine hundred students outside Jackson, Mississippi. Its president was the white civil rights activist and former chaplain at Beloit College in Beloit, Wisconsin, Adam D. Beittel.

The student body at Tougaloo, in fact, had been protesting racial discrimination in Jackson beginning in the 1950s, well before the Thompson-sponsored exchange program took place. Many students had been arrested and jailed for leading a boycott of restaurants that did not serve African Americans and for attempting to attend segregated churches and concerts in and around Jackson, and Beittel frequently raised the money to bail them out of jail.

But by September 1964, the powers-that-be in Mississippi had had enough. The Mississippi State Sovereignty Commission—established by the state legislature in 1956 to defend the state against "encroachment" from the federal government, particularly over civil rights—persuaded Tougaloo's Board of Trustees to dismiss Beittel as college president.

While president, he had hosted a series of exchange programs with several northern schools beginning in 1960, including Ripon College.

For us, the exchange programs were eye-openers, and they were as well for the students from Tougaloo who had never been out of the South. We were shocked to see first-hand the racial segregation that we had only read about in newspapers being played out in the daily lives of our southern contemporaries. "Water out of a fountain labeled 'colored,'" recalled fellow Ripon student Jim Hess, "tasted just as good as 'white' water to me."

Police brutality—long a mainstay of life for African Americans in the South—was also part of the experience. Walking on a street in downtown Jackson one day, Dick Grimsrud and two other students—Carla Mettling from Lawrence University in Appleton, Wisconsin, and an African American student from Tougaloo named Kenneth Hayes— were arrested for jaywalking and taken to the police station, where the situation quickly escalated. Mettling and Hayes were hustled upstairs, but Grimsrud was kept behind with the arresting officer. Later, on an elevator, the officer asked Grimsrud a question and slapped him for not saying "sir" when he responded. Then, he kicked and beat the 20-year-old Grimsrud. Mettling was taken aside by another officer and lectured on "the evils of the Negro." Only later would they be told that the charges against them had been dropped.

William Alexander, a psychology professor at Ripon who accompanied the students to Tougaloo, said on returning to Wisconsin that the exchange-program experience had been valuable because it meant that the Ripon student body could no longer pretend to be "ignorant" of what was happening in the South.

"A clear majority of students at [Ripon College] have become more fully cognizant of the nature of the problem confronting all Americans," he said, "both those in the North and those in the South."

To Alexander, that may have been the case. But few students at Ripon were moved enough by the tales of what had happened in Tougaloo to think about what they could to do to help ameliorate the situation in Alabama.

Only about a dozen or so of us, however, were inspired enough to approach Chaplain Thompson for advice. Thompson's initial response was circumspect. He said that he was in no position to finance a trip to Selma, although he would certainly contribute some of his own money. We suggested paying for the trip with money allocated by the Student Senate, whose president—truth be told—happened to be a good friend of ours, David Schwarz, a fellow philosophy major.

On Monday, March 15, while violent clashes between demonstrators and the police were taking place near the Alabama state capitol in Montgomery, Schwarz called a special meeting of the Student Senate.

At nearby Beloit College, the student body, which had already been involved in the civil rights movement through SNCC and the local Civil Rights Interest Group (CRIG), had had little trouble raising nearly $600 to send eight students to Selma. But we knew that seeking financial support from the much more conservative student body at Ripon would be fruitless. Plus, time was not on our side. So we took what we thought would be a more predictable and expeditious route: appealing to the Student Senate for funds. We thought we would need about $400.

At the meeting, which began in the Harwood Memorial Union building at 7:00 p.m. when most students were either studying or heading to the local pub for a beer, Chaplain Thompson rose to our defense, saying that the voting rights legislation that President Johnson was about to send to Congress would not pass unless the pressure that was being generated in Selma was maintained. He said it was important for Ripon College to be represented in Selma.

Also at the meeting that evening was Patrick Hunt, assistant dean of men, who said he had received a call the previous evening from the coordinator of the National Student Association (NSA)—a coalition of college and university student governments—at the University of Wisconsin in Madison, who had asked him if there were any students at Ripon who might be interested in joining a delegation from Wisconsin to travel to Selma.

Some members of the Student Senate argued that the money could be better spent elsewhere, such as writing a check to the NAACP or inviting a speaker to campus to lecture on the issue. This caused James R. Bowditch, of the English Department, to blow up, saying that throwing money at the problem would be the worst thing that we could do. The physical presence of people who care could make all the difference, he said.

In the end, after less than an hour of discussion, the Senate agreed by 13–9 to allocate $400 for the trip to Selma, and in the absence of President Pinkham, the dean of the college, Robert Ashley, assented on behalf of the school administration. Chaplain Thompson was made executor of the funds. He asked those of us who were interested in going to Selma to meet him in his office by 11 p.m. to make the necessary arrangements. We agreed that we would leave for Madison (in my blue Ford Falcon), and eventually Selma, the next day.

Chapter 3:
Protesting the Protests

The news that the Student Senate had allocated $400 to finance a college-sponsored trip to Selma spread like wildfire throughout Ripon College. Students who had earlier been deaf to what was happening down South now found a reason to be outraged.

Leading the protest was Richard Singer, a junior who used his show at the college radio station, WRPN, to urge students to demonstrate their opposition to this alleged misuse of student funds.

At 10 a.m. the next day, about 400 angry students—roughly half of the student body—heeded Singer's call and began to converge on Smith Hall, where a meeting involving President Pinkham, Dean Ashley, Chaplain Thompson, and Senate President David Schwarz was being held to discuss the Senate's decision. Never before had the school seen such a display of public indignation over an issue.

At the same time, about a thousand miles away, in Selma, local law enforcement officials were cracking down on several voting rights protests. And in Montgomery—in an incident that would make national headlines—police officers on horseback charged a small group of demonstrators that had broken off from a larger contingent of some 600 mainly young white protestors from the North and began beating them with canes and nightsticks.

Roy Reed, a reporter for *The New York Times*, wrote in the March 17 edition of the paper that one officer in a ten-gallon hat had jumped off his horse and "while the horses partly hid him from view, began clubbing the demonstrators. Several still refused to move, and the man's nightstick began falling with great force on their heads." One young man was struck so hard that the sound of the nightstick "carried up and down the block."

Photos of the attack and its victims appeared on the front pages of *The New York Times* and the *Washington Post*.

As the protests in Alabama were unfolding, the student protesters at Ripon College were claiming that the Student Senate had acted inappropriately—i.e., without the full consent of the student body. But more importantly, they were saying that what was happening in Alabama was none of the school's business. As Larry Wilkes, a senior from Connecticut put it, those in the North who cared about civil rights should let southerners handle the situation as they saw fit. Another senior, Tom Fischer, said it was "ridiculous" to go to Selma. And members of the Sigma Chi fraternity voted 22–7 to protest the allocation of the funds for our trip. As Fred Rueger, the president of the Ripon chapter of the fraternity, observed, individuals going to Selma on their own dime was fine; representing the school with school funds was not.

A few students publicly supported what we were planning to do. One was James E. Reed, a sophomore from

Seattle, who wrote in the student newspaper, *Ripon College Days*, that those arguing that "we Northerners don't have the right to go meddling in other people's affairs" at first sounds reasonable. But that African Americans in the South do not enjoy the same rights as others, he said, is not a local problem but a national issue "because we are one nation and one people."

"The denial of the right to vote to Mississippi Negroes can be a legitimate concern of someone living in Chicago," Reed wrote. "And if this individual is sensitive to the demands of the situation, he has every right—legal and otherwise—to 'meddle in Mississippi affairs.' Perhaps the basic reason that the problem has been so bad for so long is that sensitive people in the North have felt it was none of their business. . . . What is going on on the South today is our problem as well as the South's."

For its part, the school administration concluded that the Student Senate had acted within its rights in allocating the funds for our trip. But one member of the administration—David L. Harris, dean of men—went further, wholeheartedly endorsing our plan to participate in the ongoing demonstrations down South, including voting rights march from Selma to Montgomery.

College Dean Robert Ashley said that he had "mixed feelings" about the trip. "I question whether or not any good will be accomplished by the people who go." But he said he respected our "convictions."

Jean Van Hengel, the dean of women, said that the action taken by the Student Senate was legal and proper and "perfectly within their jurisdiction." She said she was upset by the "hasty and emotional demonstration" that was held on campus by students opposing the Senate decision. "I'm not sure it accomplished anything," she said.

Van Hengel also said, however, that while the civil rights protests in the South had played an important role in arousing people's interest and concern and "forcing attention upon the seriousness of the problem, I am not sure whether continuation of the Selma demonstrations is needed."

Dean Harris was less circumspect, saying he applauded the Senate's decision and thought that the student demonstration against it was misguided. "Wouldn't you know that once they got off their apathy," he said of the student protesters, "it would be for the wrong reasons?" He said he was ashamed at the "unseemliness" of the protest.

Students traveling to Alabama were members of the Ripon family, Harris said. "We should have been there to shake their hands and see them off," he said. "This way, they left with memories of a screaming crowd, with few people knowing precisely what they were concerned about."

Harris congratulated the Senate for its vote to fund the trip, calling it "courageous." He said that the Senate had finally concerned itself with "something of vital significance to all Americans."

"There is also a great educational opportunity here," he said. "We can go down to Selma and learn something. Do the students really want another jazz concert [funded by the Senate], or do they want a complete, well-rounded education?"

Doug Lyke, publisher of the local newspaper, the *Ripon Commonwealth Press*, also expressed his support for what we were doing. Bucking the prevailing mood among the townspeople at the time, he wrote that "we admire those Ripon College people who felt strong and sincere enough about Civil Rights to want to participate in the Selma demonstrations."

"Let not the rest of us judge their actions unless we really are qualified," Lyke wrote.

Meanwhile, Chaplain Thompson had his hands full attempting to calm the crowd that confronted him when he emerged from his hour-long meeting with President Pinkham on Tuesday, March 16. He explained that the trip to Selma was necessary to show the school's support for civil rights. Then, in a backhanded compliment, he praised the protesters for showing interest in something other than "beer and sex."

The crowd, however, showed no signs of dispersing, so we loaded up the two cars we were taking to Madison, where we would be board one of several buses headed for Selma. After briefly threatening to block our departure, the crowd withdrew and we were on our way: six students—Dick Grimsrud, Noel Carota, Alexandra Corson (now Dujardin), Nancy Cox (now Carter), Ruth Lake and I—and four college representatives—Chaplain Thompson; James R. Bowditch, of the English Department; and Patrick Hunt, assistant dean of men, and his wife.

Carter recalls being appalled at the time by accounts of violence in the South against people for riding on a bus, attempting to integrating a school or eating at a department store lunch counter. So when Chaplain Thompson announced that the University of Wisconsin was saving 10 seats for Ripon College on a bus to Selma, she signed up immediately, assuming that there would be a long list of students who wanted to go. "Alas, there wasn't."

She said that that, before we left the school, a "swarm" of protesters surrounded us, "circling menacingly, some yelling. . . ."

"Somehow, the threats provoked a new emotion in me," Carter said. "I just didn't care what they thought. This is not to be confused with courage; I just realized their opinion didn't matter to me. If I didn't go I would be a quitter.

Unacceptable. In my family you do the right thing. Period. It came to me that my own opinion of myself mattered. It was a new thought."

In Madison, we boarded a bus that ostensibly was headed for Selma. But just south of Chicago, we were informed that the situation in Alabama had become too dangerous for us to proceed, citing the beating of white college students in Montgomery the day before, as well as the ongoing violence and tension in Selma, where a memorial service had just been held for James Reeb, the white Unitarian minister from Boston who had been clubbed to death by a group of white segregationists.

Disappointed, we were told by the organizers of the trip (mainly from SNCC) that our new destination would be Washington, D.C. There, the organizers said, we would join protesters outside the White House who were demanding that President Johnson send federal troops to Alabama to protect the civil rights activists there from the wrath of the state and local law enforcement establishment.

Carter recalls that, before we were told we were heading for Washington, D.C., we were also informed that Dallas County Sheriff Jim Clark had attack dogs ready to stop the marchers in Selma, and that "if any of us wished to turn back now, a ride would be available with no hard feelings. Nobody stirred."

The next day, we arrived in the nation's capital in the middle of a snowstorm—having left Wisconsin supposedly for the warmer South. And the next day, we were ushered to a sidewalk in front of the White House to join twenty to thirty other students wrapped in sleeping bags sitting in the slush, surrounded by dozens of policemen. We were dirty and tired. But most of all, we were angry. We wanted to be in Selma where the real action was.

Chapter 4: Running Out of Money

Leading the protests in front of the White House was Paul Moore Jr., the suffragan Episcopal bishop of Washington, D.C.

"The thrill of seeing so many citizens, black and white, exerting their power directly to the President was intoxicating," Moore wrote later.

Intoxicating, too, Moore said, was the meeting that he and about a dozen other protest leaders secured with the president.

"We took our seats around the Cabinet table," he wrote, "and in a few minutes the President entered. . . . He greeted us courteously. . . . We tried to convey the frustration of the civil rights people and of black America at the apparent lack of sympathy on the part of the White House and to build the case for federal troops to protect the Selma march."

A couple of days later, on March 20, Johnson came through, notifying Gov. Wallace that he was mobilizing the Alabama National Guard to protect the planned march from Selma to Montgomery, due to begin the next day.

But we had a problem. We were running out of money. So we did what seemed natural at the time: we called on our representatives on Capitol Hill—Sen. William Proxmire (D-Wisconsin), who had been elected in a special election in August 1957 following the death of Sen. Joseph McCarthy, and Rep. John A. Race (D-Wisconsin), who was elected in 1964 on the coattails of Johnson's presidential victory.

After meeting us, Race, whose district included Ripon, sent a letter to President Pinkham at Ripon College saying that he admired the students he had met and was confident that Pinkham did as well.

But it was Proxmire who really cleared the way for us to continue on to Selma by asking his chief of staff, Paul K. Barkla, to accompany us as we solicited contributions from sympathetic members of Congress.

An Episcopalian, Proxmire also arranged for us to meet Bishop Moore in his office at the National Cathedral.

I recall walking into Moore's office and seeing him for the first time. How could I forget? He was larger than life in every way (6' 4" tall) and charismatic. He greeted us with a bear hug (unusual for the day) and told us that he would "loan" us $50 each for the trip to Selma from his "discretionary fund," which we assumed (correctly, as it turned out) had been set aside for liberal causes.

Moore had grown up a son of privilege—a great-nephew of the Republican senator and political kingmaker from Ohio, Mark Hanna, and a grandson of the founder of Bankers Trust. He had graduated from St. Paul's School and Yale University, as did his father before him. But after earning the Navy Cross, a Silver Star, and a Purple Heart in World War II, he devoted the rest of his life to advocating on behalf of the poor and the marginalized members of society, ministering for years in the slums before being named suffragan bishop of Washington, D.C., in 1964. He later became bishop of New York (1972–1989) and in 1976, he voiced his support for the ordination of female priests. He was also a vocal and highly effective opponent of the war in Vietnam. He passed away in 2003 at the age of eighty-four.

After meeting Moore, and with $200 in "loans" from the Episcopal Church and another $25 from the Reverend Harris T. Hall of St. Peter's Episcopal Church in Ripon, four of us—Chaplain Thompson, Dick Grimsrud, Noel Carota and I—rented a car and took off for Atlanta.

I'm not sure who made the decision, but apparently on the assumption that the trip to Selma would be too dangerous for the "girls" to undertake, the three female students who had begun the trip with us were ordered to return to Ripon.

Alexandra Dujardin recalls being "steamed" at being left behind, noting that she had been determined to march on Selma "come hell or high water." And now that was not going to happen.

Like Carter, she also remembers being subjected to taunts and other hostile actions by some of her fellow students at the school before we left, saying she was "accosted" by an angry group of her sorority sisters who demanded—to her surprise—that she turn in her sorority pin. "I complied," she said, "and that was the end of my sorority affiliation."

For her part, Carter said that her sorority sisters begged her not to go on the trip because it would "reflect badly on the group." Some of them even shunned her when she refused their request.

"The next morning, I was accosted in the cafeteria while heaping scrambled eggs and toast on my plate," she remembers. "Some students hurtled across the room to call me a 'nigger-lover' or 'whore' or simply hiss. I was told that what happened to someone else, somewhere else in the U.S.A., was none of my business. It seemed like everyone was staring at me, and I sat at a table alone. . . . The experience was humiliating."

Chapter 5: Tensions High in Selma

Arriving in Atlanta, Chaplain Thompson, Dick Grimsrud, Noel Carota turned in our Hertz rental car and boarded a bus for Birmingham, Alabama—a city known then as "Bombingham" because of its history of racially motivated bombings by white segregationists who had terrorized the African American residents of the city for years.

But now, as we changed buses at the Greyhound bus station in Birmingham on March 20, 1965, I was more concerned about our own well-being. We certainly must have stood out as "outside agitators" with our rolled-up sleeping bags and northern dialects. Four years earlier, several Freedom Riders at this very bus station had been singled out for attack with baseball bats, iron pipes, and bicycle chains by a mob of white racists, aided by the Birmingham police. I remember wanting get the hell out of there and board the bus to Selma as quickly as possible.

That evening, we arrived in Selma and were welcomed by several African American parishioners at the West Trinity

Baptist Church, where we spent the night. The women of the congregation prepared meals for us and our fellow would-be marchers.

From there, Noel Carota telephoned his mother in Massachusetts to say that he had arrived safely in Selma. Later, he told us that his mother had been one of thirteen conservative activists who had gathered at the Parker House in Boston in 1963 to launch a "Draft Goldwater" campaign.

After "checking in" at the West Trinity Baptist Church, we made our way to Brown Chapel A.M.E. Church several blocks away, where a rally was being held to fire up the crowd for the march to Montgomery the next day. The speakers included James Bevel, an aide to Martin Luther King Jr. who had first proposed the march; Andrew Young; and John Lewis. But it was the comedian Dick Gregory who electrified the crowd by joking that it would be just their luck to discover on arriving in Montgomery "that Wallace is colored."

The organizers of the march, according to John Lewis, had spent several days in a "swirl of activity, much like preparing an army for assault," planning for the march. Thousands of "outsiders" had come to Selma to participate, he said, and thousands of dollars were being spent on everything from food to security. Four tents large enough to sleep hundreds of marchers on stops along U.S. Highway 80 over the next five days were rented at $430 each. Seven hundred air mattresses were purchased. Seven hundred blankets were donated by local schools and churches. And two 2,500-watt generators had been acquired to light the campsites at night.

Walkie-talkies, flashlights, pots, pans—the list seemed endless. A crew of twelve clergymen called the "fish and loaves committee" was charged with transporting food to each campsite each evening. Ten local women cooked meals in church kitchens around Selma. Ten others made sandwiches.

On orders from President Johnson, more than 1,800 armed members of the Alabama National Guard would line the fifty-four-mile route of the march, along with more than one thousand U.S. Army troops, one hundred FBI agents, and one hundred federal marshals. Helicopters and light planes would patrol the skies watching for snipers. And federal demolition teams would be assigned to inspect bridges and other potential targets for explosives.

President Johnson told Gov. Wallace that he was disappointed at Alabama's failure to carry out its normal law enforcement functions, adding that the federalized National Guard units—reinforced by army regulars—"will help you meet your responsibility."

The whole idea was enough to drive Wallace into what *TIME* magazine called "paroxysms of rage," appearing before the Alabama state legislature "to rend the air with 20 minutes of bombast," the magazine reported in its March 26, 1965 issue. The proposed march, he declared, was Communist-inspired and abetted by a "collectivist press" and "propagandists masquerading as newsmen."

At a press conference at his ranch in Texas on Saturday, March 20, meanwhile, Johnson told reporters that during the five-day march, "the eyes of the nation will be on Alabama, and the eyes of the world will be on the nation." He said that after the dust had settled, the United States would emerge a stronger, more united country.

But over the weekend of March 20–21, tensions remained high in and around Selma despite the promise of a massive federal presence, with white segregationists continuing to look for ways to disrupt or blunt the impact of the event.

Former Birmingham Mayor Art Hanes, who in 1962 had closed city parks in violation of a federal order to integrate, announced plans for a reverse march by whites from Montgomery to Selma, which were only canceled after Gov. Wallace asked citizens to "stay away from the scenes of tension."

In Selma, a number of residents had asked for permission to stage a counter-demonstration—a request that Mayor Joe T. Smitherman and Dallas County Sheriff Jim Clark eventually turned down.

"We fully understand the motives which have prompted this request," the two officials said in a joint statement, noting that the request had come from "a large number of our friends and fellow white citizens from Alabama and other states. . . ." They said that the "abuses" of the Negro and "transient white demonstrators . . . have plagued our city for nine weeks." But in the end, they said, "our best course to follow is to try to minimize and curtail all demonstrations, so that our community can continue to operate on as normal a basis as possible . . . We assure you that as a united community, this, too, 'We Shall Overcome,' so that we may resume our vital task of building a progressive and more prosperous community for all of our citizens."

In Montgomery, meanwhile, about 200 pro-segregation protestors assembled in front of the Federal Building under the leadership of the Organization for Better Government, carrying signs that read "Outside Clergy, Go Home," "Pious Phonies, Go Home," and "LBJ and MLK, Get Off Our Backs."

One of the leaders of the protest, Rev. Russell Pate, said that Martin Luther King Jr. and clergy from other states were making a mockery of religion. "I do not believe in integration," he said, "and I believe I have the Bible to back me up." He blamed the downfall of the Roman Empire on interracial marriage and warned that the same fate could face the United States.

The Methodist bishop of Alabama, Rev. W. Kenneth Goodson, said that in his view the Selma-to-Montgomery march would do a "great disservice to the cause of human freedom. . . . I counsel all Methodists against participation."

Chapter 6: Ordered to Remain Nonviolent

Just after dawn on Sunday, March 21, 1965, we awoke stiff and aching from a long night on the hard pews of the West Trinity Baptist Church, and after breakfast, Chaplain Thompson, Noel Carota, Dick Grimsrud and I made our way to Brown Chapel A.M.E. Church, where the march was scheduled to begin at 10 a.m.

On the way, we learned that a white student from Boston University had been attacked by a local white resident and slashed across the face with a razor blade.

We also learned—at least according to *The Selma Times-Journal*—that most of the demonstrators were "clergymen and beatnik whites." The newspaper reported as well that Robert M. Shelton, the Grand Wizard of the United Klans of America, had announced plans to hold a mass meeting in Montgomery on Sunday to protest the Selma-to-Montgomery march, adding that his protests would be "peaceful."

A block or so from Brown Chapel, we passed the First Baptist Church, the headquarters of SNCC. Several veteran civil rights workers in bibbed denim overalls were mingling outside with new a few white recruits from the North.

Later, we would learn that some SNCC leaders, including its militant executive secretary, James Forman, were threatening to boycott the march over what they believed to be the relative weakness of Martin Luther King Jr.'s Southern Christian Leadership Conference (SCLC) and the ineffectiveness of such protests. In the end, after several days of negotiations, it was agreed that individual SNCC members would be allowed to participate in the march but that SNCC as an organization would not.

Later in the day, Dick Grimsrud attempted to engage Forman in conversation. But the civil rights leader rejected his offer, making it clear he was not interested in chatting with some white college kid from the North.

Over the years, Forman would become increasingly frustrated with what he saw as the gradualist and relatively timid approach taken by King and other civil rights leaders in addressing economic and racial injustice. He flirted with the Black Panthers and wrote a book, *The Making of Black Revolutionaries*, in which he devoted an entire chapter to laying out his reasons for dismissing God and other "religious crap." Even in Selma, he did not hide the fact that he had problems with the theory and practice of nonviolence, saying in a fiery speech at Brown Chapel on the evening of March 15, for example, that "if we can't sit at the table [of democracy], let's knock the fuckin' legs off." By January 1966, he had lost all patience with nonviolence—"even as a tactic."

We arrived at Brown Chapel at around 8 a.m., well before the planned start of the march, eager to see King and the other civil rights "celebrities." In a nearby field, Andrew Young was offering last-minute instructions to the march marshals on the importance of remaining nonviolent—an admonition that would have made Forman deeply uncomfortable had he been there.

"If you're beaten," Young told the marshals, "put your hands over the back of your head. Get to know the people in your unit, so you can tell if somebody's missing or if there's somebody there who shouldn't be there. And listen! If you can't be nonviolent, let me know now."

The crowd waiting for the march to begin was a motley assortment of factory workers, school teachers, ministers, nuns, labor leaders, college students, firemen—people from all backgrounds, from all over the United States, black and white, Native American and Asian. An estimated 3,000 protestors would eventually show up for the beginning of the march.

Among the dignitaries in attendance were Ralph J. Bunche, undersecretary for special political affairs at the United Nations and a Nobel Peace Prize laureate; A. Philip Randolph, the African American labor organizer; and Rabbi Abraham Heschel, a leading Jewish theologian and philosopher.

As for King, he had spent the night at the home of Dr. Sullivan Jackson, a local dentist who, with his wife, Jean, were devout and longstanding supporters of the civil rights movement. His home was next door to the West Trinity Baptist Church, where we had slept that night. FBI agents would later report that King's entourage arrived at Brown Chapel at 10:58 a.m., almost an hour after the march was scheduled to begin.

It wasn't until 12:46 p.m., after King and members of the clergy had spoken, that the crowd began to move from Brown Chapel slowly down Sylvan Street, with King and his senior aide Ralph D. Abernathy, along with Bunche,

Heschel, and Lewis, leading the way. A fellow marcher pointed to Walker's Cafe, where Rev. James Reeb had suffered the assault by several whites on March 9 that would end his life.

At Alabama Avenue, we turned right and saw the first of many local white citizens we would encounter along the route. Here, they lined the street and were silent. But as we turned left onto Broad Street—the city's main thoroughfare and also the road to Montgomery—loudspeakers blared "Bye, Bye, Blackbird," and white onlookers began to jeer. Later, a private plane flew overhead dropping hate leaflets on us.

Six abreast, we approached the Edmund Pettus Bridge. It was the third time since "Bloody Sunday," March 7, that voting rights protesters were about to cross the high, arching steel structure over the Alabama River, headed for Montgomery. I remember thinking as we walked over the bridge that we would all die instantly if some maniac were to dynamite the bridge from below.

The police, meanwhile, had closed off the two eastbound lanes of the four-lane highway, enabling us to proceed safely and smoothly. But the two westbound lanes remained open to traffic, which included a black Volkswagen with "martin luther kink," "walk, coon," and "coonsville, u.s.a." whitewashed on its fenders and doors. Several white children lined the road waving toy guns and chanting "Nigger lover!" and "White nigger!" as loudly as they could.

Another Volkswagen navigating the westbound lanes carried two Episcopal seminarians, Jonathan Myrick Daniels and Judith Upham, who were returning to Selma even though the Episcopal bishop of Alabama, Charles C. J. Carpenter, had advised all Episcopalians from outside the South to stay away.

"This 'march' is a foolish business and sad waste of time," Carpenter was quoted as saying, "[which reflects] a childish instinct to parade at great cost to our state."

Daniels and Upham, who had been in Selma earlier in the month seeking to integrate St. Paul's Episcopal Church, had returned to their studies at the Episcopal Theological School in Cambridge, Massachusetts, for several days. Now, they were back in Selma to fulfill part of what they saw as their calling to devote their lives to the cause of civil rights. As Daniels put it, "Something had happened to me in Selma which meant I had to come back. I could not stand by in benevolent dispassion any longer without compromising everything I know and love and value. The imperative was too clear, the stakes were too high. . . ."

I don't recall seeing the Volkswagen carrying Daniels and Upham traveling in the opposite direction, toward Selma. But they would say later that they had saluted the last of the marchers coming down the Edmund Pettus Bridge to the flat land on the other side of the Alabama River, before heading to the George Washington Carver Homes, opposite Brown Chapel, where they would spend the night.

Across the bridge, as we passed diners, gas stations, and Craig Field Air Force base, several cars continued to drive by us with signs that were decidedly unwelcoming: "Yankee Trash Go Home," for instance, and "I Hate Niggers."

Small groups of white onlookers yelled insults and threats, and some waved Confederate flags. One woman stopped her car briefly, exited, stuck out her tongue, climbed back in, slammed the door, and drove off.

Selma Mayor Joseph T. Smitherman told reporters that he was "glad to get these people out of town. But I am afraid some of them will come back."

As darkness approached, after walking about seven miles, we turned off U.S. Highway 80 onto a small road leading up to a farm owned by a black man named David Hall, who had agreed to allow the marchers to pitch tents and spend the night. Did he fear retaliation from local whites for doing so? "The Lord," he answered, "will provide."

By dusk, four large canvas tents had been set up for the select few—a total of three hundred—who would be allowed to march the next day, while the rest of us returned to Selma.

Those returning to Selma also included John Lewis, whose doctors had insisted that after his beating at the Edmund Pettus Bridge on "Bloody Sunday," he should sleep in a real bed every night during the march and not in a tent out in the cold.

"My head was still bothering me badly enough that I agreed with them," he said later. "I would walk the entire fifty-four-mile route, but I spent each night back in Selma, with a doctor nearby. . . ."

Lewis said that, nonetheless, he was never tired. "You really didn't get weary," he said. "You had to go—it was more than an ordinary march. To me, there was never a march like this one before; there hasn't been one since."

Chapter 7: Covering the 'Race Beat'

The role that the national news media played in ensuring the success of Martin Luther King Jr.'s voting rights campaign throughout the South cannot be overstated. And no one knew the importance of the media better than King himself, who often berated reporters for not doing their "duty" to portray racial injustice in the starkest of terms.

"The world doesn't know this happened, because you didn't photograph it," King once told *Life* photographer Flip Schulke when he dropped his camera and began helping several black children being manhandled by Alabama law enforcement officers. "It is so much more important for you to take a picture of us getting beaten up than for you to be another person joining in the fray."

Some members of the national news media, however, like Renata Adler of *The New Yorker*, were not inclined to provide King with the kind of positive coverage that he hoped for.

"It was unclear what such a demonstration [as the Selma-to-Montgomery march] could hope to achieve," Adler wrote.

"Few segregationists could be converted by it, the national commitment to civil rights would hardly be increased by it . . . and for the local citizenry it might have a long and ugly aftermath."

But most reporters who were assigned to the "race beat" understood full well the importance of the march in the short term and its potential historical significance.

I was too young to know personally any of the reporters who covered the march, including Adler and Paul Montgomery, of *The New York Times*, who, at 28 years old, was one of the best. Later, however, Montgomery and I would cross paths when we were both posted in Brussels as foreign correspondents in the 1980s.

Born in Brooklyn, Montgomery was hired by the *Times* as a copy boy in 1959 and soon became a reporter, assigned initially to the metropolitan desk. In early 1965, as the civil rights struggle in the South was heating up, he was sent to Selma.

He was one of the few reporters assigned to cover the "race beat" who was not from the South. He did not know how to drive—a fact that the paper's national news editor, Claude Sitton, would learn only after the young reporter had taken up his post in Selma. Tongue in cheek, Sitton wondered whether the Metro section editors who had loaned Montgomery to him knew that there were no subways in the South and that you could not hail a taxicab from a cotton field. [Ibid]

Yet Montgomery, along with fellow *Times* reporter Roy Reed, would have little trouble dealing with the situation at hand, walking the fifty-four miles from Selma to Montgomery through rain and baking sun and filing elegant and riveting reports from the field over the course of four days and five nights.

"There were civil rights leaders and rabbis, pretty coeds and bearded representatives of the student left, movie stars and infants in strollers," Montgomery wrote in a dispatch filed on the first day of the march, Sunday, March 21. "There were two blind people and a man with one leg. But mostly there were Negroes who believe they have been denied the vote too long."

Less colorful but nonetheless instructive were the daily updates on the march filed by Joseph A. Califano Jr., of the Defense Department, who reported back to the various government offices and agencies in Washington, D.C., that had an interest in ensuring the overall safety of the event: the White House, the State Department, the Justice Department, and the Defense Department.

At noon on the second day of the march—Monday, March 22—Califano reported that the marchers had stepped off at 8:06 a.m. in cold weather (twenty-eight degrees). "The marchers were tired, having spent most of the night around the fire to keep warm," he wrote. "There were about 392 people in the column, of which approximately 45 are white. . . . The spectators have been mostly negro."

Califano also reported that a bomb had been found at a school in Birmingham and that a demolition team had been sent to the scene. "There is no further information on this at present."

The incident that Califano referred to was one in a series of planned bombings by segregationists in Birmingham and the surrounding area apparently intended to coincide with the Selma-to-Montgomery march.

According to an AP story in *The Selma Times-Journal*—the local newspaper that reporters from outside Alabama relied on for providing detailed and reliable accounts of civil rights-related activity in the region—six bombs had been discovered in and around Birmingham in two days.

The story, by AP reporter Jim Purks, said that home-made bombs had been found in the parking lot of an African American funeral home; near the former home of the Reverend A. D. King, the brother of Martin Luther King Jr.; at a Catholic church in an area of the city called "Dynamite Hill" because of past racial bombings; and at Western Olin High School, an African American school in suburban Ensley. All of the bombs, the story said, were successfully disarmed by army demolition teams.

By March 1965, in fact, Purks had become something of an expert on the bombings in Birmingham, having covered initially the most notorious such incident—the dynamiting by the KKK of the Sixteenth Street Baptist Church in 1963.

Walking nearby just after the explosion, Purks hastily scribbled a series of unconnected notes in his reporter's notebook: "[S]everal cars outside twisted and wrecked, windows in 2nd floor broken—Negroes looking. . . . People walking over crumpled glass. Pieces of rock. 'My grandbaby 11 years old—pulled rocks off her'. . . . Clock stopped at 10:25. . . . Patches of blood among the glass—one piece of glass."

It was *The New York Times,* however, that would provide the most extensive coverage of the civil rights movement of any "non-Southern" newspaper.

Sensing the increasing importance of the story to a national audience, the paper hired Roy Reed, formerly of the *Arkansas Gazette,* to cover the voting rights campaign in Selma (launched by Martin Luther King Jr. in early January 1965), along with John Herbers (and later, Paul Montgomery).

Colleagues called Reed unfailingly accurate, deeply reflective, and uncommonly polite. He could write magically, they said. And like a number of other reporters for the *Times* who had preceded him in the South, he spoke "Southern."

On the first day of the Selma-to-Montgomery march, Reed filed a report saying that the march had already taken on enormous historical significance. "The marchers are well aware," he wrote, "that the armed forces of the United States are poised to protect them and that no matter how peacefully or violently the thing is carried off, it will be long remembered."

On day two of the march, Reed reported that the 300 or so "freedom marchers" had "plodded 16 more miles through the sunny Alabama countryside . . . before stopping for the night in the heart of Lowndes County—which many Negroes regard as hostile territory."

Reed said that the marchers sang "we are not afraid" as they crossed the Dallas-Lowndes county line at 12:13 p.m. "But Lowndes is lonesome country," he wrote, "and the marchers, if not afraid, are at least a little nervous."

He said that the rolling farmland gave way to marshes and small swamps, and that the marchers had been advised to watch for water moccasins sunning themselves on the road.

"But what the marchers are really watching for," Reed wrote, "are embittered white men, the kind who flew a small plane over the march this morning and threw out leaflets advertising: 'Operation Ban—selective hiring, firing, buying, selling—an unemployed agitator ceases to agitate.'"

Califano, of the Defense Department, wrote in a report filed at 2 p.m. that the marchers—arranged in six, 50-man groups walking three abreast and including 37 whites— had stopped for lunch at the start of the two-lane highway near Benton. He said that John Lewis, who had returned to

Selma to spend the night of March 21–22, had rejoined the marchers. "The age of the marchers runs generally between twelve and twenty," Califano reported. "One-third are female."

Leading the procession were King and his wife, Coretta, along with LeRoy Collins, director of the Community Relations Service, representing President Johnson.

At dusk, King and the rest of the marchers arrived at the day's campsite—an open field next to a grocery store owned by Rosie Steele, a 78-year-old widow, near the edge of Big Swamp Creek. His feet were in "poor condition," his wife later reported, and he was treated by a doctor.

Before bedding down for the night, however, King was told that a plot to assassinate him had been uncovered. The suspected assailant, according to his wife, was "a man disguised as a minister." But King refused to alter his plans, which called for continuing to march then flying to Cleveland the next day to raise money. "While we maintained unarmed guards," his wife wrote, "we understood the FBI was on hand guarding Martin all the time."

Local law enforcement officials like Lowndes County Sheriff Frank Ryals had little use for King and his followers, calling them "beatniks and screwballs and people like that."

"This march is uncalled for," he said. "It's a lot of expense for nothing. It's disrupting people in their homes and on the highway. . . . We have been getting along fine here. And we will continue to unless they come in here with a whole lot of this unlawful stuff and this provocation."

Not surprisingly, Ryals enjoyed the overwhelming support of the county's white population. But he also won over nationally syndicated columnists Rowland Evans and Robert Novak, who argued that the provocative presence of Stokely Carmichael, of SNCC, in Lowndes County had made it impossible for Ryals to abandon his "hereditary segregationism."

Evans and Novak wrote that Ryals—"no belly-bumping Southern sheriff, but a soft-spoken farmer criticized by local Klansmen as too soft"—had become "increasingly alienated from the Negro" because of the push for African American voting rights in the county.

Earlier, Evans and Novak had claimed that Martin Luther King Jr. had relinquished command of the Selma movement demonstrations to John Lewis and James Forman ("two hothead extremists"), adding that SNCC had been "substantially infiltrated" by "beatnik left-wing revolutionaries, and—worst of all—by Communists."

The local press in Alabama also had a problem with beatniks. A front-page story in the March 22 issue of *The Selma Times-Journal,* for instance, said that the participants in the Selma-to-Montgomery march included priests, nuns, ministers, rabbis, and "beatniks types." Also present, it said, were white women, Negro civil rights leaders, and a Negro pushing his baby in a stroller. "Some were well-dressed," it said, "some wore Levi's."

Some members of the media were more sympathetic, including four students at Grinnell College—a small liberal arts school in central Iowa and, like Ripon College, a member of the Associated Colleges of the Midwest (ACM)—who were so moved by the events in Selma on "Bloody Sunday" that they decided to drive south immediately and report on what they saw.

One of the students, Henry Wilhelm, later recalled that as staff members of the Grinnell College newspaper *Scarlet & Black,* they had sensed the importance of what was unfolding in Selma. "And two days later," he said, "[we] climbed into my VW bug and drove straight to Selma," arriving twenty hours later.

The stories and pictures they filed to their editor back at Grinnell, John Wolf, were fresh and remarkably insightful, given their age.

"One drives into Selma and encounters a never-never land," wrote Robert Hodierne, another student. "It's kind of an Alfred Hitchcock version of Alice in Wonderland." He said that Selma is an old town with old customs. "The customs are hard to change. . . ."

Hodierne, who later became an award-winning reporter/ photographer, argued in a special edition of *Scarlet & Black* dated March 20, 1965, that Selma represented a major turning point in the civil rights movement because, for the first time, it involved religious leaders from across the country.

"In the past, the churches made statements supporting civil rights but had never been active," he wrote.

Hodierne wrote that Selma's public safety director, Wilson Baker, was unique among southern police in that he attempted "impartial and objective law enforcement"— an assessment that may have been too generous given that Wilson had been and remained a proud segregationist throughout his entire life.

"It goes without saying that these [white] people [in Selma] hate Negroes," Hodierne wrote. "Even more they hate the press which exposes them to the world. But even more, they hate the northern college students. The four of us are an unfortunate combination—northern college student pressmen."

Hodierne said that he and Harold Fuson, also a reporter for *Scarlet & Black*, had managed to obtain press credentials "though means which would make a red-neck indignant and probably make Sheriff Clark furious." As for Wilhelm and the fourth student, John F. Phillips—both photographers—they were fearless in going everywhere with their cameras but without press credentials, with everyone simply assuming they were members of the press.

"In the few words I have here," Hodierne wrote, conceding that there were limits to their ability to accurately portray what was happening right in front of them, "I cannot begin to describe the Selma demonstration. It is a situation that will require millions of words and hundreds of pictures. We have lived with demonstrators, police and townspeople, yet I'm not sure any of us could begin to draw a clear picture of it all. You have to come to Selma to know Selma."

Chapter 8: The Clergy Heeds the Call

On the third day of the march—Tuesday, March 23—the heavens opened up, flooding the campsite that the marchers had used the night before, halfway between Selma and Montgomery. And just after 8 a.m., with the rain expected to continue for most of the day, they stepped off in a cold drizzle onto U.S. Highway 80 heading east.

Among those now participating in the march were large numbers of Christians, Jews, and others from the religious community who had heeded Martin Luther King Jr.'s call to come to Alabama to support the voting rights campaign.

The Episcopalian contingent was particularly impressive—perhaps reflecting decades of pent-up guilt over the denomination's sad stance on race relations. It included Jonathan Daniels, the young Episcopal seminarian from Boston, who stood guard at the campsite as part of a security force organized by the Reverend Morris V. Samuel Jr., another Episcopalian, from Los Angeles.

Also part of the contingent were roughly five hundred other Episcopalians, including the Right Reverend John E. Hines, the presiding bishop of the Episcopal Church. It didn't take long for them to turn their attention in Selma to another pressing civil rights issue—beyond voting rights—that needed to be addressed: the longstanding ban on African Americans worshipping at the city's Episcopal church, St. Paul's, located in the relatively prosperous white section of the city.

Daniels and about two dozen other Episcopal seminarians and clergy began their quest for church justice one day by walking from Brown Chapel to St. Paul's to meet the rector, the Reverend T. Frank Matthews, who, in a brief session with them, forcefully defended the parish policy of prohibiting interracial worship—even though doing so directly contravened a resolution adopted by the General Convention of the Episcopal Church several months earlier prohibiting discrimination on the basis of race, color, or ethnic origin.

Matthews told the group that at his church it was up to the ushers to decide whether to admit African Americans. But most of them, he said, would bar any integrated group from entering, and he could do nothing about it if he wanted to keep his job.

For Daniels and the other Episcopalians, the only choice, it seemed, was to challenge the policy by showing up with an interracial group for Sunday worship.

Led by Rev. John B. Morris, executive secretary of the Episcopal Society for Cultural and Racial Unity (ESCRU), and Malcolm Peabody, president of the ESCRU board of directors, the group was met at the church door by a phalanx of ushers intent on, as Morris joked at the time, "guarding the church from the Church." Only members of the clergy and white lay people would be allowed to enter, the ushers said—a condition that Morris and the others refused to accept. So they kneeled for a moment of prayer and left.

Another attempt at integrating the church came on Saturday, March 20, the day before the start of the Selma-to-Montgomery march. It was led by Rev. C. Kilmer Myers, the suffragan bishop of Michigan, who had sought permission from the bishop of the Alabama diocese, the Right Reverend Charles C. J. Carpenter, to celebrate Eucharist at St. Paul's with an integrated congregation, arguing that, as a bishop, he had the right to celebrate Eucharist at any Episcopal parish he visited.

But Carpenter refused to order Matthews and the church vestry to honor Myers's request.

Two years earlier—in April 1963—Carpenter had caused a stir by signing, along with seven other religious leaders in Alabama, an open letter to Martin Luther King Jr. calling for an end to the mass demonstrations that were being led by King in Birmingham.

"We recognize the natural impatience of people who feel that their hopes are slow in being realized," the letter, published in the *Birmingham News* on April 12, said. "But we are convinced that these demonstrations are unwise and untimely. . . . [They] have not contributed to the resolution of our local problems." Racial matters, it said, should properly be pursued in the courts. "When rights are consistently denied," it said, "a cause should be pressed in the courts and in negotiations among local leaders, and not in the streets." It said that the demonstrations were being led "in part by outsiders."

In response, while confined to a Birmingham jail for violating a court injunction against street protests, King scribbled on scraps of paper smuggled into his cell what would become perhaps the most important written document of the civil rights era: "Letter from Birmingham Jail."

The letter, typed up later by an aide and published in full by the Christian Century, set out the case for pursuing nonviolent civil disobedience as a means of addressing racial injustice and offered a blistering critique of "white moderates," who, he said, "paternalistically" believed that they could set a timetable for another man's freedom.

King said in his 20-page response dated April 16 that, yes, he was not from Alabama but that he had come to Birmingham "because injustice is here."

"Injustice anywhere is a threat to justice everywhere," he wrote in one of his most widely quoted lines. "We are caught in an inescapable network of mutuality, tied in a single garment of destiny. Whatever affects one directly, affects all indirectly."

Today, those lines appear prominently with thirteen other quotations from King's speeches, sermons, and writings inscribed on a stone wall at the Martin Luther King Jr. Memorial in Washington, D.C.

King said he was sorry that Carpenter and the other clergymen, while deploring the demonstrations, had failed to show similar concern for the conditions that had prompted the demonstrations. "It is unfortunate that demonstrations are taking place in Birmingham," he said, "but it is even more unfortunate that the city's white power structure left the Negro community with no alternative."

He said that no gain in the civil rights movement had ever been made without persistent legal and nonviolent pressure from concerned citizens. Freedom, he said, is never voluntarily given by the oppressor; it must be demanded by the oppressed.

King told his "Christian and Jewish brothers," moreover, that he was extremely disappointed with the behavior of what he called the "white moderate."

"I have almost reached the regrettable conclusion that the Negro's great stumbling block in his stride toward freedom is not the White Citizen's Counciler or the Ku Klux Klanner, but the white moderate," King wrote, "who is more devoted to 'order' than to justice; who prefers a negative peace which is the absence of tension to a positive peace which is the presence of justice; who constantly says: 'I agree with you in the goal you seek, but I cannot agree with your methods of direct action'; who paternalistically believes he can set the timetable for another man's freedom; who lives by a mythical concept of time and who constantly advises the Negro to wait for a 'more convenient season.' Shallow understanding from people of good will is more frustrating than absolute misunderstanding from people of ill will. Lukewarm acceptance is much more bewildering than outright rejection."

King also said he had wept at the "laxity" of the church. "If today's church does not capture the sacrificial spirit of the early church," he wrote, "it will lose its authenticity, forfeit the loyalty of millions and be dismissed as irrelevant social club with no meaning for the twentieth century."

Now, two years later, on the morning of March 20, 1965, seeing no sign of cooperation from Carpenter or the leadership of St. Paul's in Selma, Rev. Myers, the suffragan bishop of Michigan, led a group of about 200 would-be worshippers to the church but was blocked at the entrance by the police. There, the group—consisting mainly of ESCRU members and supporters—recited the penitential office from the Episcopal Prayer Book and then walked silently back to Brown Chapel, where Myers celebrated communion on a makeshift altar set up on the sidewalk—a gesture designed to symbolize, he said, the presence of Christ in temporal affairs.

The presence of hundreds of "outside" clergy in Selma, in fact, underscored the failure of the white clergy in the South to deal with the race issue as the overwhelming majority of southern ministers, priests, and rabbis put their traditional way of life above any potential improvement in the lives of African Americans.

A year and a half earlier, a delegation sent to Selma by the National Council of Churches (NCC) would find only one kindred soul who shared its interest in promoting dialogue between the city's black and white communities: Father Maurice Ouellet, a Catholic priest of the Society of St. Edmund.

According to the NCC, Ouellet was the only white clergy member in Selma who publicly supported the civil rights movement, and for his stance on race issues, he was constantly harassed by white residents, as well as by then-mayor Chris Heinz, who urged him to move out of the city. But Archbishop Thomas J. Toolen, of the Catholic Archdiocese of Mobile-Birmingham, rejected a request to transfer the Ouellet to another city, asking him instead to stop his "secular" activities.

Another attempt at mediation came from the Reverend Ralph E. Smeltzer, a Church of Brethren pastor from Elgin, Illinois. Traveling to Selma in 1963, however, he received a hostile reception from his fellow Christians, including the pastor of Selma's largest Methodist church, George Kerlin, and the church congregation, which Smelter called a bastion of segregationists and strong supporters of Alabama Governor George C. Wallace.

Smeltzer found Rev. Matthews of St. Paul's to be what he called a "congenial back-slapper" but also someone who was opposed to "outside people" coming to Selma and "whipping people up." Historically, according to Smeltzer, quoting Matthews, there had never been any racial tension in Selma; in fact, Smeltzer said, Matthews claimed that Selma "really has no racial problem."

Later, Matthews wrote in St. Paul's church bulletin that calm would only return to Selma when "troublesome immigrants have packed their bags and gathered their photographers and reporters and have left to wreak havoc in some other unsuspecting community."

The Selma-to-Montgomery marchers, meanwhile, continued to make their way through the rain and mud in Lowndes County, with Andrew Young in the lead, having replaced King, who had flown to Cleveland for a speaking engagement.

"The rain has made it difficult for the trucks to get out of last night's bivouac," Joseph Califano, of the Defense Department, reported back to Washington, D.C., at 10 a.m. "One latrine truck is still stuck. . . . The group is orderly; there have been no incidents." At 11:05 a.m., he continued, the marchers had crossed the intersection of U.S. Highway 80 and Route 97, about sixteen miles west of the Montgomery city limit.

Most of the marchers, whose number was limited at this point to 300 in compliance with a federal court order restricting the number of marchers on the two-lane road portion of U.S. Highway 80 through Lowndes County, wore ponchos made from large sheets of plastic. Hats were patched together from cereal boxes. But one of the government's representatives on the march—John M. Doar, head of the civil rights division at the Justice Department—was not so fortunate, as he walked through the torrential rain soaked to the skin. He said that the marchers did not complain about the rain but did raise objections over one state trooper who, they said, had been "high-handed" in directing traffic outside the campsite. Another trooper was heard to shout at an African American driver in a passing car, "Come on up over here, nigger."

By 2:15 p.m., the marchers had closed in on their campsite for the night: a high-ground pasture near the junction of U.S. Highway 80 and Route 21, which the FBI said in a report was a "sea of mud."

We were not aware at the time—but would learn later—that the farm land was owned by A. G. Gaston, a remarkable African American entrepreneur from Birmingham and a strong but silent supporter of the civil rights movement. At the time of his death in 1996 at 103 years old, he was reported to have been worth more than $130 million.

Gaston was born into poverty in the small town of Demopolis, Alabama, the son of a railroad worker and a woman who cooked for a prominent white family. When he was thirteen, his family moved to Birmingham, where his mother worked for A. B. Loveman, a wealthy Jewish department store owner, whose work ethic and attention to saving and investing later would become a model for the rising African American entrepreneur.

After serving in the army in World War I, Gaston earned a living as a coal miner in Fairfield, Alabama. His success at selling box lunches made by his mother to his fellow miners led him to sell popcorn and peanuts on the side and eventually to loan money to his fellow workers.

Soon, Gaston would establish a funeral service—the Booker T. Washington Burial Society—and sponsor gospel singers and Alabama's first regular African American radio program. Over time, he would branch out into other ventures, including a business college, a bottling company, a savings and loan association, a construction firm, and the A. G. Gaston Motel. In the late 1950s and early 1960s, civil rights leaders including King and Abernathy rented out the best suite at the motel at reduced rates to use as a war room for planning protests. And in retaliation, a bomb most likely planted by white segregationists blew off the motel's facade in 1963 (the same year that Gaston put up $160,000 to bail out King from a Birmingham jail).

At the Selma-to-Montgomery campsite on Gaston's property, just south of U.S. Highway 80, several tents had already been erected by the time the marchers arrived. But the field was a quagmire. Hay was brought in to soak up some of the water. And security—such as it was—had broken down.

At last the rain stopped, and air mattresses were distributed. A small American flag was planted in front of one of the tents. "It looked so good to me," recalled Unitarian minister Richard D. Leonard from New York City, "that I put my mattress down close to it and spent many minutes just contemplating it."

Leonard said he slept from 8 p.m. to 1:30 a.m. and then in fits and starts until around 5 a.m. when the sky began to brighten. "As I sat on my mattress and looked out on the sea of mud," he said, "and realized that I would eventually have to climb back into cold, wet socks and barely recognizable shoes, open at the soles and caked with mud, for another fifteen-mile walk, perhaps in the rain, I had no trouble identifying with Job in the Old Testament sitting on his dung heap and asking why he was born."

The Alabama State Legislature, for its part, decided to weigh in later in the day, adopting a series of resolutions denouncing the march and its participants. One resolution said that there had been evidence—vehemently denied by the participants in the march—of "much fornication" among the demonstrators and that "young women are returning to their respective states apparently as unwed expectant mothers." Another resolution—also scoffed at angrily by the marchers—said that "supposedly religious leaders from other parts of the United States" had been "drinking strong drink promiscuously" and using "vulgar language."

That evening, Martin Luther King Jr. addressed an audience of 2,200 paying guests in Cleveland, telling them that the money being raised would be used to help defray the $50,000 cost for the Selma-to-Montgomery march. He also said that after ensuring enactment of the Voting Rights Act of 1965 later in the year, he would begin to protest the "unjust conditions" of race nationwide, outside of the South.

"We must act now before it is too late," King said at a dinner in his honor at the Hotel Sheraton-Cleveland. "We cannot afford not to live up to the American dream. . . . [W]e all must learn to live together as brothers or all perish together as fools."

The "real heroes" of the civil rights struggle, he said, were those participating in the Selma-to-Montgomery voting rights march.

It was just after midnight when King boarded a flight back to Alabama to rejoin the march, which was still slated to end at the state capitol in Montgomery on Thursday, March 25.

Chapter 9: Trouble with Success

By the time I headed south to join the Selma-to-Montgomery voting rights march, in the spring of 1965, hundreds of white university and college students and other activists—many from the North—had already been working in the civil rights movement for years.

Among the more prominent were SNCC members Bob Zellner, Bill Hansen, John Perdew, Dotty Miller, Peter de Lissovoy, Constance Curry, Casey Hayden, and Sam Shirah, along with Zev Aelony, of CORE, and Anne Braden, of the Southern Conference Educational Fund (SCEF), a small New Orleans-based civil rights group whose laudable but nearly impossible task was to solicit support among white southerners for the cause.

For some, notoriety would come—but for the wrong reasons. Michael Schwerner and Andrew Goodman, for example, were murdered by members of the Ku Klux Klan near Philadelphia, Mississippi, along with James Chaney, an African American, in June 1964.

Loners, too, would also pay the ultimate price in their bid to shake things up, including William L. Moore, a white postal worker from Baltimore who walked across Mississippi carrying signs protesting racial discrimination. He was shot to death on a road near Attalla, Alabama, in April 1963.

My first visit to the South came in the spring of 1962 when I volunteered to work at the Back Bay Mission in Biloxi, Mississippi—founded in 1922 as an outreach initiative of the First Evangelical Church (later the United Church of Christ). Its mission was to serve the impoverished and marginalized residents of the city, black and white.

But like other "do-gooder" organizations, the Back Bay Mission was also inescapably, and almost daily, involved in the ongoing struggle against racism and the institutions that nurtured it.

As a volunteer from the North, I was quickly introduced to the uncomfortable workings of the state of Mississippi by people like the man who ran the Mission, Rev. Richard P. Ellerbrake.

Just 28 years old, Ellerbrake had been an advocate for racial equality as pastor of St. Paul's United Church of Christ in Biloxi. He was also a member of the Mississippi Advisory Committee to the U.S. Commission on Civil Rights, and in that role he railed ceaselessly against the Mississippi State Sovereignty Commission, created by the Mississippi legislature in 1956 to defend the state against "encroachment" by the federal government and to portray the state-backed policy of racial segregation in a favorable light.

But over time, the commission also became a vehicle for a much more nefarious campaign: employing investigators and informants to disrupt civil rights activities across the state. One expert on its activities said that from

1956 to 1973 it "spied on civil rights workers, acted as a clearinghouse for information on civil rights activities and legislation from around the nation, funneled money to pro-segregation causes and distributed right-wing propaganda."

Unlike the KKK, however, it rejected the use of violence to achieve its objectives. Yet for five critical years—from 1960 to 1964—it provided funding for the White Citizens' Council, a white supremacist organization that incited violence and pursued the agenda of the KKK "with the demeanor of the Rotary [Club]," as one historian put it.

Its interest in Ellerbrake was triggered by a letter he had sent to its director, Albert Jones, in which he objected to the commission's decision to allocate $20,000 in public funds to the White Citizens' Council. He called the decision a flagrant violation of the democratic principle that public funds should only be used "for that which is in the best interest of the public."

"Roughly half of Mississippi's 'public' are colored citizens," Ellerbrake wrote in the letter, dated July 8, 1960. "I doubt that they approve such an expenditure; nor do many intelligent white citizens, who see in it only the continued foment of discord and group hatred upon the people of Mississippi."

On July 11, after receiving the letter, Jones telephoned the mayor of Biloxi, Laz Quave, and asked him what he knew about Ellerbrake.

"[Quave] stated that Rev. Ellerbrake was very definitely an integrationist and persistent in his efforts to bring about equality among the races," according to an internal commission memo that Jones wrote about his conversation with Quave. "Mayor Quave stated that he thought [Ellerbrake] came to Biloxi, Mississippi, from the State of Minnesota.

Mayor Quave stated that he had nothing to do with Rev. Ellerbrake, in any manner."

Jones also reported that he had spoken with Howard McDonald, a member of St. Paul's congregation, who said that he did not know Ellerbrake but that he had "very little respect for Ellerbrake's ideas regarding segregation."

Jesse E. Stockstill, a fellow member of the commission, urged Jones to reply to the letter from Ellerbrake and drafted a possible response. It condemned Ellerbrake for embracing "leanings to nefarious Communistic Organizations that are sweeping this Nation. . . ."

Stockstill, a 76-year-old attorney from Picayune, Mississippi, argued that *Brown v. Board of Education*, the 1954 Supreme Court decision that struck down state segregation of public schools, was a "farcical undertaking to force the wholesale mixing of Negro and white races in schools, transportation facilities, public parks, hotels, restaurants, and all other facilities which have been segregated heretofore for 95 years. . . ."

The aim of segregation, Stockstill wrote, was to protect the "pure White Anglo-Saxon blood of the people of America," to maintain a "safe degree of health for the inhabitants of the Nation (now sacrificing the millions of dollars spent by the States to eradicate venereal disease among the Negroes, as well as cases where they have transmitted it to Whites)," and to ultimately prevent the "downfall and degradation of the pure White races of this Nation from the inevitable miscegenation that will surely be inflicted upon all inhabitants, including all races, which will be to the everlasting decline and final downfall as a Nation."

Other members of the commission, however, while agreeing with the sentiments expressed in the Stockstill draft, were against sending the letter, arguing that it could be used in a lawsuit contesting the commission's decision to allocate money to the White Citizens' Council, so it was never sent.

In the end, the commission decided not to take action against Ellerbrake. But eventually he would be forced to resign as pastor of St. Paul's, in the summer of 1962, in the wake of mounting pressure from the church membership over his association with the U.S. Civil Rights Commission.

Meanwhile, the Mississippi State Sovereignty Commission continued to thrive, receiving $50,000 in appropriations from the state legislature for the two-year period ending June 30, 1964—meaning that the taxpaying African American residents of Mississippi were being forced to support an organization whose aim was to repress them economically, socially, and politically.

It is not surprising, given the times, that other southern states, notably Louisiana and Alabama, would use the Mississippi commission as a model for creating similar institutions to fight racial integration and the "encroachment" of the federal government in their affairs. Cooperation among the three states—Mississippi, Louisiana, and Alabama—was formalized with the founding of the Southern Association of Investigators in 1966 and the Interstate Sovereignty Commission in 1968.

Local white pro-integration advocates like Ellerbrake continued to play a role in the movement. But in the summer of 1964, their work was overshadowed by the invasion of more than a thousand out-of-state volunteers who had been recruited to participate in a ten-week voter registration drive in Mississippi. Ninety percent of the participants were white, and most of them were young and from the North. It was in those early days of what has since become known as "Freedom Summer," in fact, that Schwerner, Goodman, and Chaney were murdered.

The groundwork for the initiative had been laid earlier. At the third annual general conference of SNCC, held April 27–29, 1962, for instance, some 250 delegates and observers from twenty-two states gathered in Atlanta, Georgia, to discuss broadening the work of the organization beyond campus protest activities to community organizing and voter registration. Nearly one-third of the participants at that meeting were white.

By 1963, white activists had begun to play a wider and more important leadership role in the movement, with the hiring, for example, of Casey Hayden and Mary E. King to expand SNCC's publicity operations—two years after Bob Zellner had become the first white southerner to be named a SNCC field secretary.

Charles Sherrod, an African American project director for SNCC, argued that using whites as voter registration volunteers was necessary "to strike at the very root of segregation . . . the idea that white is superior. . . . We can only [break that image] if [local blacks] see white and black people working together, side by side, the white man no more and no less than his black brother, but human beings together."

Others in the movement, however, disagreed, saying that there were already too many white people in the movement.

Hollis Watkins, a SNCC staffer, reflected the views of many when he said that whites coming from the North to Mississippi would destroy the grassroots civil rights institutions that were being built by the local population.

"For the first time," he said, "we had local people who had begun to take the initiative themselves and do things. For the first time, we had local Mississippians who were making decisions. . . . We felt that with a lot of students from the North coming in, being predominantly white, that they would come in and overshadow the grassroots organizations. . . ."

Finding room for a relatively small number of individual white volunteers in the movement was not difficult, and by the fall of 1963 about 20 percent of SNCC's staff was white. But sending large numbers of white students into black communities that historically had feared and distrusted whites, in the "Freedom Summer" of 1964, was another matter.

"At this point," according to a SNCC report, written in 1963, "it is too dangerous for whites to participate in the project in Mississippi—too dangerous for them and too dangerous for the Negroes who would be working with them."

The report also cited the "higher pitch" of "terror" in Mississippi than in nearby Georgia, saying that "this means not only more outright violence but more difficulty in obtaining a place to meet and more difficulty in convincing local leaders (ministers, teachers, doctors, and other professionals) to take an active stand."

Even in Georgia, according to Anne Braden, white workers were running into problems in black communities because of their race. White students, she said in December 1962, did not have "an easy time communicating with Negroes who have known whites only as oppressors." John Pardew of SNCC said that poor blacks were frequently "afraid of me as a white."

Yet plans to import 1,000 or more northern white volunteers to Mississippi in the summer of 1964—drafted by SNCC project director Bob Moses and Allard K. Lowenstein, a white civil rights activist from New York— were, nevertheless, set quickly into motion.

Moses argued that the only hope for blacks was to change the power structure in Mississippi by provoking a crisis between the federal government and the state government. That could only be done, he argued, by swamping the state with out-of-state volunteers. His assumption was that the state alone would not be able crush such a massive show of force and, moreover, that public opinion nationwide would not tolerate law enforcement assaults against defenseless white students.

But the Council of Confederated Organizations (COFO), a loose coalition of major civil rights organizations, decided in November 1963 to recruit only 100 northern white students for the "Freedom Summer" project, despite a plea from COFO co-director Moses that to have white people "working alongside of you . . . changes the whole complexion of what you're doing, so it isn't any longer Negro fighting white, it's a question of rational people against irrational people. . . . I always thought that the one thing we can do for the country that no one else can do is to be above the race issue."

Support for the project, meanwhile, continued to grow, with Lowenstein and others formulating plans of their own to bring thousands of students to Mississippi in the summer of 1964 to force a showdown between state and federal officials. The National Council of Churches was also planning to organize its own projects. And John Lewis, who had been elected chairman of SNCC in June 1963, said that SNCC wanted to create such a crisis in Mississippi that the federal government would have to intervene. "Out of this conflict, this division and chaos," he said, "will come something positive."

Finding white students in the North who were willing to spend their summer in the dangerous South was, surprisingly, not difficult.

"They all wanted to come to where the action was," said Casey Hayden, who had moved to Mississippi in 1963 to work for SNCC. "These were the early sixties. Kids on college campuses were reading existentialists. The black students were . . . like existentialist heroes. . . . They wanted to get close to it."

Hayden's husband at the time—the liberal activist Tom Hayden, who also worked in Mississippi—has said that, for the leaders of the civil rights movement, the aim was to "mobilize the North" to put pressure on Congress and the administration, so that "they would finally do something about these strongholds of segregation in the South."

"The conclusion was that . . . it would be necessary to bring down the white sons and daughters of the country's middle class from the liberal North," Hayden said, "to experience the true nature of southern segregation."

Bob Zellner, of SNCC, noting that "only" one white person (William L. Moore, the postal worker from Baltimore) had been killed fighting for civil rights in the South prior to June 1964, explained it this way: "We knew that if black people were brutalized and arrested, neither the country nor the government was going to care. But if the son of white lawyer so-and-so or the daughter of white senator such-and-such got beaten or arrested—or God forbid, killed—people would have to pay attention and demand that the government do something about it. . . . We would have to pull out all the stops. A thousand volunteers from middle-class families, black and white, from all over the United States would converge on Mississippi. That would get attention and possibly protection for people attempting to register to vote."

For many of us in the North, however, the decision to travel south had little to do with strategy or existentialism. Rather, it was a visceral response to persistent racial injustice. The murder of white activists like Schwerner and Goodman touched a nerve. But the violence being perpetrated daily against African Americans was different.

News of one case, in particular, spoke to us like no other.

It involved Louis Allen, an African American logger from Liberty, Mississippi, who in September 1961 had witnessed what he claimed initially was the killing in self-defense of another African American and fellow voter registration activist, Herbert Lee, by a white state legislator, E. H. Hurst.

Amite County Sheriff E. L. Caston said at the time that he and other local officials had investigated the incident and found, according to the Mississippi State Sovereignty Commission, that Lee had attempted to attack Hurst with an eighteen-inch tire iron, which prompted Hurst to strike Lee on the head with his .38-caliber revolver. The gun discharged, according to Allen and the others, killing Lee instantly.

A coroner's jury the same day cleared Hurst after hearing testimony from five witnesses—two whites and three African Americans, including Allen. A hearing at the county courthouse on September 26 also exonerated Hurst after it had taken testimony from the same five witnesses, ruling that he had acted in self-defense.

But Allen later told SNCC activists Julian Bond and Bob Moses that he had falsified his testimony out of fear for his life. "If he had implicated a powerful white man in a murder of a black man," Bond said years later, "he was risking his life. . . . I tried to encourage him to tell the truth, but it was like saying 'Why don't you volunteer to be killed?'"

Eventually, Allen decided to approach the FBI, saying that in reality, Hurst had shot Lee without provocation. Word of what Allen had done spread quickly through Liberty's white population. He was threatened repeatedly and even shot once and beaten by the county's newly elected sheriff, Daniel Jones. Again fearing for his life, Allen decided to escape to Milwaukee to move in with relatives. But on the night before he was scheduled to leave—January 31, 1964—he was ambushed at his property outside Liberty and killed by two shotgun blasts to the head. No charges were filed at the time.

Since then, the FBI has reopened the case following an investigation by Tulane University history professor Plater Robinson, and Jones has been targeted as the prime suspect. But again, no charges were filed.

News of Allen's murder spread rapidly to the dormitories of mainly white colleges and universities in the North. It underscored the gravity of the situation, but it also reminded the students of what dangers lay ahead.

Peter Orris, a freshman at Harvard University, said that he and the other white students who attended training sessions at Western College for Women in Oxford, Ohio, in mid-June 1964 spent hours listening to Bob Moses and other SNCC leaders "give us a feeling of exactly what kind of a tense atmosphere we were going into, what kind of violence we should expect, how to avoid violence, as well as nonviolent responses to violent situations."

Many white Mississippians, of course, were resentful of "outsiders" coming to the state (where in 1962, incidentally, only 6.2 percent of eligible African American voters were registered to vote) in order to fundamentally change their way of life. They regularly harassed the volunteers with drive-by shootings and Molotov cocktails—all with the implicit (and sometimes explicit) support of the local authorities.

In the end—after 10 weeks of voter registration work and the creation of Freedom Schools and community centers in small towns throughout the state—about 17,000 African Americans were moved enough to fill out voter registration forms, but only 1,600 were permitted to register. [Carson . . .] Four civil rights workers had been killed. A total of 80 Freedom Summer workers were beaten. At least three African Americans from Mississippi who supported the project were murdered. Thirty-seven churches were bombed or burned. And 30 African American homes or businesses were attacked.

Most observers, however, said that the project had been a success, arguing that it had, after all, generated widespread press coverage nationally, which, for the movement, was unprecedented. Quite literally, according to one study, its triumph could be measured in column inches of newsprint and running feet of videotape. "Easily the most spectacular and sustained single event in recent civil rights history," the study said, "it provided summer-long, nationwide exposure of the inequities of white supremacy in the deepest of the Deep South states."

But Bob Moses, who had played a pivotal role in initiating and implementing the project, was not convinced that it had been worth it. "Success?" he told a group of reporters. "I have trouble with that word. When we started, we hoped no one would be killed."

Chapter 10: A Sea of Mud

It was a brisk and sunny morning as the marchers set off shortly after 7 a.m. on Wednesday, March 24—the fourth day of the five-day march from Selma to Montgomery.

After spending the night camped in a field at the Gaston farm just south of U.S. Highway 80, about twenty miles west of Montgomery, they were joined by hundreds of other protesters as they closed in slowly on the Alabama state capital. And I was among them.

I had marched with about 3,000 other protestors on the first day of the march and, with all but three hundred, had returned to Selma that evening to wait until now, when we were allowed to rejoin the march as U.S. Highway 80 widened to four lanes and the limit on the number of marchers was lifted. By late morning, there were about 1,200 of us; by mid-afternoon, we were four to five thousand.

Califano, of the Defense Department, wrote in a dispatch back to Washington, D.C., at 10 a.m. that the only notable incident that morning involved the driver of a support vehicle who had been been punched in the nose after stopping at a gas station run by whites. A small contingent of national guardsmen, Califano said, had been sent to the scene to investigate.

Throughout the afternoon, cars and buses discharged new marchers along the route. A brief but heavy rain shower soaked everyone. But we were in a jubilant mood, singing freedom songs as we passed a billboard with large letters exhorting citizens to "Help Get the U.S. Out of the United Nations."

But animosity among the local white population toward the marchers, not surprisingly, continued to grow.

The city of Selma, for instance, filed a lawsuit on behalf of the local community against Martin Luther King Jr. and other "nonresident" civil rights leaders, seeking $100,000 in damages for the loss of revenue resulting from the boy-cott of the city buses and the police protection needed in the weeks of civil rights demonstrations leading up to the march.

"We believe that a court of law is a proper forum for the settlement of just grievances," Selma Mayor Joe T. Smitherman said, "and not the streets and highways of our city and state."

J. A. Pickard, the city's superintendent of schools, attacked "outside agitators" for causing a sharp drop in attendance at R. B. Hudson High School and other segregated African American schools in the city.

"The effects of the demonstrations in and around Selma during the past weeks have been devastating to the Negro schools of the Selma City School System," Pickard said. "Particularly in the early days of the movement, students defied their parents and school teachers by participating in demonstrations. After constant harangue by outside agitators, many parents and their children no longer realize that they must work and study to better themselves, but expect to be given privileges, normally earned through considerable effort, purely because they demonstrate."

A. R. Meadows, the Alabama state superintendent of education, said that parents would be fined $100 and sentenced to hard labor for up to ninety days for failing to send their children to school.

One Selma resident said in a letter to the editor in *The Selma Times-Journal* that the religious leaders who had come to the city from other parts of the country were participating in, as he put it, "one of the greatest fiascoes ever witnessed in America—the march to Montgomery to secure rights which have already been granted."

"Like a Ringling Brothers circus parade with its menagerie of clowns, clergymen, politicians and beatniks with everything but a calliope," the reader wrote, "they will march down Highway 80. . . . They have not bound together a divided community, but have driven its citizens further apart. They have not manifest a spirit of love but of judgement. . . . Some day they will leave. They will have eased their consciences, satisfied their flair for the dramatic, and inflated their egos. But they leave behind a community and a church sorely wounded by what they did and did not do. And upon us . . . will fall the responsibility of trying to build back and restore a community spirit of love and understanding and brotherhood which they helped to destroy."

National news magazines and religious journals reported favorably on what they saw as a new brand of social activism among the nation's clergy. But some condemned the clergy's involvement. A young Baptist minister and the future founder of the Moral Majority, Jerry Falwell, told his parishioners at the Thomas Road Baptist Church in Lynchburg, Virginia, that preaching the gospel of Jesus Christ was a full-time job. He said that minsters were not called by God to be politicians but to be "soul winners."

Along the route of the march, as we approached Montgomery, I saw fewer and fewer white men and women protesting our presence—perhaps because the *Montgomery Advertiser* had run an ad by the City Commissioner's Committee on Community Affairs calling on local residents to ignore the march and not overreact.

For his part, Richard D. Leonard, a 37-year-old Unitarian minister from New York City, who had marched now for three days, was becoming concerned about the "gruesome appearance I was presenting as a minister," as cars and buses continued to drop off "cleanly scrubbed" passengers (like me) to join the hike on day four. He had not shaved or changed shirts and was not able to get a comb through his matted hair. But he was heartened at the news that large numbers of people from around the country were due to arrive in Montgomery later in the day to join the final leg of the march, set for Thursday, March 25.

One of the more committed activists on the march was Casey Hayden, a cofounder of SNCC, who, according to those who knew her, was simple, gentle and very southern, with impeccable manners. She was deeply concerned about social issues and seemed to know instinctively what was right, they said.

She was also married to the high-profile, left-wing activist Tom Hayden. The couple, who "sparkled together," met for the first time at a meeting of the National Student Association (NSA) in 1960 and again at a SNCC conference in Atlanta later that year. From the beginning, she was a supporter of what was called in SNCC's founding document the "philosophical or religious idea" of nonviolence as the "foundation of our purpose, the presupposition of our belief and the manner of our action."

"My life in the sixties was strewn with crowded overnight car trips and red-eye airplane flights," she wrote later. "I and others like me moved fast and improvised, carrying ideas and names and contacts, connecting folks to each other, welding, one by one, those crucial linkages. We moved so fast the dross burned off. We burned down to our essential selves, and our relationships were intense. I was part of a small group who were the tip of the wedge of change, carrying the weight of opening space for all who came after us."

At the SNCC leadership conference in March 1962, she and Bob Zellner organized a workshop on the role of white students in the movement. "I liked the leverage white students would provide," she wrote later. "Press and northern politicians would pay attention."

But by 1965, SNCC had entered a period of transition—from a nonviolent, interracial organization to a more militant, Afro-centric institution.

"I watched, conflicted and depressed, as that fabric unraveled," Casey Hayden wrote. Tensions were on the rise between whites who still believed in interracial cooperation and blacks who were seeking their own identity.

Hayden said she listened to SNCC Chairman John Lewis at a SNCC conference in Atlanta in February 1965, where he indicated that what the organization needed was not more whites but black leaders who were strong, militant and experienced. [Ibid]

After the Selma-to-Montgomery march, while she continued to draw her paycheck from SNCC of $9.64 a week, she left for Cleveland, and eventually for Chicago, to work with the Economic Research and Action Project (ERAP)—

an initiative created by Students for a Democratic Society (SDS) to organize poor whites in urban areas.

"I was trying to follow the new [segregated] line in SNCC," Hayden wrote, "viewing my move as an experimental effort to find ways for whites to leave SNCC and work on the white side. I hoped for an alliance now between black and white, even though we were working in separate communities."

But now, at mid-afternoon on the fourth day of the march, the "separate communities" we were part of were still working closely together, arriving tired but exuberant at the City of St. Jude—a Catholic-run complex with a church, hospital and school—where we would stay the night before concluding the march the next day by walking several miles to the state capitol in Montgomery.

After having flown to Cleveland to speak the previous night, Martin Luther King Jr. had rejoined the march, and walking behind him was the Reverend Morris H. Tynes from Chicago, who joked with his friend as they walked. "Moses, can you let your people rest for a minute?" Tynes asked. "Can you just let the homiletic smoke from your cigarette drift out of your mouth and engulf the multitude and let them rest?"

Years later I would come across a letter written by Tynes—and signed by King and several other civil rights leaders—calling on high school and college students, through their churches and synagogues, to travel to Washington, DC, on April 18, 1959, to demonstrate in support of the "immediate and peaceful integration of the schools of our nation."

An estimated 26,000 had heeded the call, marching down the National Mall that day and demanding, in the words of their petition, that the president and Congress put into effect an "executive and legislative program which will insure the orderly and speedy integration of schools throughout the United States."

Learning about that event was a reminder to me of how long the struggle for racial justice in the United States had been going on—well before I and many others got involved. Some say that the origins of the movement as an organized force date back to the Montgomery bus boycott of 1955–1956 and to the refusal of Rosa Parks to give up her seat to a white man. Others, like Danielle L. McGuire, in the remarkable book *At the Dark End of the Street*, have argued that the beginning of the movement dates back to 1944 when Parks, an organizer for the NAACP, was sent to Abbeville, Alabama, to investigate the rape of a 24-year-old mother and sharecropper by seven white men armed with knives and shotguns.

Now, twenty-one years later, on March 24, 1965, newspapers across the country were reporting on the war in Vietnam and the successful flight of the Gemini 3 spacecraft, along with the Selma-to-Montgomery march. Not surprisingly, *The Selma Times-Journal* devoted considerable space to the march and the public reaction to it, particularly among the local white population.

It reported, for instance, that Rep. William L. Dickinson (R-Ala), a member of Congress from Montgomery, had asked Gov. Wallace to receive the marchers "courteously and graciously" when they arrived at the state capitol on March 25. Otherwise, he said, "these thousands of civil rights demonstrators may decide to camp by the thousands indefinitely on the capitol grounds, getting more and more publicity for Martin Luther King at the expense of the state and the people of Alabama in the process." He said that Wallace should tell the marchers, "as he has many times told the rest of the nation," that anyone who is qualified to register to vote can vote in Alabama.

A Detroit resident said in a letter to the editor of *The Selma Times-Journal* that he would like to apologize to the residents of Selma for the behavior of his fellow northerners, calling them "jackasses wandering around the countryside with blinders on."

"I must side with Governor Wallace and [Dallas County] Sheriff [Jim] Clark in demanding that the Northern church and political do-gooders return to their own troubled areas in the North," the writer, Jerry Woodman, said. "I'm sorry for all the Yankee agitation that has caused so much trouble in such a pleasant Southern city as Selma."

One Selma resident—Ella Holladay Harris—urged all Americans to write to President Johnson protesting what she called the "discrimination now being leveled against Alabama."

But the newspaper also published an AP story noting that the Ralph D. Abernathy, an aide to Martin Luther King Jr., had told journalists that he considered the Selma-to-Montgomery march to be the "greatest demonstration for freedom in the nation since Abraham Lincoln signed the Emancipation Proclamation"—an exaggeration perhaps, but nonetheless heartfelt.

It had been raining off and on during the day, so when we arrived at the City of St. Jude on the outskirts of Montgomery after several hours of walking along U.S. Highway 80, the field where we would camp for the night was now deep in mud. One hiker described the experience as an adventure in "mud skiing." Thousands poured into the grounds from Selma and Montgomery through lax security, planning to march the final few miles the next day. And now, instead of being subjected to jeers and insults from white segregationists along the route, we were being cheered by people on both sides of the street in the African American section of the city.

No one seemed to know exactly who had given us permission to use the St. Jude grounds for the final campsite that night. It was certainly not the Catholic Church, since its leaders were far from united on the question of employing church resources in the campaign for social justice, which included, of course, the Selma-to-Montgomery march.

We had heard that Father Paul J. Mullaney, the director of St. Jude, had said that the permission had come from Archbishop Thomas J. Toolen, which seemed odd, if not unlikely, given his longstanding and very public opposition to the march.

Toolen's record on race was mixed. A year earlier, as schools in Alabama continued to oppose implementing the Supreme Court's 1954 decision striking down state laws establishing separate schools for black and white students, Toolen took the bold step, which angered many white parents, of desegregating all Catholic schools in Alabama, effective immediately. But he also denounced the tactics of civil rights protestors, saying that "outsiders" like the dozens of Catholic priests and nuns who had come to Selma from New York, Michigan, and other states were just there to stir up trouble.

Still, parishioners at St. Elizabeth's Church in Selma— under the leadership of Father Ouellet, of the Edmundite order—continued to work closely and proudly with SNCC, housing and feeding visiting marchers and carrying on a tradition initiated by Edmundites of working in Selma on behalf of the city's African American community for nearly thirty years by building, for example, a hospital and a school dedicated to their care and education.

Ouellet's superior, the Very Reverend Eymard Galligan, had decided in the fall of 1963 that he wanted the Edmundites to play a more active role in Selma, particularly in promoting racial integration, so he wrote to Toolen saying he hoped that the Edmundites would be allowed to "actively help the Negro people in their struggle, knowing full well the dangers involved and the consequences." But Toolen replied by saying that picketing and marching by all priests and nuns in his diocese was and would remain strictly prohibited.

Yet the struggle within the Catholic Church over the race issue would continue. A month before the Selma-to-Montgomery march, in February 1965, Father John Crowley, director of the Edmundites' southern missions, took out a full-page ad in *The Selma Times-Journal* citing the "evils" of racial discrimination and insisting on the need for street protests to remedy the situation.

"[Racial discrimination] denies to a citizen his human and civil rights," Crowley wrote, "and thus undermines the principles on which our nation was founded. . . . Fair-minded citizens reject the evils of segregation."

The Edmundite leader argued that the United States was "fortunate" to have African American leaders in its midst who were, he said, by and large "temperate" and dedicated to American ideals.

"It is when their so-obviously just claims are ignored, their needs completed unattended, their just demands refused," the Catholic cleric wrote, "that the streets become their only means of protest. The Negroes in Selma . . . have no other power. . . . That is why we support wholeheartedly those non-violent efforts to obtain their full rights as Americans."

Archbishop Toolen blew up, firing off a letter to Father Galligan saying that he and the Edmundite Fathers had come to a "parting of the ways."

"Both Crowley and Ouellet have shot off their mouths entirely too much," he wrote. "I have put up with as much as I am going to. . . . I have always felt closer to the Edmundite Fathers than any other Community in the Diocese, but Selma has cured this." He said he wanted Ouellet "out of Selma." And soon the man called by Martin Luther King Jr. the "most righteous white man in Selma" was gone.

Chapter 11: Anger Turned to Good

The mood among the celebrities taking the short flight from Atlanta to Montgomery on the afternoon of March 24, 1965, was upbeat—but apprehensive.

Leonard Bernstein, the American conductor and composer, sat in the front. Behind him was Oscar-winning actress Shelley Winters, who joked with comedian Alan King. In the back of the plane James Baldwin and his brother David were silent. Across from them was Floyd Patterson—"The Gentleman of Boxing"—and Peter, Paul, and Mary were seen munching on cold fried chicken and a salad behind him.

Waiting at the Montgomery airport to load the celebrities onto a bus for downtown and the Greystone Hotel, near the Alabama state capitol, was Ossie Davis, the actor and activist. In the lobby of the hotel, Harry Belafonte gestured wildly, assigning rooms to the other stars who had arrived earlier.

Over the course of the afternoon, more planes landed at Montgomery's Dannelly Field carrying more celebrities, including Tony Bennett, Sammy Davis Jr., Tony Perkins, Nina Simone, Bobby Darin, Mike Nichols, and Elaine May. After freshening up at the hotel, they were off in two busloads to St. Jude's, where a "Stars for Freedom" rally—organized by Belafonte—would be held that night for the exhausted marchers and thousands of other supporters.

Belafonte, who had just turned 38 years old, was at the peak of his career. Dubbed the "King of Calypso," he had recorded his breakthrough album *Calypso* in 1956—the first LP to sell more than a million copies. He was also the first African American to win an Emmy (1959) and had racked up other triumphs in Hollywood and on Broadway.

But his greatest achievement, he would recall, was his work as a civil rights activist. By March 1965, he had already been involved in the movement for more than a decade, appearing, for instance, with Duke Ellington at a fund-raising event in December 1956—"Salute to Montgomery"—and marching with Martin Luther King Jr. at countless freedom rallies across the country. In 1963, he helped organize the "March on Washington" (where King delivered his "I Have a Dream" speech at the Lincoln Memorial). And not insignificantly he provided critical financial backing for King's Southern Christian Leadership Conference (SCLC) and for SNCC, as well as for the entire King family, especially early on in their lives when, as a preacher, King was supporting a growing family on an annual income of only $8,000.

"Whenever we got into trouble or when tragedy struck," King's wife, Coretta Scott King, recalled, "Harry has always come to our aid, his generous heart wide open." He also raised thousands of dollars to bail out civil rights protesters, including King, and so concerned was he for the safety and well-being of the King family that he personally took out life insurance policies worth $100,000 each for each of his four children.

But Belafonte's most dramatic and daring achievement came in the summer of 1964, following the murders of Michael Schwerner, James Chaney, and Andrew Goodman near Philadelphia, Mississippi.

It began in the evening of August 4, 1964, when the phone rang in Belafonte's 21-room apartment on the Upper West Side of New York. "We've got a crisis on our hands down here," the man on the other end of the line, SNCC's James Forman, told him. "We need help."

The bodies of Schwerner, Chaney, and Goodman had just been found in a shallow grave, which prompted many white students from the North who had taken part in the Freedom Summer not to leave the state, as might have been expected, but instead to request permission to stay longer to carry on the fight. But money was running short.

Forman told Belafonte that if the students were to leave Mississippi now, the KKK would claim that it had driven them out. "The press would play it that way," he said. "And if they all stay, we can get thousands of more voters registered. The problem is we don't have the resources to keep them all here." He said he needed at least $50,000, adding that he said he expected to burn through the meager remainder of his budget in the next seventy-two hours.

Belafonte had already opened his personal checkbook to the tune of about $50,000 to help establish SNCC a few years earlier, and he was prepared to do so again. But he recalled the experience of his idol, the singer, actor, and activist Paul Robeson, whose generosity on behalf of various social causes had almost ruined him financially. So Belafonte vowed to raise most of the money from outside sources, and quickly.

The Chicago newspaper columnist and broadcaster Irv Kupcinet offered to help by hosting a fund-raiser at his home, where rich Chicagoans would throw checks and cash at Belafonte totaling $35,000 during a hastily arranged visit to the Windy City. A trip to Montreal yielded another $20,000, and he and his wife, Julie, collected an additional $15,000 at a fund-raiser at their apartment in New York.

Now, however, he had to figure out a way to get the money to Mississippi. "I couldn't just wire it and have a black activist go to the local Western Union office to ask for his [money], please," he said later. "He'd be dead before he drove a mile away. So would a white college volunteer. . . . The money would have to be brought down in cash. And unless I could come up with a brighter idea, I'd have to take it down myself."

So Belafonte—failing to come up with that brighter idea—contacted his longtime friend and fellow entertainer Sidney Poitier, who understandably was reluctant to join him on his potentially risky mission down south. But Belafonte eventually convinced his friend, joking that while "the chances of a Klansman taking a potshot at me were actually pretty high . . . it'll be harder for them to knock off two black stars than one. Strength in numbers, man."

Unaccompanied, the two men then boarded a plane at the airport in Newark, New Jersey, for Jackson, Mississippi, toting a black doctor's bag filled with $70,000 in small bills.

At the Jackson airport, Forman and two SNCC volunteers met them and took them to a private airstrip with a dirt runway, where they were put on a small Cessna flown by an unfriendly white pilot ("Was he a Klansman, leading us into a trap?") some one hundred miles north to Greenwood, Mississippi, where SNCC had its state headquarters.

Two more SNCC volunteers, in two cars, were waiting for them for the drive to town, and as they were starting their engines the driver of the car carrying Belafonte and Poitier—SNCC field secretary Willie Blue—saw a long row of headlights at the far end of the pitch-black airfield. "That's the Klan," he said. But instead of turning away, he and the driver of the other car drove full-speed toward the outline of three or four pickup trucks in the distance.

Nearing the trucks, the two SNCC cars then swung around to take an alternate route to town, and the trucks fell in line behind them. "Why aren't you driving faster?" Belafonte asked Blue, who was keeping strictly to the forty-five-mile-an-hour speed limit. "Faster, man!"

But Blue refused, saying he was not about to drive at full speed because that was exactly what the Klansmen wanted him to do. "They got a state trooper there waiting in his car with the headlights off, ready to arrest us for speeding," Blue said. "He takes us to the station, lets us out in an hour, and even more of the Klan be waiting for us. That's how they work. That's how those boys [Schwerner, Chaney, and Goodman] got killed."

Belafonte later recalled that one of the pickup trucks kept ramming the back of the car as Blue maneuvered his vehicle toward the middle of the two-lane road to keep the truck from pulling alongside. "We can't let them pull up beside us," Blue said. "They'll shoot."

After two or three "terrifying" minutes, which "seemed like forever," Belafonte said, a convoy of cars appeared ahead. "That's them," Blue said, signaling that a SNCC brigade was coming to the rescue. "My heart was still pounding, but I started to breathe again."

As the pickup trucks slowly retreated, a dozen or so shots rang out in the night air. But no one was hit, fortunately, and the SNCC convoy led the cars into Greenwood, where hundreds of SNCC volunteers had assembled at their headquarters in an old barn to greet Belafonte and Poitier.

"Screams of joy went up from the crowd," Belafonte recalled. "Sidney and I had heard a lot of applause in our day, but never anything like those cheers. . . . To have two of the biggest black stars in the world walk in to show solidarity with them—that meant a lot to them, and to us."

He said that once the crowd had settled down, he held up the black satchel he had brought with him and turned it upside down on a table in front of him, letting bundles of cash roll out to the shouts of the roomful of tired but now-inspired and overjoyed SNCC volunteers.

Belafonte said that when he got home to his wife and children—waiting in the family's apartment in New York City—he asked himself why he had taken on the civil rights movement as his personal crusade.

"I knew the reason I'd gotten involved in general—any black American with a pulse and a conscience had done that by the summer of 1964," he wrote, "at least to the extent of writing the occasional check. A lot of white Americans had, too. All of us sensed this was a point at which history simply had to turn. We couldn't tolerate more lynchings and beatings. We couldn't abide more 'whites-only' signs on the hotels and restaurants and gas stations and water fountains and bus stations in the segregated South. We couldn't let black Americans be treated as slaves in all but name anymore."

This wasn't anything new, he said. Everyone knew that. "But why did I feel so personally offended?" he asked. His mother had much to do with it. Yet long after his initial involvement in the movement, he would continue to struggle with "piecing the parts together."

"Why this little boy, among all others, should use his anger to push himself up, make a name for himself, and then make it his mission to smash racial barriers and injustice with such grim determination, I'm not sure I can say," Belafonte wrote. "Perhaps, in the end, where your anger comes from is less important than what you do with it."

Chapter 12: Stars Come Out for Freedom

What I remember most about the night of March 24, 1965—aside from the world-class entertainment that Harry Belafonte had made possible at the City of St. Jude outside Montgomery—was the mud. It was what Belafonte would remember most as well.

The megastar entertainer had succeeded in persuading many of his fellow entertainers to drop what they were doing and fly to Montgomery to perform at a "Stars for Freedom" rally on the last night of the Selma-to-Montgomery march. He had lined up transportation for them from the airport, and he had found rooms for them at the Greystone Hotel in downtown Montgomery (now the Hampton Inn & Suites Montgomery), which boasted "circulating ice water, fans and bed lamps." All their expenses would be taken care of, he said, and they were.

"In all, that evening would cost me $10,000," Belafonte later wrote. "I could handle that. What I couldn't control was the rain."

By early evening, the temporary campsite that had been set up in the field directly behind the City of St. Jude was so inundated that the microphones and klieg lights that Belafonte had brought in kept sinking in the mud. A local teenager, however, came up with an idea that would save the day: retrieving a load of empty coffins from a local black funeral home, which were laid two rows deep in the mud, with a layer of plywood secured on the top, forming a makeshift stage. "Yes, *coffins*," John Lewis recalled.

Thousands of people, in fact, had made their way to St. Jude—mainly African Americans. And eventually, according to the U.S. Justice Department, some 30,000 would be on hand for the show.

In the darkness, I heard cries for help from people in the crush of humanity pressing against the stage. Several young girls collapsed and were lifted from the muddy field onto the lighted stage. Some two dozen people—none seriously ill or injured, thankfully—were carried off to the hospital on stretchers.

Finally, the entertainment—scheduled to begin at 9:00 p.m. but now two hours late—got under way as the jerry-built sound system suddenly came to life, with Belafonte opening the show with his calypso hit, "Jamaica Farewell."

The spectacle of two dozen or so "Stars for Freedom" now assembled on or near the makeshift stage was truly impressive and included, in addition to Belafonte, who emceed the proceedings, Tony Bennett, Sammy Davis Jr., Shelley Winters, Floyd Patterson, Nina Simone, Odetta, Nipsey Russell, Mike Nichols, Elaine May, Leonard Bernstein, Dick Gregory, and the Chad Mitchell Trio. They sang, told a joke or two, or just saluted to the crowd.

Simone sang "Mississippi Goddam," which she wrote in response to the murder of Medgar Evers in 1963. And

Sammy Davis Jr., who had closed his Broadway show *Golden Boy* for the night to be in Montgomery, told the crowd after singing several songs that it was "the biggest thrill of my life" to be there.

Charles E. Fager, a participant in the Selma-to-Montgomery march who worked with King, wrote that "Montgomery that night had become the place to be and be seen. . . ."

The comedic team of Nichols and May offered the audience a sketch based on a "telegram" from Gov. Wallace to President Johnson claiming he could not afford to call in state troops to protect the marchers because the cost of keeping hundreds of civil rights protesters in jail had grown so high, "to say nothing of the upkeep on cattle prods and bull whips."

For his part, Leonard Bernstein told the crowd he had come to Montgomery because "I just wanted to come down to be with you." The author James Baldwin, who was living in France but had returned to the United States for the week, said that the march marked "the beginning of the end of Negro enslavement."

Rallying the rain-soaked crowd—described by *The New York Times* as a "bedraggled band of Alabama Negroes and sympathizers"—Martin Luther King, Jr. shouted, "What do we want?" The crowd's response: "Freedom! Now!" He told them that the next day they would be engaging in "the greatest march that has ever been made on a state capitol in the South." And he exhorted "every self-respecting Negro" to join in.

But it was King's wife, Coretta, who stole the show, despite her reluctance to speak even after Belafonte insisted that she do so. Later, she recalled how dark it was that night, except for the lighted stage, and how she and her husband had struggled hand-in-hand through the crowd to get to the makeshift stage before being lifted onto it.

"I told our companions on the march," she wrote, "that this was in the area where I had grown up and spoke of how returning to Montgomery ten years after we first went there had very special meaning for me. Then I spoke directly to the women about what all this means for the future of our children." Then she read from Langston Hughes's powerful poem "Mother to Son": "Well, son, I'll tell you: / Life for me ain't been no crystal stair / It's had tacks in it / And splinters / And boards torn up / And places with no carpet on the floor / Bare / But all the time / I'se been a-climbin' on / And reachin' landin's / And turnin' corners / And sometimes goin' in the dark / Where there ain't been no light / So, boy, don't you turn back / Don't you set down on the steps / 'Cause you finds it's kinder hard / Don't you fall now / For I'se still goin', honey / I'se still climbin' / And life for me ain't been no crystal stair."

Some in the crowd, however, like the Episcopal seminarian Jonathan Daniels, thought that the festivities were bordering on a shameless publicity stunt. He said that, yes, the entertainers were "good" and some of them were even "thrilling." But during the show, he said, he felt "as if I were at a circus."

A reporter covering the event asked comedian Elaine May what she thought. "The only real circus," she replied, "is the state of Alabama and George Wallace."

Chapter 13: Loving the Hell Out of Alabama

On the morning of March 25, 1965—on what would be the last day of the march—a mass of humanity streamed into the muddy field behind the City of St. Jude, where hundreds of federal troops stood guard. Army helicopters clattered overhead.

I grabbed a cup of coffee as the tents we had slept in were taken down, and we prepared to join the rest of the marchers for a scheduled 8:30 a.m. departure. A light rain began to fall.

Harry Belafonte's wife, Julie—a ballet dancer—lined up the entertainers who had performed the night before. She had been told to move them to the head of the march. Seeing the original three hundred marchers wearing orange plastic jackets, however, she said that *they* were the real stars. "We can't march here [at the front]," she said, as she led the celebrities around behind.

Also falling in behind the original "foot soldiers" who had marched every day since Sunday were Martin Luther

King Jr., Ralph Bunche, Ralph D. Abernathy, Rev. Fred L. Shuttlesworth and other civil rights leaders. Behind them was the grandfather of Jimmie Lee Jackson, who had been killed by an Alabama state trooper in nearby Perry County and whose death had triggered the march. There, too, was Rev. Orloff Miller, a friend of James Reeb, who had been beaten to death in Selma earlier in the month. And behind them were the rest of us, now numbering about 10,000.

Califano, of the Defense Department, wrote in a report filed at 10 a.m. that marchers had been scheduled to step off at 9 a.m. but were running late "because of a lack of organization." He said the marchers were due to arrive at the capitol in Montgomery at around noon. Then, they would conduct a rally until 3 p.m. and attempt to send twenty marchers to meet Gov. Wallace, if he would have them, and disperse between 3:30 p.m. and 4:30 p.m.

That there was a "lack of organization," however, was an understatement. The delay in setting out as scheduled was also due to mixed signals—or no signals at all—that had been received by the military. Army jeeps positioned at a roadblock, for instance, prevented King's car from entering the City of St. Jude. His aide, Bernard Lee, told the soldiers that the march could not begin without King. Andrew Young jumped from the car to deliver the same message, imploring the sergeant in charge to allow the car to make a left turn. Bunche also intervened.

"I'm Dr. Bunche, undersecretary of the United Nations," he told the sergeant. "Sorry, sir," the sergeant replied. "This is not the United Nations. My orders are no left turn."

As King was getting out of the car to ask Lee what was wrong, a Montgomery police officer on a motorcycle arrived on the scene. "You danged fool," he said to the sergeant, pointing to King. "This is the man. Let him through!"

Death threats against the civil rights leader, meanwhile, continued to come in, prompting several black ministers to wear the same blue suit King wore to confuse any would-be sniper.

At 11 a.m., under sunny skies, some 10,000 marchers, led by King, moved out. At his side was his wife, Coretta, who later recalled that it was a "genuine love of justice" that drove the marchers on despite the risks. "A human torrent of brotherhood," she wrote, "engulfed the 'Cradle of the Confederacy.'"

I recall vividly marching through the African American section of Montgomery, north along Oak Street, and seeing mothers, fathers, and children cheering from ramshackle houses, urging us on.

A 17-year-old student from Hudson High School in Selma, Charles Mauldin, shouted to the onlookers, "Come march with us! You can't make your witness standing on the corner. We're going downtown. There's nothing to be afraid of." And many of them did join us, swelling our numbers to around 25,000.

From Oak Street, we headed up Mobile Street—crossing Jefferson Davis Avenue, named after the leader of the Confederacy, which amused us to no end—into Montgomery's downtown business district. Then, at Court Square, where Rosa Parks had boarded a segregated bus on December 1, 1955, and refused to give up her seat to a white passenger, triggering a citywide boycott of Montgomery's public transportation system by its African American population, we turned east onto Dexter Avenue where we could now see the Baptist church by the same name where King had served as pastor from 1954 to 1960.

As we passed the church, the street widened as we approached the whitewashed state capitol—with

Confederate flags waving above the dome—up a slight hill a block away. A line of Alabama state troopers stood between us and the capitol, where Dexter Avenue came to an end at Bainbridge Street. On the steps of the capitol, where Jefferson Davis was sworn in as president of the Confederacy in February 1861, a second line of troopers stood guard.

"This is a revolution," Andrew Young called out to us over the loudspeakers, "a revolution that won't fire a shot. . . . We come to love the hell out of the state of Alabama."

Some of the entertainers who had appeared at the "Stars for Freedom" rally the night before—Harry Belafonte; Peter, Paul, and Mary; Joan Baez; Odetta; the Chad Mitchell Trio—led the crowd in folk songs and spirituals, including "Blowin' in the Wind," "Go Tell It on the Mountain," and "This Land Is Your Land."

Then the speeches began—Ralph Bunche, A. Philip Randolph, Ralph D. Abernathy, Fred L. Shuttlesworth, John Lewis, James Farmer, Amelia Boynton—and as they did, Coretta Scott King looked over at Rosa Parks and thought about the many years of struggle, beginning with the Montgomery bus boycott a decade earlier.

"I realized we had really come a long way from our start in the bus protest," she wrote years later, "when only a handful of people, relatively speaking, were involved—all black people who were fighting for their dignity and the right to sit down in a bus. Now ten years had passed. We had desegregated the buses; we had desegregated public transportation, interstate as well as intrastate. Our right to use public accommodations had been guaranteed. We had progressed toward school integration."

But most important, she said, the issue had gained national attention. "When I looked out over the big crowd," she wrote, "I saw many white people and church people. There were more church people involved than in any demonstration we had ever had, and I said to Martin later that it was perhaps the greatest witness by the church since the days of the early Christians. I still believe that."

Finally, it was King's turn to speak and to bring the two-hour program—and the march—to an end.

"Last Sunday, more than 8,000 of us started on a mighty walk from Selma, Alabama," he began. "We have walked on meandering highways and rested our bodies on rocky byways. . . . Some of literally slept in the mud. We have been drenched by rains. Our bodies are tired and our feet are somewhat sore.

"They told us we wouldn't get here," he continued. "And there were those who said that we would get here only over their dead bodies. But all the world today knows that we are here and we are standing before the forces of power in the state of Alabama saying, 'We ain't goin' let nobody turn us around.'"

King said that the Selma movement had become a shining moment in the conscience of man. "If the worst in American life lurked in its dark streets," he said, "the best of American instincts rose passionately from across the nation to overcome it. There never was a moment in American history more honorable and more inspiring than the pilgrimage of clergymen and laymen of every race and faith pouring into Selma to face danger at the side of its embattled Negroes."

He paid his "profound respects," in particular, to the white Americans who "cherish their democratic traditions over the ugly customs and privileges of generations and come forth boldly to join hands with us.

"So I stand before you this afternoon with the conviction that segregation is on its deathbed in Alabama," he said, "and the only thing uncertain about it is how costly the segregationists and Wallace will make the funeral."

He said that some were asking how long it would take to achieve freedom and justice for all people.

"How long? Not long, because no lie can live forever. How long? Not long, because you shall reap what you sow . . . How long? Not long, because the arc of the moral universe is long, but it bends toward justice."

Chapter 14: Too Many People Just Talking

Among those in the audience listening to Martin Luther King Jr. at the end of the Selma-to-Montgomery march was a 39-year-old white mother of five, Viola Liuzzo, who had driven from her home in Detroit to participate in the march. "I want to be part of it," she told her husband before leaving.

Liuzzo had thought about making the trip after watching television coverage of "Bloody Sunday." It took her about a week, however, to make the decision to leave her family and head south. Once she did, she took off immediately, alone, in the family's powder blue 1963 Oldsmobile, telling her husband, Anthony, that there were "too many people who just stand around talking." She arrived in Selma on Friday, March 19, after three days on the road—a day before we arrived in the city following a five-day trek from Ripon, Wisconsin, by way of Washington, D.C.

A student at Detroit's Wayne State University, Liuzzo had participated in a sympathy march for the Selma protestors on March 16. She had also joined other students to discuss "Bloody Sunday" and other events in Selma with Rev. Malcolm Boyd, a chaplain at the school.

Boyd, an Episcopal priest who had worked in the South for several years seeking to ease tensions between the races, told Liuzzo and the others that some Wayne State students were planning to travel to Alabama to participate in the Selma-to-Montgomery march (although, in the end, they would not make the trip).

"He's made me do a lot of thinking," Liuzzo said later, referring to Boyd, who in 1961 had protested segregation in the public transportation system in the South, riding interstate buses with dozens of other black and white civil rights activists as one of CORE's "Freedom Riders."

On the morning of March 19, Liuzzo pulled up at Brown Chapel A.M.E. Church in Selma and was met by two African American teenagers who identified themselves as civil rights workers. They asked to borrow her car to pick up people arriving for the march at Montgomery's bus and train stations, as well as at Dannelly Field. Without hesitating, she gave them the keys.

Later that day she returned to Brown Chapel, after settling into a room that had been assigned to her across the street, to check on her car. There, she met Leroy Moton, a 19-year-old SCLC volunteer from Selma who was in charge of moving people around Montgomery in rental cars or private vehicles that had been volunteered for that purpose. He assured Liuzzo that her car was safe, and she agreed to turn it over to him for the duration of the march. On Saturday, he drove her to the City of St. Jude. She spent the rest of the day running a first-aid station for the protestors.

Up early the next day, Liuzzo asked one of the St. Jude priests, Father Timothy Deasy, if he would accompany her to the top of the church tower to take a look out over the city, and he agreed. But as she and Deasy reached the small room at the pinnacle of the tower, a strange feeling came over her, and she rushed out onto the street, where she had a full-blown panic attack. "Father," she said, "I have a feeling . . . something is going to happen today. Someone is going to get killed." After saying a prayer or two, she felt better and joined the march to downtown Montgomery.

After the march, she returned to St. Jude to retrieve her car, which she had loaned to Moton, who arrived at the complex around 6:00 p.m. with a carload of passengers— one heading to the airport and others back to Selma.

Together with Liuzzo behind the wheel, they drove west on U.S. Highway 80, dropping off the passenger at Dannelly Field, and then continued on to Selma, where they deposited the remaining four passengers.

After a quick bite to eat, they set off for Montgomery to pick up more marchers who were returning to Selma. At a traffic light near the Edmund Pettus Bridge, they were spotted by four Klansmen in a red-and-white Chevrolet Impala. Later, it would be revealed that they had spent the day looking for an opportunity to kill Martin Luther King Jr. But now, instead, they decided to attack Liuzzo and Moton to send a message to northern whites, southern blacks, and like-minded liberals.

Moton would later recall that after crossing the Edmund Pettus Bridge, Liuzzo spoke about how she hoped to become more involved in the civil rights movement when she returned to Detroit. It was dark, he said, and U.S. Highway 80, where the marchers had walked proudly and under the protection of federal troops earlier in the week, was now deserted.

"Mrs. Liuzzo was singing ["We Shall Overcome"] and talking," Moton said later, "but I didn't say a word. I almost say to her, we better turn around and go back. But then I say to myself, she probably wouldn't do it anyhow."

About twenty miles east of Selma—now in Lowndes County—the pair noticed a car following them at some distance with its headlights on high beam. After a few minutes, it pulled up alongside Liuzzo's car at high speed. There was gunfire, and fourteen bullets shattered the glass on the driver's side, killing Liuzzo instantly and sending the car off the road into a ditch. "I'm one hell of a shot," one of the Klansmen was reported to have said. "That bitch and that bastard are dead and in hell."

But Moton had survived the attack, and after playing dead, he ran out onto the highway and after some time flagged down a flatbed truck full of marchers from Selma. "A woman's been killed," he told the driver, a young minister from Richmond, California. "She's been shot!"

Liuzzo was the third civil rights activist who had been killed in Alabama in less than a month—after Jimmie Lee Jackson, who was shot by an Alabama state trooper in Marion, and James Reeb, the Unitarian Universalist minister from Boston who was beaten to death by white segregationists in Selma.

The next day condolences poured in to the Liuzzo family from around the country. President Johnson telephoned them to express his and Mrs. Johnson's sorrow at their loss. Vice President Hubert Humphrey paid a personal visit to the Liuzzo home in Detroit. And Rev. Malcolm Boyd told a reporter that Liuzzo epitomized a strong person in the movement "who didn't ask to be a leader."

"People like Mrs. Liuzzo make up the moral backbone of the movement," Boyd said. "They are committed to freedom that they are really ready to die for."

The Grand Wizard of the United Klans of America—Robert M. Shelton of Tuscaloosa, Alabama—was asked if he knew anything about Liuzzo's murder. "I don't have any knowledge of any participation in any acts of violence by any members of our organization," he said.

But in May 1965, three of the four men who had fired on Liuzzo and Moton that night—William Orville Eaton, Eugene Thomas, and Collie Leroy Wilkins Jr., all members of the KKK—were indicted on a state charge of murder and brought to trial. The fourth, Gary Thomas Rowe Jr., turned out to be an undercover FBI informant and was protected from prosecution. An all-white jury was unable to reach a decision on guilt or innocence, and a mistrial was declared. A second trial later that year ended with a verdict of not guilty. But in a subsequent federal trial, they were found guilty of conspiring to violate the civil rights of Liuzzo and were sentenced to ten years behind bars.

Chapter 15: An Heroic Christian Deed

After the Selma-to-Montgomery march, I caught a Greyhound bus packed with fellow marchers and headed north—pursuing along the way local newspapers filled with extensive coverage of the final day of the march and of the murder of Viola Liuzzo.

Some reports were skeptical, if not downright dismissive, of the march. The *Birmingham Post-Herald*, for instance, which I picked up at the bus station in Birmingham during a brief stopover, said in a front-page story that the march had been a failure. It quoted Gov. Wallace as saying that it had cost $1 million—an apparent reference to expenditures by the federal government to protect the marchers—and that known communists were among the marchers.

Wallace was quoted as saying that the delegation that had been named to deliver a petition on voting rights to him, headed by Rev. Joseph Lowery of Birmingham, included people who belonged to organizations "cited as subversive" by the House Un-American Activities Committee, as well as known felons and "some nonresidents." He said he would not be intimidated by people "who come up here in a mob."

But The Courier-Journal in Louisville, Kentucky, provided front-page coverage that was more favorable to the march, focusing on the fact that Wallace had refused to meet the Lowery-led delegation. An editorial said that Wallace and his followers were racists. "The march from Selma to Montgomery was risky," it said. "Was it worth it? Yes. It was an eloquent answer to those who believe that brutality can prevail against aroused conscience, and a living dramatization of the determination of those who are dedicated to a new day of justice in Alabama."

In Indianapolis—as the bus now closed in on my hometown of Chicago—I bought a copy of *The Indianapolis Times*, which highlighted coverage of the Liuzzo murder. The paper called it a "race killing" by a "night rider." It also provided extensive coverage of King's speech on the steps of the Alabama state capitol.

The *Chicago Daily News* used its front page on March 26 to highlight President Johnson's pledge to defeat the Ku Klux Klan, following the arrest of four KKK members in connection with Liuzzo's death.

"They struck by night as they generally do," Johnson was quoted by the newspaper as saying, "for their purposes cannot cannot stand the light of day." He said his father had fought the KKK in Texas, and that he would continue to fight them because "I believe them to threaten the peace of every community where they exist." He urged members of the shadowy organization to "get out . . . now and return to a decent society—before it is too late."

Eventually, I arrived back at Ripon College. I was happy to be "home." But for Chaplain Thompson, it was not a happy homecoming. For leading our small band of "outside agitators" to Alabama, he was rewarded with hate mail from local residents and was even declared persona non grata at his own church for two years—even as he continued to speak out in favor of what one would have thought was core value of the Christian church: nonviolence.

On returning to Ripon, Thompson told the local newspaper, *The Ripon Commonwealth-Press*, that we had just participated in "history in the making."

"As long as long as there are places in the United States where these rights are denied, it is up to us as Americans to do something about it," he said. "We can send money, but there are times when our physical presence is needed."

For my part, I was welcomed back on campus by students and faculty who were curious about the trip. I was eager to share what I had learned, and like Nancy Carter, I recall being, as she put it, "mildly surprised to find people eager to hear about our experiences."

But little on the campus had really changed. I was not naive enough to think that one trip to Selma could spark a full-blown revolution. But I had hoped that the lines between the students who thought that the racial problems in the South were none of our business and those who thought otherwise would somehow be less clearly drawn.

"People seemed to have turned their feelings around," Carter recalled, "or maybe their behavior simply became more decorous in light of so much national news coverage."

James R. Bowditch, of the Ripon College English Department, said in an Op-Ed piece in the school newspaper that the students seemed to have decided that "little of importance has happened or is happening in Alabama and across the nation."

"Perhaps if we sit tight, ignore the Medgar Everses, the Jimmie Lee Jacksons, the Reebs and Liuzzos, the bombings and the cross burnings (we are so isolated, you know)," he wrote, "the whole mess will disappear. If we can persuade ourselves that those who cause disturbance by trying to integrate a public restaurant, enter a white church, register as full citizens or march to call attention to systematic and deliberate injustice are merely rabble-rousing exhibitionists, then perhaps we can turn our attention to less painful matters. Above all, if we can convince ourselves that the true patriot is he who keeps his nose out of others' affairs, then perhaps we can really enjoy the coming spring. Perhaps."

As for me, I continued to speak out about the issue, perhaps not as aggressively or as convincingly as I should have, explaining to anyone who would listen what it had been like "down South" and making the best case I could for sending what money we could to support the ongoing work of organizations like SNCC—but more importantly, for sending people.

Chapter 16: Another Name for Lawlessness

Other activists from the North, meanwhile, remained behind after the Selma-to-Montgomery march to continue to "agitate" for justice—like Jonathan Myrick Daniels, the 26-year-old Episcopal seminarian, who had come to Alabama as part of a delegation from the Episcopal Theological School (ETS) in Cambridge, Massachusetts.

After the march, Daniels and his fellow seminarian Judith Upham made their way back to Selma, thinking about the "danger," no doubt, that King had referred to when he had talked about the white activists who had come from other parts of the country to stand "at the side of its embattled Negroes." It was not until the next day, however, that Daniels and Upham would learn—like the rest of us—about Viola Liuzzo's murder on U.S. Highway 80.

Those who knew Daniels, and those who, like him, experienced life in Alabama in the 1960s, remember it as being a frightening time. Dozens of civil rights activists—black and white—were killed by white segregationists throughout the South, and countless others were beaten or otherwise verbally and physically intimidated.

Even seasoned civil rights activists like Julian Bond, the longtime civil rights leader, said that for him and others, it was a "scary time," particularly for those working to register African Americans in Lowndes County. To African Americans, the county was known simply as "Bloody Lowndes."

But Bond, a cofounder of SNCC, which supported the work of Daniels and others throughout the South, told me before he passed away in 2015 that he also remembered the spring and summer of 1965 as a hopeful time, with the enactment, for instance, of the Voting Rights Act of 1965, signed into law by President Johnson on August 6.

The legislation—approved overwhelmingly by members of Congress who were shocked into action by the events in Selma—suspended literacy tests for prospective voters in twenty-six states, including Alabama; replaced local officials serving as voter registrars with federal examiners; and empowered the attorney general to take action against state and local authorities who imposed a poll tax on voters.

Before signing the bill, President Johnson met with civil rights leaders and others in the Oval Office at the White House, including John Lewis, the 25-year-old chairman of SNCC, who had been beaten badly by Alabama state troopers at the foot of the Edmund Pettus Bridge in Selma on "Bloody Sunday" in early March.

Lewis recalled that Johnson, his feet propped up on a chair and his hands folded behind his head, suddenly leaned forward and told him, "Now, John, you've got to go back and get those folks registered. You've got to go back and get those boys by the balls. Just like a bull gets on top of a cow.

You've got to get 'em by the balls, and you've got to *squeeze*, squeeze 'em till they *hurt*."

Recalling that he had heard that Johnson enjoyed speaking in graphic, down-home terms, Lewis said, "But I wasn't quite prepared for all those bulls and balls."

A less profane priority for Jonathan Daniels, meanwhile, was working with other like-minded clergy and laymen in Selma to break down the longstanding barriers between blacks and whites by, for example, integrating the city's only Episcopal church, St. Paul's.

He and other Episcopalians had come to Selma despite strong opposition from Alabama's Episcopal bishop, Charles C. J. Carpenter, who had made it clear that civil rights activists, especially Episcopalians, would not be welcome in his diocese.

"Civil disobedience," Carpenter said, "is just another name for lawlessness."

Efforts to integrate St. Paul's were being spearheaded in the spring of 1965 by the Reverend John B. Morris, executive director of the Episcopal Society for Cultural and Racial Unity (ESCRU), whose members had arrived in the city en masse in response to Martin Luther King Jr.'s call for support.

Morris and the other Episcopalians, including Daniels, were probably not aware that the vestry at St. Paul's met in special session on March 11 to review its policy on race relations and had voted twelve to two to allow visiting Episcopal clergy to be seated at the rear of the church for services but to leave it up to the ushers to decide whether to seat other visitors.

Shortly after arriving in Selma, Daniels and about two dozen other seminarians and clergy took their case directly to St. Paul's then-rector, the Reverend T. Frank Matthews, who, in an hour-long meeting with the group, defended the longstanding ban on blacks, arguing that church policy was church policy.

When Morris and the Reverend Malcolm Peabody, president of the ESCRU board of directors, led an interracial group to St. Paul's on March 14 (a week before the Selma-to-Montgomery march would begin), they were informed by the ushers that only clergy and white laypeople would be allowed to attend the Sunday service. So they left the church—disappointed but not surprised—after praying together for a few minutes at the front of the brownstone edifice.

Opposed to the ban on interracial worship were two prominent members of the church and of Selma's white establishment: Miller Childers, an attorney who would later be named judge of the Dallas County Court and the District Court of Dallas County, and Harry W. Gamble Jr., another lawyer whose grandfather had earlier served as rector of the church.

Childers and Gamble told me on a visit to Selma several years ago that they recall seeing Daniels among the group of Episcopalian protesters who had showed up at the church that Sunday. They said they were disgusted by what the ushers had done in turning them away.

The church vestry, according to Childers, had been meeting almost daily to discuss what to do in response to the widening civil rights protests that had been shaking up normal life in Selma since the beginning of the year. He said he was one of only two members of the vestry who initially voiced concern over the church's policy of ignoring the edict issued by the General Convention of the Episcopal Convention the previous October amending Canon 16, which prohibited the exclusion of worshippers on the basis of race, color, or ethnic origin.

Church records show that on March 19, the vestry—perhaps influenced by the negative media publicity that had begun to surround the refusal of the church to allow blacks to worship at St. Paul's—narrowly rejected a resolution directing the church to abide by the newly amended Canon 16. But on March 22—the day after the Selma-to-Montgomery march had begun—the vestry approved the resolution by eight to three, with one abstention, effectively ending the church's century-plus record of racial segregation.

It is likely that the vestry had also been influenced by the persistence of Daniels and the other Episcopalian pro-testors in calling for an end to the ban, which included a procession of about two hundred ESCRU members on March 20 from Brown Chapel to St. Paul's, led by Rev. C. Kilmer Myers, the suffragan bishop of Michigan, who had branded the Episcopal Church a "racist, caste-ridden" insti-tution. Refused entry, the group celebrated communion on a makeshift altar set up on the sidewalk and then left.

On the Sunday after the Selma-to-Montgomery march—March 28—Daniels and his fellow seminarian, Judith Upham, along with nine other whites and five blacks, were admitted to St. Paul's for the 11 a.m. service. They were seated in the front row, where they listened to Matthews speak on the "Ministry of Reconciliation" without ever mentioning race relations or the controversy within the church.

Gamble told me he recalls Daniels being "very low key and cordial," and not challenging or "in-your-face."

As for Childers, he and his family had paid a heavy price for having supported a reversal of St. Paul's policy of racial discrimination. His children were taunted by other children at school, he said, and friends and acquaintances avoided eye contact on hearing of his stand on the issue at St. Paul's. Asked why he did what he did in opposing the ban on blacks, Childers said, "I thought it was the right thing to do."

In May, after two months in Selma, Daniels returned to the Episcopal Theological School (ETS) in Cambridge, Massachusetts, for final examinations and graduation. In early July, after a brief vacation, he returned to Selma, this time by car, writing later that "something had happened to me in Selma, which meant I had to come back. I could not stand by in benevolent dispassion any longer without compromising everything I know and love and value. The imperative was too clear, the stakes too high. . . ."

In Selma, Daniels found lodging with Alice and Lonzy West and their family in the African American section of the city, across from Brown Chapel. He continued to work to fully integrate St. Paul's Episcopal Church. He sought to open channels of communication with the white community. He encouraged blacks to register to vote. And he involved himself in projects aimed at improving health care, housing, and other social services for blacks in Dallas County.

But he became increasingly frustrated with what he saw as his inability to make progress with local whites on race relations—and with the relatively routine nature of the work. "It may be too much to say I'm beginning to despair of Selma," he told Upham, who was now in St. Louis, "but at any rate I am not optimistic." So in mid-July, he decided to shift his work to neighboring Lowndes County, where SNCC was active in protesting racial discrimination and registering African Americans to vote.

On August 13, while picketing whites-only businesses in the small Lowndes County town of Fort Deposit, Daniels and about two dozen other protesters were arrested and taken by truck to the county jail in Hayneville, where most of them, including Daniels, were held for six days.

Released on August 20, Daniels and three others—Father Richard F. Morrisroe, a white Roman Catholic priest from Chicago, and two young black girls—went immediately to a local grocery store to buy a soda. Standing in the doorway was Thomas L. Coleman, a part-time deputy sheriff, armed with a shotgun, who ordered them to leave, aiming his gun at one of the girls, sixteen-year-old Ruby Sales. Daniels pushed her to the ground, and when Coleman opened fire the young seminarian took the full blast of the weapon straight on and died instantly.

A second blast from Coleman's gun struck Morrisroe in the back as he ran from the scene pulling the other girl, Joyce Bailey, with him. After several months in the hospital, Morrisroe recovered and returned to work on behalf of social justice in the Chicago area.

The next day, Coleman turned himself in, but six weeks later he was acquitted by an all-white jury after only two hours of deliberation. He died at his home in Hayneville in 1997 at the age of 86.

On hearing the news of Daniels's death, Martin Luther King Jr. called his selfless defense of Ruby Sales in Hayneville "one of the most heroic Christian deeds of which I have heard in my entire ministry. . . ."

The Very Reverend Samuel T. Lloyd III, former dean of the Washington National Cathedral, told me that Daniels, recognized as a martyr by the Episcopal Church in 1994, took a stand against racial injustice at a time when the church was, in his view, "sluggish" on civil rights. "He stood for what we hope the church stands for today," Lloyd said, "and he gave his life for it."

Rachel West, then nine years old, has said that what she remembers most about Daniels—"a part of our family" and of "every black family in Selma"—was his boyish smile. "His eyes were clear and steady," she wrote. He was friendly, she said. But most of all he was gentle. "I know there were times when he must have been frightened," she said, "but he never showed it."

She said that one day, when she was playing outside with her friends, her mother, Alice, called to her, crying. "Our friend is dead," she recalls her mother saying. "They killed Jonathan."

"I must have cried the whole night," Rachel wrote. "Of all the things that happened during that movement, nothing touched me as deeply as his death. . . . He had died trying to make peace. I'm sure that if he had had a choice, he would have preferred to have lived awhile; he was a very young person. But I also think that he preferred to die for a cause.

"From that first day he walked in with his suitcase and little knapsack," she recalled, "it was like an old friend coming home. We children loved him. . . . When Jonathan came to us, I knew for certain that there were really good white folks in this country, and with them on our side we would win our freedom."

Her mother, Alice, told me that Daniels was "like a member of the family"—even though her neighbors were at first distrustful of this young white seminarian from the North. But they soon grew to like him, she said, eventually considering him to be part of the African American community.

She said she is proud of having been active in the civil rights movement at an early age, and she considers her most important contribution to the civil rights movement housing and feeding many of the civil rights workers who came to Selma in the 1960s. She said that Daniels, who stayed with the West family for several months, was the most well-liked of what she called the "outside agitators" who boarded with her family in their five-bedroom, two-bathroom apartment, which was known as the Freedom Rights Home.

She recalled that Daniels would leave the family apartment early in the morning for civil rights work in Lowndes County and return late at night. On that fateful day in August 1965, she said, he hugged and kissed her before he left. She said he said a special prayer for the West family before walking out to his car. But he came back. "He hugged me again," she said, "and said, 'Goodbye, Mrs. West. Please hug and kiss your children for me when they wake up.'" It was the last time she saw him.

She said that the Episcopal Church flew her and her family to Keene, New Hampshire—Daniels's hometown—to attend his funeral. "I couldn't believe it," she said, "seeing Jon lying there in his casket. All the black people in Selma loved him so." One of her grandsons, she said, is named Jonathan Myrick West.

In the days following Daniels's murder, memorial services honoring the fallen Episcopal seminarian were held in cities across the United States, including St. Louis, Chicago, Atlanta, and Boston.

Rev. Malcolm Boyd, a civil rights activist who had befriended Daniels in Selma earlier that summer, said at a requiem mass at the Episcopal Church of the Atonement in Washington, D.C., on Sunday, August 22, 1965—two days after Daniels was killed—that he was "the most alive young man in the church I have met. . . ."

"Theologically, he knew what he was doing," said Boyd, who was the Episcopal Church's chaplain-at-large for colleges and universities, "and in the church . . . he was one person who was not afraid of getting involved."

But the main religious service in Daniels's honor was held two days later in his hometown of Keene, New Hampshire, where more than 1,000 mourners filed past his casket at St. James Episcopal Church on Monday, August 23, and another four hundred on the morning of August 24, prior to the 1 p.m. service.

After the service—attended by some 800 people—a small group of mourners gathered around his grave after internment at Monadnock View Cemetery, next to his father, and sang softly and with tears in their eyes "We Shall Overcome."

Prominent in the group was Stokely Carmichael, the charismatic SNCC field secretary, who later shared with Boyd, also in attendance, some notes that he had made on the program during the service that day.

"Jon was not a religious man," Carmichael wrote. "He lived a religious life. Jon did not die for us all. His life was taken from him. Jon lived for us all. Jon did not get his strength from rituals. He got his strength from people. From whence cometh my strength? My strength cometh not from the hills. My strength cometh from men like Jon. Jon was not a follower of Christ. He lived like Christ."

The previous night, at a mass meeting of African American residents in Lowndes County, Carmichael had said that crying over Daniels's death was not for him. "We ain't going to resurrect Jon," he said. "We're going to resurrect ourselves."

Carmichael had also exhorted the crowd to action, saying that African Americans were more committed to change now than ever before. "We're going to tear this country up," he said. "We're going to build it back up, until it's a fit place for human beings."

His friendship with Daniels, he said later, was forged earlier that month when they were arrested with some two dozen other civil rights workers in Fort Deposit, Alabama, while picketing local stores for equal job opportunities.

"I was a little uneasy even about the picket itself," Carmichael later wrote, "which would be . . . the first direct action not directly related to voting in the county. But, I thought, hey, a public demonstration in the middle of the day. The media will be there. What can happen?"

The demonstration, in fact, turned out to be shorter than planned because a group of men from the Ku Klux Klan had been waiting for them. "We were immediately surrounded by a mob larger than the demonstration," he said, adding that it was one time he was not sorry to be arrested. At the jail in Hayneville, he said, the guards were quick to single out Daniels and Father Richard F. Morrisroe—the only two whites among those who were arrested—for abuse.

Initially, Carmichael said, he had opposed Daniels and other whites working in Lowndes County. "This was not because we had any formal policy of excluding them," he said. "We simply did not encourage them. At that time [in Lowndes County], it was really like operating behind enemy lines."

Ruby Sales, whose life Daniels saved by shielding her from the shotgun blast outside the grocery store in Hayneville on August 20, said that one reason for the hesitancy among some blacks to allow white activists to work in Lowndes County—a Klan stronghold—was that their presence would incite local whites to violence.

"I was very afraid of unleashing uncontrolled violence because of Lowndes County's history," Sales told an interviewer. "But ultimately it was decided that the movement was an open place and should provide an opportunity for anyone who wanted to come and struggle against racism to be a part of that struggle."

Carmichael said later that he had been devastated by Daniels' murder. "He'd been in Selma a while and would always seek me out for serious discussions whenever I was there," he recalled. "I appreciated his intelligence and seriousness. In this he was a little different from the usual white activists you met. He was somewhat more thoughtful and analytic. Tried to think things through, didn't trot out glib slogans but was looking for lasting solutions. . . . He was shocked and pained by the racism, injustice, and poverty he was seeing. . . . I thought Jon was an impressive guy, very responsible. . . . But what I should have said [to him] very firmly was, please, stay the heck away from Lowndes."

As a SNCC project director, and having known Daniels so well, Carmichael was asked to personally inform the young seminarian's parents of their son's death. So he flew to New York City to pick up his mother for the drive to Keene.

"I had never seen my son like that," his mother, Mabel, recalled. "Silent, grim, like a heavy, heavy weight was pressing on him. Even when his father died, that had really hit him, but this was different. . . . [It was] the only time he ever asked me to go with him on movement business. He told me the young man was his friend."

She said that her son said nothing during the entire trip. "He didn't even play the [car] radio," she said. When they arrived in Keene, he and Daniels's parents went into another room in the house. "I believe Stokely was crying," his mother said. "He never told me what was said. The trip back in the car was just as silent. I do think this was the hardest thing my son ever had to do in the movement."

Others who knew Daniels also said that his death and the acquittal by an all-white jury of his white assassin, Thomas L. Coleman, had clearly traumatized Carmichael. "He became distrustful of practically all whites," wrote Jack Nelson, the veteran civil rights reporter for *The Los Angeles Times*. "I could see the changes in him, watching as he turned bitter and cynical, cursing his country and saying that democracy was a failure."

It is unclear, however, to what extent Daniels' murder triggered—or contributed to—Carmichael's eventual rejection of nonviolence as a means of achieving racial justice.

His immediate reaction to the murder was to bring in ten of SNCC's most experienced field secretaries to Lowndes County to work on voter registration. "We want to show the people that we are not afraid of Lowndes County," he said, "and that they can't run us out." He said he wanted to see at least four thousand African Americans registered to vote—up from none in March—by the time the additional field secretaries left the county.

Carmichael later wrote that after Daniels was murdered, African Americans in Alabama saw no other choice than to prepare to defend themselves, and so they did.

"Jon's murder grieved us," he wrote. "His wasn't the first death we'd experienced. But it was in some ways the closest to me as an organizer. . . . But we couldn't let that stop the work. That's precisely what the killers intended. However, from then on, a little too late, the [SNCC] project staff took the strong position, nonnegotiable, that to allow whites in would be tantamount to inviting their deaths. That became our policy. And we armed ourselves. . . . We made a mistake with Jonathan. One that I always remember with regret."

The radicalization of the civil rights movement became clear the following year when, at a SNCC meeting near

Nashville, Tennessee, in May 1966, Carmichael was elected its new leader, replacing John Lewis, a staunch advocate of nonviolence.

Earlier that year, several SNCC dissidents working in Atlanta with the Vine City Project under the leadership of Bill Ware had put forward a paper calling for severing all ties with white activists. It would become, in retrospect, the opening volley in a pivotal struggle among blacks over the control of SNCC and the future direction of the movement.

"If we are to proceed toward liberation," the paper argued, "we must cut ourselves off from white people." It said that whites should only play a minor role at best in civil rights activities or political organizing among African Americans. "We must form our own institutions, credit unions, co-ops, political parties, write our own histories."

Not surprisingly, the paper caused an uproar among some members of the SNCC leadership, and Carmichael was forced to defend white workers against criticism from within the organization, underscoring his relatively complicated views on interracial cooperation.

But by June of that year, he had abandoned any hope he might have had of working toward racial integration (although he would maintain his commitment to forming biracial progressive coalitions whenever possible), pinning his hopes instead on achieving economic and political power for all African Americans.

"What had happened in Alabama is that we started building something, and we made whites irrelevant to everything we did," Carmichael said in a June 1966 interview published in the *Movement*, SNCC's monthly magazine, in which he outlined what he and his colleagues had done to create an all-black political party in Lowndes County—later a model for the Black Panther Party, which was launched in Oakland, California, at the end of the year. "When you talk about going for power, moral force and nonviolence become completely irrelevant. When you go for power, you go for it the way everyone in the country goes for it."

Carmichael went on to criticize white liberals for "cutting out" when the chips were down, leaving poor blacks holding the bag. "But if you didn't depend on them for anything," he said, "you could do anything you wanted to do."

Some critics, like James T. Patterson, the historian, have dismissed "Black Power," which Carmichael employed for first time publicly in Greenwood, Mississippi, in June 1966, as "a vague and combative slogan."

But Carmichael—an alumnus of the nonviolent civil rights movement who turned militant, reflecting the mood among many African Americans at the time—understood its deeper significance, noting at a rally of supporters in Selma on November 7, 1966, that they did not have to waste their time arguing over the meaning of Black Power. "They understood [it]," he said.

For the rest of this life, until his death in 1998 in self-imposed exile in Guinea at the age of fifty-seven, Carmichael would argue that seizing political power and not depending on legal remedies or moral suasion was the only way that racial justice in the United States could be achieved.

Chapter 17: 'He's Coming to Start Riots'

Several years ago, I attended a seminar at Concordia College in Selma an historically black educational institution, which has since closed. In the back of the room was an elderly, bearded, black man who frequently rose from his seat to shout at the top of his lungs, "Black Power!" "Black Power!" "Black Power!"

I did not recognize him at first. Curious, I asked the man next to me who he was. "That's Mukasa Dada," he replied. "Who?" I asked. "Maybe you know him better," he said, "as Willie Ricks."

Indeed I did. It was difficult, in fact, *not* to have known him when I ventured south in the mid-1960s. He was everywhere: Georgia, Alabama, Louisiana, Mississippi. Stirring up crowds. And stirring up trouble.

Martin Luther King Jr. called him a "fiery orator." His preacher-like speaking style earned him the nickname "The Reverend."

An associate of Stokely Carmichael, Ricks was one of the most charismatic and effective organizers that the movement had ever known: the brains and brawn behind countless sit-ins, marches, demonstrations, and boycotts throughout the South. And it was Ricks, one of the most militant members of SNCC, who thrust "Black Power" into the forefront of the consciousness of countless African Americans—not only in the South but across the country.

Earl Johnston Jr., director of the now-defunct Mississippi State Sovereignty Commission—a state-funded intelligence agency that was charged with working to preserve racial segregation—once reported to his fellow commission members that he had heard that Ricks was on his way to Jackson, the state capital.

"He's coming to start riots," Johnston wrote in an internal memo. "Our informant states he hopes this does not happen, because there will be trouble if Ricks comes here."

Perhaps his most notable public appearance, however, would not come in Jackson but in Greenwood, Mississippi, when, in June 1966, he urged Carmichael to use the phrase "Black Power" as a slogan for the movement for the first time. And he did.

At an outdoor rally that evening, Carmichael mounted the speakers' platform and after arousing the audience with a powerful attack on the Mississippi state justice system shouted, "We have been saying 'freedom' for six years and we ain't got nothing. What we are gonna start saying now is 'Black Power!'" Whereupon Ricks jumped to the platform and shouted to the stirred-up crowd, "What do you want?" And the the crowd roared, "Black Power!" Again and again, Ricks cried, "What do you want?" and the "Black Power" response from the crowd grew louder and louder until it reached a fever pitch.

According to Carmichael, who has often been (inaccurately) credited with (or blamed for) introducing the phrase, the notion of black power was nothing new.

"We'd been talking about nothing else in the Delta for years," he wrote. "The only difference was that this time [in Greenwood, Mississippi] the national media were there. . . . As I passed [Ricks], he said, 'Drop it now. The people are ready. Drop it now.'"

In fact, the phrase had been around for years. Richard Wright had used it in the title of his book on African politics, published in 1954. The African American singer, actor, and activist Paul Robeson used it, too. And Harlem politician Adam Clayton Powell Jr. had also employed it, telling students at Howard University in a May 1966 baccalaureate address, for instance, "to demand these God-given rights is to seek black power."

But it was Ricks, a 23-year-old SNCC field secretary at the time, who pushed "Black Power!" as a slogan to replace King's more docile admonition to his followers: "Freedom Now!"

An early activist, Ricks joined the struggle for racial justice as a high school student in Chattanooga, Tennessee. Following the murder of a close friend during a civil rights protest, he grew increasingly militant. Soon, he was calling himself a black nationalist and supporting armed self-defense for his fellow African Americans. His attitude toward whites has been described as hostile.

A reporter for *The New York Times*, Roy Reed, who knew Ricks on a first-name basis in the 1960s, has said that Ricks told him one day that there would be revolution in the United States and that, in fact, it was already under way and that it would lead to the deaths of many white people. Then, looking the reporter straight in the eyes, he said, "When the revolution gets here, and if I ever see you in the sights of my gun, I'll pull the trigger."

Years later, Reed, who died in 2017, wrote that he knew Ricks was serious.

After the seminar in Selma several years ago, I asked Ricks what he thought about white people today. He said he has never had anything against individual white people, and that his motivation for supporting the expulsion of whites from SNCC was rooted in the belief that the struggle for black rights needed to be led by blacks and that white liberals should organize poor whites and fight racism in their own communities.

The next day, Ricks told me that he believes that blacks need to create their own future. He said he admired Martin Luther King Jr.—"a servant of the people"—but, along with Carmichael and others, he simply had had a disagreement with him over strategy.

For his part, King has called "Black Power" an "unfortunate choice of words." After Carmichael and Ricks had spoken to the crowd in Greenwood, Mississippi, he asked them—along with Floyd McKissick, the leader of the Congress of Racial Equality (CORE)—to a meeting to discuss the issue. For five hours, he said, he pleaded with them to abandon the "Black Power" slogan.

"It was my contention that a leader has to be concerned about the problem of semantics," King said. "The slogan 'Black Power' carried the wrong connotations. . . . I conceded the fact that we must have slogans. But why have one that would confuse our allies, isolate the Negro community and give many prejudiced whites, who might otherwise be ashamed of their anti-Negro feeling, a ready excuse for self-justification?" He said that the words "black" and "power" together give the impression that the issue being talked about is black domination rather than black equality.

King said that behind the "Black Power" slogan's "legitimate and necessary concern for group unity and black identity" lies the belief that there can be a separate black road to power and fulfillment. "Few ideas are more unrealistic," he said. "There is no salvation for the Negro through isolation. . . . In a multiracial society no group can make it alone."

But Carmichael and McKissick were adamant, arguing that King's proposal to use "Black Consciousness" or "Black Equality" as slogans lacked the "ready appeal and persuasive force" of "Black Power." The meeting ended with the staff members of King's Southern Christian Leadership Conference (SCLC) agreeing that the "Black Power" slogan was unfortunate and would only divert attention from the evils of racism and with the staff members of CORE and SNCC insisting that it should be spread nationwide.

And indeed it was, with Carmichael exploiting his strident rhetoric and evolving black power philosophy to oust John Lewis—a civil rights pioneer, cofounder of SNCC, and staunch advocate of nonviolence—as the chairman of the organization. Its new objective, he said in an interview with SNCC's monthly magazine *The Movement* in June 1966, was to make whites "irrelevant to everything we did." In the interview, he also outlined what he and his colleagues had done to create an all-black political party in Alabama's Lowndes County, which would later become a model for the Black Panther Party, launched in Oakland, California, at the end of the year.

The distinguished African American historian Clayborne Carson, director of the Martin Luther King Jr. Research and Education Institute, has said that Carmichael's popularization of black power as a driving force of the civil rights movement opened a new chapter in the transformation of the political consciousness of African Americans, particularly among those—mainly in the urban centers of the North—whose hopes were raised by the nonviolent civil rights struggle but that remained unfulfilled.

"It was during the year of Carmichael's chairmanship that SNCC acquired unprecedented importance as a source of new political ideas," Carson wrote. "SNCC did not itself change the direction of black politics, but it did reflect a shift in the focus of black struggles from the rural South to the urban North and from civil rights reforms to complex, interrelated problems of poverty, powerlessness and cultural subordination. . . . Millions of black people were prepared to adopt the rhetoric of black power in order to express their accumulated anger and to assume new, more satisfying racial identities."

For the rest of this life, Carmichael would argue that seizing political power—and not depending on legal remedies or moral suasion—was the only realistic path to racial justice in the United States.

Yet internal divisions within SNCC and the rise in racial violence hampered the ability of the organization, according to Carson, to transform black discontent into programs for achieving black power.

"[A]s it became more isolated from former white allies and more openly identified with uncontrollable urban black militancy," Carson wrote, "[SNCC] encountered ruthless government repression [and] their message would reach an ever-decreasing number of blacks."

Chapter 18: A Good Fight in Chattanooga

Willie Ricks was born in Chattanooga, Tennessee, on February 18, 1943. His parents were sharecroppers from northern Alabama, and his early years were spent stealing hubcaps and engaging in other forms of petty crime. He he has said, however, that he was basically a "nice lil' guy. I didn't do nothing too bad."

He said he hung around pool halls drinking and "just being wild." He dropped out of high school, and in late 1959 and early 1960, he began working with other students at Howard High School, including his twin sister Betty Joyce, to organize sit-ins and other forms of protest at department stores, movie theaters and lunch counters in downtown Chattanooga.

At first, they were ignored. But soon, as the protests escalated, gangs of white students began to organize counter-demonstrations and to attack their black counterparts. Thousands of people eventually poured into the downtown streets of Chattanooga, throwing bricks, rocks and other objects at the black protesters.

"We had a good fight," Ricks later recalled, describing the black-led demonstrations in Chattanooga in early 1960 as a "major rebellion."

It was about this time he first heard the word nonviolence. "I was looking [at] that man [who said it] and I as like . . . that's the craziest shit I've ever heard in my life."

By late February, then-Mayor P.R. Olgiati had had enough and ordered the fire department to break up the demonstration, prompting the use of high-powered fire hoses against peaceful civil rights protestors for the first time in the South.

"Everybody got wet," Olgiati said. "I got wet, too. But it broke it up, see."

Ricks said that he joined SNCC, which was established at Shaw University in Raleigh, North Carolina, in April 1960, even as his involvement in protests in Chattanooga were continuing and confrontations between blacks and whites were escalating.

An item published in the March 1961 edition of the SNCC newsletter *The Student Voice* said that "harassment" had begun to "plague" demonstrations at segregated movie theaters in downtown Chattanooga "as arrests and ducktail hair white youths moved in on the [black] students."

"Rocks were hurled in the first racial tiff after shoving incident at a downtown movie," the item said, adding that the incident had been triggered by the arrest of 18-year-old Willie Ricks on charges of disorderly conduct. It said that Ricks had already been fined three times in connection with direct action "Stand-Ins" at the Rogers Theatre on Market Street. The movie being shown at the theatre at the time was "Hell is a City."

The Ricks family, according to the report, had also received threatening phone calls on a number of occasions. On March 15, the report said, a cross was burned in the front yard of their home, compliments of the Ku Klux Klan.

From Chattanooga, where he earned a reputation as one of the city's most effective organizers, Ricks was recruited by the Rev. C.T. Vivian, a pastor in Chattanooga and an early SNCC leader, to move to Atlanta to organize mass protests in southwest Georgia.

At 35 years old, Vivian had already spent more than a decade on the front lines of the civil rights movement, working initially in Nashville alongside other leaders of the movement, including Diane Nash, James Bevel and John Lewis.

Vivian joined SNCC in 1960, and the following year he and other members of the organization traveled to Mississippi to participate in the so-called Freedom Rides on buses throughout the South, which challenged the failure of the state and local authorities to enforce rulings by the U.S. Supreme Court outlawing racial segregation on public buses. He and other SNCC protesters were arrested in Jackson, Mississippi, and transferred to the Mississippi State Penitentiary in Parchman—also known as Parchman Farm—where they were beaten and tortured.

Ricks remained in Atlanta working out of the SNCC office and recruiting students at area colleges and universities and spearheading non-violent direct action aimed at desegregating local restaurants, movie theaters and other public and private facilities.

He has said that, to him, the most important aspect of his work has been to sit down with and talk to people, "winning their confidence and letting them show you the need to come together to protest this or that."

Gwendolyn Robinson, a student at Atlanta's Spelman College, recalled meeting Ricks in 1962 when she was a freshman at the school.

"I began to go to the SNCC office between classes or at other times—although it was against Spelman's rules," she has said. "To have been caught going there could have been grounds for suspension or even expulsion."

She said that Ricks would alternate between "cajoling and lambasting" her and her fellow students for not participating in SNCC-sponsored sit-ins and other protest demonstrations in downtown Atlanta. "He'd stand there in his blue-jean overalls talking about how the SNCC folks were making history while we studied it," she said.

It was not until the following year, however, that Ricks, who had just turned 20 years old, would take his unorthodox and often confrontational tactics to a new level.

Alabama Gov. George C. Wallace had begun the new year by proclaiming in his inaugural address on January 14, 1963, "segregation now, segregation tomorrow, segregation forever," which became a rallying cry for those opposed to the ongoing work of Ricks and other civil rights activists throughout the South.

It was partly Wallace's hard-line stance that led many SNCC staffers, including Ricks, to travel 150 miles west to Birmingham, Alabama, in early 1963 to lend their support to what would become known as the Birmingham Campaign.

Martin Luther King Jr., who led the campaign, would later call Birmingham "probably the most thoroughly segregated city in the United States."

Former U.S. Secretary of State Condoleezza Rice, who was born in Birmingham in 1954, has written that the city was steeped in racism. It was "a very scary place," she wrote, noting that her father would sit on the front porch of their home at night with a loaded shotgun in his lap—not believing in nonviolence, she said, in the face of violence.

"What I can remember most from this time," Rice wrote in *Extraordinary, Ordinary People: A Memoir of Family,* "is the sound of bombs going off in neighborhoods, including our own."

An earlier, less successful iteration of the Birmingham Campaign was launched in the city in the mid-1950s by the Rev. Fred L. Shuttlesworth, pastor of the Bethel Baptist Church, who had created the Alabama Christian Movement for Human Rights (ACMHR) in 1956 (after the city had banned the NAACP) to challenge the city's segregation policies through lawsuits and protests. Later, he helped found the SCLC, headed by King.

In 1962, after his arrest and imprisonment for violating the city's segregation laws, Shuttlesworth invited King to come to Birmingham to lend his prestige to the movement, and on April 3, 1963, Shuttlesworth issued a "manifesto" formally launching the Birmingham Campaign.

The manifesto, among other demands, called for the desegregation of rest rooms, lunch counters and water fountains in downtown stores; the hiring of blacks by local businesses; and the creation of a biracial committee to devise a timetable for the desegregation of other aspects of city life.

Over the next few weeks—until mid-May—SCLC led a series of marches, sit-ins, boycotts and other forms of non-violent direct action which eventually forced the municipal government to scrap its discriminatory laws.

Thousands were arrested and jailed, including King, who in mid-April wrote his now-famous "Letter from Birmingham Jail" in response to an open letter by seven local religious leaders published in the *Birmingham News* on April 12.

The religious leaders—Christians and Jews—had called for an end to the mass demonstrations being led by King. "We recognize the natural impatience of people who feel that their hopes are slow in being realized," they wrote. "But we are convinced that these demonstrations are unwise and untimely . . . [They] have not contributed to the resolution of our local problems."

Racial matters, they said, should properly be pursued in the courts. "When rights are consistently denied a cause should be pressed in the courts and in negotiations among local leaders, and not in the streets." It said that the demonstrations were being led "in part by outsiders."

In response, while confined to jail for violating a court injunction against street protests, King set out the case for pursuing nonviolent civil disobedience as a means of addressing racial injustice.

King said in his letter, dated April 16, that, yes, he was not from Alabama but that he had come to Birmingham "because injustice is here."

"Injustice anywhere is a threat to justice everywhere," he wrote in one of his most widely quoted sentences. "We are caught in an inescapable network of mutuality, tied in a single garment of destiny. Whatever affects one directly, affects all indirectly."

King said he was sorry that the clergymen, even as they were deploring the demonstrations, had shown no concern for the conditions that had prompted the protests. "It is unfortunate that demonstrations are taking place in Birmingham," he said, "but it is even more unfortunate that the city's white power structure left the Negro community with no alternative."

After more than a week in jail, King was released on April 20. Street protests and sit-ins at segregated lunch counters continued over the next two weeks.

One of Willie Ricks' mentors, James Forman, the executive secretary of SNCC, had arrived in the city in early April with the purpose of, as he later put it, making the demonstrations "as militant as we could."

He had played a major role in moving SNCC from being an organization that served simply as a gathering place for the leaders of local student movements to being an effective organizer of mass protests throughout the Deep South. But Shuttlesworth had told Forman that he did not appreciate him coming to Birmingham and establishing a "SNCC chapter," which included Willie Ricks, who, according to Forman, was "an excellent student organizer."

Nevertheless, Forman and Shuttlesworth were able to work together with other movement leaders to pressure the local white establishment to give in to their demands.

Forman has written, however, that he and Ricks grew frustrated with the prevailing strategy of encouraging the arrest and jailing of as many demonstrators as possible in order to fill the city prisons to overflowing. He said that on May 6, for example, several hundred protesters led by the comedian, Dick Gregory, were arrested shortly after leaving the Sixteenth Street Baptist Church to march downtown. "I did not see much strategy in people walking from the church into waiting police vans," Forman wrote.

So the next day, he and Dorothy Cotton, of SCLC, gathered some people together to "get downtown and create some disturbance," as Forman later wrote. Hundreds turned out.

"We decided to call our demonstrations 'Operation Confusion' [and] split the people into about fifteen groups and sent them downtown by different routes," Forman wrote in his memoir, *The Making of Black Revolutionaries.* "Some headed for the bus station, others to the post office. And we sent a small decoy group straight down the usual street of the marches, to fool the police. It worked. . . . [T]he police were thrown into confusion."

He said that, in downtown Birmingham, he and Ricks put themselves at the front of a group and began weaving people in and out of stores and around corners. People were singing, picketing and sitting-in. No arrests were made, and the police were taken completely by surprise.

But by that afternoon the city's police chief, Eugene "Bull" Connor, had begun closing off the streets and erecting barricades in an attempt to curtail the movement of the protesters. Fire trucks were brought out. At a local park, several students ran around the barricades, and Forman and Ricks joined them.

"The police started shooting water on people," Forman wrote. "Bricks and rocks started flying back at the police and the firemen. For forty-five minutes, there was a chase in and out of the alleys and streets. Other black people joined in the fight against the police."

The next day, May 8, King announced an agreement with local business leaders to work with the city on implementing the protesters' demands, and the mass street demonstrations were called off, infuriating Shuttlesworth and Forman, who wanted to push for greater concessions.

Forman wrote later that Attorney General Robert F. Kennedy and Burke Marshall, head of the civil rights division at the Justice Department, had pressured King into ending the protests.

"People had become too militant for the government's liking and Dr. King's image," Forman wrote. "I felt that the masses of young people who were the backbone of the protest in Birmingham and throughout the South had been cheated once more."

Chapter 19: SNCC Kids and the 'Bad Nigra'

Back in southwest Georgia, in the summer of 1963, the principal challenge facing SNCC organizers like Willie Ricks was staying out of jail. Or avoiding bombs. Or bullets. Or beatings.

It was dangerous work. Yet dozens of black and white students and other "SNCC kids," like Ricks, toiled day and night to register black voters and to organize mass demonstrations, despite the risks, in towns and cities across the the state.

Their leader was a 26-year-old African American by the name of Charles Sherrod, a veteran of the so-called Albany Movement in 1961–1962 and a strong proponent of bringing white students from the North to work alongside blacks in the South.

Sherrod argued that using whites as voter registration volunteers was necessary "to strike at the very root of segregation [which is] the idea that white is superior. . . . We can only [break that image] if [local blacks] see white and black

150

people working together, side by side, the white man no more and no less than his black brother, but human beings together."

Others SNCC leaders, however, disagreed, contending that there were already too many white people in the movement.

Hollis Watkins, a SNCC staffer working in Mississippi, reflected the views of many, including Ricks, when he said that whites from the North would destroy the grassroots civil rights institutions that were being built by the local population.

"For the first time," he said, "we had local people who had begun to take the initiative themselves and do things. For the first time, we had local Mississippians who were making decisions. . . . We felt that with a lot of students from the North coming in, being predominantly white, that they would come in and overshadow the grassroots organizations. . . ."

A SNCC report at the time said, moreover, that it was too dangerous for whites to work in Mississippi—"too dangerous for them and too dangerous for the Negroes who would be working with them."

The report also cited the "higher pitch" of white "terror" in Mississippi than in Georgia, where Charles Sherrod continued to press ahead with a staff of eleven "SNCC kids," including several whites.

One of those kids was Peter de Lissovoy, a former Harvard University student from Illinois, who said that Sherrod was a strict disciplinarian, although sweet and reserved.

"He scared me," de Lissovoy recalled. "Everybody had a bit of a problem with Sherrod, because that was partly what he was there for, to keep a pack of boisterous SNCC kids in line."

Another SNCC kid was John Perdew, the son of a college professor from California who dropped out of Harvard when he heard that SNCC was recruiting white students from the North to work in Georgia. He has said that he wanted to do something "adventurous and different." He drove to Albany in the summer of 1963, and "then I got my ass kicked"—spending three weeks in jail in August 1963 for participating in a civil rights march. Later, he served three months in jail on multiple charges of unlawful assembly, disorderly conduct and insurrection.

Also working out of Sherrod's SNCC office in Albany was 23-year-old Prathia Hall, who was the daughter of the husband and wife team who founded the Mount Sharon Baptist Church in inner-city Philadelphia. She was also a highly accomplished Baptist preacher.

In her preaching, Hall often spoke of her dream for the future in America—a refrain that inspired Martin Luther King Jr. to use the phrase "I have a dream" in his now-famous speech on the steps of the Lincoln Memorial in Washington, D.C., during the March on Washington in August 1963.

"Prathia Hall is one of the platform speakers I would prefer not to follow," King has been quoted as saying.

The youngest of Sherrod's "kids" in southwest Georgia—and certainly the least educated, at least formally—was Willie Ricks, who had just turned 21.

Like Sherrod, Ricks was already a veteran of the movement, having, at the age of 17, worked with other students at Chattanooga's Howard High School to organize non-violent protests in the city; recruited students for SNCC at Spelman College in Atlanta at the age of 19; and participated in the Birmingham Campaign at the age of 20.

Now in Georgia, working under Sherrod's leadership, Ricks was among dozens of SNCC workers arrested in or around Albany in the spring of 1963 on various charges related to their direction action activities.

A 27-page report by Sherrod on SNCC's "Southwest Georgia Project," submitted to the SNCC Coordinating Committee on December 27, 1963, said that SNCC personnel had been fighting segregation during the year through sit-ins, stand-ins, picketing, marching, promoting voter registration and supporting "buying and economic withdrawal projects," i.e., boycotts.

It said that Ricks had been arrested on May 17, along with SNCC's Jack Chatfield, while demonstrating in front of City Hall in Albany. Prathia Hall had also been arrested with two other SNCC women for handing out leaflets. And Sherrod himself had been arrested for failing to yield the right of way while driving a bus.

By mid-July, the report said, more than 100 people had been imprisoned, including Ricks, who had been arrested on June 20 on a charge of inciting a riot.

Handling Ricks' case in court—along with those of many of the other SNCC kids who had been thrown in jail—was C.B. King (no relation to Martin Luther King Jr.), the sole black attorney in southwest Georgia. His legal assistant was Dennis Roberts, a white law student at the University of California, Berkeley, who had come to Georgia to work on civil rights under a program sponsored by the National Lawyers Guild.

In a daily journal kept at the time, Roberts wrote that he had visited the jail and found the conditions to be atrocious.

"The cells are unbelievably filthy; smells of human excretion overwhelm you on entering," Roberts wrote on June 22. "Puddles of water covered the floor. . . . 14 Negro males were stuffed into a 4 man cell and will remain there for at least a week until they come to trial. Of course sleeping is impossible. In another 4 bunk cell (no mattresses) are seven white girls, all SNCC workers."

Roberts wrote on June 26 that the case involving Ricks concerned charges of disorderly conduct at a mass meeting, which Roberts described as "clearly constitutionally permissible conduct." But the judge nevertheless fined him $200 and ordered him to prison for 60 days "as Willie is . . . a 'bad nigra'."

"The damnedest part of this farce is that we have to watch the judge overrule every defensive pleading we filed without so much courtesy as to even pretending that he read it," Roberts wrote. "Attorney King hands it to him, he puts it aside, and says 'overruled'."

A week later, obviously depressed, Roberts wrote that fewer people were now attending mass meetings being held at churches and other venues. Fewer people were also participating in demonstrations, he said, and fewer people still were willing go to jail.

"However, this doesn't mean that [Albany Police Chief Laurie] Pritchett and the whites of Albany have defeated the Negroes of Albany," Roberts observed. "Rather, what they have done is drive some of the people underground so that weapons are being collected, and people are sitting home with guns, or hanging around bars and arguing, but not doing anything in a positive and constitutionally permissible manner. . . . . .[I]t is a matter of one more incident, another rape, or beating, or abuse, and the dissatisfied and disenfranchised, who no longer have the patience to listen to the leaders of the Movement, will take their guns, their dynamite, their gasoline bombs, and go out into the streets. . . . I wake up every morning and am a little surprised that nothing has happened the night before, but I don't know how long this can last. The sporting goods stores in town have no more rifles."

Roberts said that, meanwhile, Ricks and Perdew continued to languish in jail along with another SNCC activist, Lana Mae Thrower. He said that de Lissovoy and Phil Davis, a 24-year-old white SNCC staffer from Detroit, could have been released on bond but had elected to stay in jail with Perdew, "as it is extremely dangerous for the white males to be in jail alone as they are put in cells with local whites who take great delight in beating them."

Roberts said that Ricks was being held in the Albany city jail on a state charge of inciting a riot, and Thrower and Perdew were being detained on state charges of assault with intent to murder, a felony—Perdew for allegedly throwing a rock or brick at a police car. "The bonds for all three are about $1900 each," Roberts wrote, "and this money has been very difficult to raise."

For more than two weeks, from June 28 to July 13, Ricks survived in prison on a diet of bread and water, before being "bonded out" by SNCC on July 14.

"When I came down to get [Ricks] out [of jail]," Roberts wrote, noting that Ricks was extremely weak, "one of the officials asked me 'you come after a nigger,' and I politely told him, 'No, a Negro' and he just got a real surprised look on his face and didn't say anything more."

After his release, Ricks headed north about 50 miles to the city of Americus, in Sumter County. Not long after arriving, he was charged with contributing to the delinquency of minors for encouraging about 2,000 local black students to stay out of school on August 3 to protest the jailing of some of their fellow students.

SNCC Executive Secretary James Forman, based in Atlanta, later praised Ricks for being "busy on the scene [in Americus], working again with young people. . . ."

Forman said that August was the "longest, hottest month of all" in Americus, beginning on August 8 when about 250 people who were attending a mass meeting at the Friendship Baptist Church left the church to march a block or so to a "colored" cafe, singing "We Shall Overcome." For a while, the police stood by without acting but shortly began shooting in the air and ordering the crowd to disperse.

"The police and troopers then moved in with guns and billy clubs," Forman wrote, "slugging their way through the group to arrest SNCC Field Secretary Don Harris—whom they considered its leader. He was beaten and dragged to a squad car. SNCC workers Ralph Allen and John Perdew were also beaten and arrested." All were charged with attempting to incite insurrection, inciting a riot, obstructing a lawful arrest and holding an unlawful assembly.

The next day, 175 people turned out to protest the arrests; many of them were beaten and arrested as well. Another group of 25 people knelt in prayer at the police station on August 11 and were also arrested. On August 17, thirty-five more people were arrested while praying in front of the police station.

Throughout the fall, when not behind bars, Willie Ricks focused on voter registration. On one occasion, he was arrested in Albany on a charge of disorderly conduct. Arrested with him were two young black girls—Shirley Gaines (16) and LaVette Christian (11). Their "crime": accompanying several African Americans to the Dougherty County courthouse to register to vote.

Gaines and Christian, in fact, were among dozens of local young girls who were at the front lines of the Albany protests throughout 1963, including LeVette's 14-year-old sister, Joanne. She was arrested thirteen times and spent a total of 60 days in jail.

Toward the end of the year, on December 24, Ricks accompanied another prospective voter to the county courthouse, and on entering the building they took a seat on a bench and waited for the registrar to call them. According to a SNCC report on the incident, the deputy sheriff happened to be there and approached Ricks, swearing at him and telling him to get up.

Ricks stood up, the report said, and the officer then told him to move to another bench nearby.

"Willie stood there," according to the report. "[The deputy sheriff] then grabbed Willie and dragged him about 3 or 4 feet from the bench and threw him the rest of the way. . . . After that, Willie started to write down what had happened. [The deputy sheriff] said, 'You write down anything and I'll knock the hell out of you.' Then he walked away. Then, the custodian came up to Willie and said, 'This is my courthouse and don't you try to take over.' Willie then stood by the door to the registrar's office, about 3 feet from the door and against the wall. John Senn, deputy registrar, swore at him and told him he was in the way. He then slammed the door in Willie's face."

James Forman wrote later that by the end of 1963 SNCC had developed and continued to develop projects throughout the South and elsewhere at an "overwhelming pace."

"Everywhere there were projects developing and repression mounting," he wrote. "[W]e had projects going in Alabama, Mississippi, Georgia, Arkansas, Tennessee and Maryland and were planning new ones in North and South Carolina and Texas. . . . [We were] constantly seeking new ways to attack white supremacy—imaginative forms and styles that would involve more black people in mass actions."

For Willie Ricks, attacking white supremacy often meant going it alone. In April 1964, for instance, he was arrested in Leesburg, Georgia, for distributing leaflets at an all-black public school urging the students' parents to vote. A warrant for his arrest was served as he escorted an elderly African American woman to the Lee County courthouse to vote, and he was sentenced to 31 days in jail.

On his release, he said that he had been held in a cell at the Albany city jail with a white man who had beaten and broken the jaw of another SNCC activist, Bill Hansen, in 1962.

"He told me the reason he beat Hansen was that the sheriff promised to drop six or seven counts of burglary against him if he 'roughed up Hansen good'," Ricks said, according to a report in the SNCC newsletter *The Student Voice*.

Hansen, who later served as director of SNCC's Arkansas project, had been arrested and jailed for taking part in a demonstration near Albany.

At other times, Ricks worked closely with other SNCC supporters, which was the case in July 1964 when he joined John Perdew and several others in Americus to integrate a local restaurant called the Hasty House.

One member of the group, Sam Mahone, said later that it was Perdew who suggested testing the just-enacted Civil Rights Act of 1964 by attempting to eat at a local segregated restaurant on the night of July 3.

"Not really thinking of the consequences, six of us piled into John's car, a red 1956 Ford convertible," Mahone said. "Once parked, we entered the restaurant and took our seats while Kitty [Newsome] decided to go to the rest room on the side of the building. . . . As the waitress ignored us for more than fifteen minutes, we suddenly realized that Kitty had not returned. . . . We all then decided to go outside to look for him [and outside] noticed about a dozen whites armed with tire irons and baseball bats approaching. As we were attacked and beaten, but it was John, the only white person in our group, who suffered the most. Somehow, with Bob [Mants] behind the wheel, we all managed to get into the car and race away. . . . [But it was several days] before we learned that Kitty had been attacked behind the restaurant, severely beaten, and chased away."

Chapter 20: Changed Lives in Mississippi

On the night of February 28, 1963, Jimmy Travis, a 21-year-old SNCC field secretary, was at the wheel of his car heading west out of the Mississippi Delta town of Greenwood when several bullets ripped through the driver-side window.

"I yelled out that I had been shot," Travis recalled. He said that one of the two other passengers in the car, Bob Moses, who ran the SNCC office in Greenwood, grabbed the wheel and brought the car to a stop. "I was scared. I didn't know what had happened."

What had happened was that the shots had been fired from a white 1962 Buick that had been following the three civil rights workers for some time. One bullet had struck Travis in the head; another had hit him in the shoulder. Miraculously, he survived.

That incident, on a lonely stretch of Mississippi highway, would trigger an unprecedented influx of SNCC staffers and volunteers into Greenwood to show "with their bodies," as one staffer put it, that they would not be cowed by white terrorists, who had plied the Mississippi Delta with impunity for generations.

What they were up against were well-funded white suprematist organizations like the White Citizens' Councils, whose first chapter was founded in Indianola, Mississippi, just west of Greenwood, by Robert B. "Tut" Patterson, in the wake of the 1954 Supreme Court ruling outlawing segregation in public schools.

The organization fought openly against integration by enlisting the support of local businessmen and other respected (by whites) members of the community. They held public rallies where speakers railed against mixing races. They published a newspaper, which called civil rights activists "self-admitted agents provocateurs" and "wandering minstrels of racial friction." They took out ads in newspapers comparing the Civil Rights Act of 1984 to the Communist Party's racial equality platform.

Sara Criss, a Greenwood native who served as the Mississippi Delta correspondent for The Commercial Appeal in Memphis for 30 years beginning in the 1950s, said that the white community at first did not pay much attention to the White Citizens' Council. But in many ways, she said, it had a greater impact on people's feelings and attitudes than the Ku Klux Klan.

"The Klan was made up more of rednecks and working class people who were very secretive about their activities," Criss wrote. "The Citizens' Council went about their work quietly and behind the scenes by putting pressure on local citizens to go along with their way of thinking. It was more or less expected of us to pay our $5.00 yearly dues to the Citizens' Council and stand behind them."

Criss, born in 1921, said that the Council opened an office in downtown Greenwood, and one day Patterson showed her pictures of riots in cities in other parts of the country. "He would point to nice-looking people in the streets and warn me that this would happen in Greenwood and that it wouldn't just be rednecks involved but probably some of my good friends."

She said that Patterson also visualized white girls marrying Negro boys if the schools were integrated and made many "other dire predictions."

Criss, who died in 2009, said in her still-unpublished memoirs that she was afraid of the Klan, "afraid that if I wrote something they did not like I would have a cross burned in my yard, or be threatened, or be included in the hate sheets being distributed. But I was also afraid of the Citizens' Council because their members were my friends and I did not want to incur their ill will either."

According to Criss, the presidents of three local banks (all of whom were probably active in the White Citizens' Council) once called the wife of the publisher of The Greenwood Commonwealth, Sumter Gillespie, and told her that if the newspaper took any stand on civil rights that they did not agree with, they would not advertise in the newspaper again.

Also created in the wake of the Supreme Court decision on segregation in public schools—Brown v. Board of Education—was the Mississippi State Sovereignty Commission, a state-supported agency whose goal, it said, was to protect the sovereignty of Mississippi and its "sister states" and from "federal encroachment."

But the commission, more importantly, also served as an internal intelligence agency that collected information on tens of thousands of individuals associated with the civil rights movement. It infiltrated most of the major civil rights organizations in the state and informed the police about planned marches or boycotts, and it encouraged the harassment by the police of those African-Americans who cooperated with civil rights groups.

The commission's staff also worked closely with—and in some cases funded—the White Citizens' Councils.

At the same time, some white residents of Greenwood and the surrounding communities resorted to less sophisticated, often brutal means of opposing racial reconciliation, as they had for generations, throughout the 1950s and 1960s.

In the summer of 1955, for instance, two white men murdered a 14-year-old black boy—Emmett Till—after he allegedly flirted with a white woman at a grocery store in Money, Mississippi, just north of Greenwood. His murder, which sparked a national outcry, has often been cited as the "Big Bang" of the modern-day civil rights movement.

However, over the next decade, little changed in and around Greenwood, with whites, for example, continuing to own about 310,000 acres of land in LaFlore County, of which Greenwood was the county seat, compared with only about 24,000 acres for blacks, who made up two-thirds of the total population of the county of 47,142. Nearly 60 percent of the whites who were eligible to vote were registered, compared with only 9 percent of blacks.

Sara Criss said that voter registration applicants were required to pass a test that included interpreting part of the state Constitution. Applicants were also required to pay an poll tax of $2.00. "Not many blacks attempted to register," she wrote, "and those who did usually failed to pass the test."

Hardy Lott, the city attorney in Greenwood, who reportedly was active in the local White Citizens' Council, was quoted as telling a reporter for The Commercial Appeal that from 1955 to 1962 fewer than 100 blacks had qualified to vote.

"It has not been the case of Negroes not registering," he said. "They just didn't make application. . . . It's not a case of discrimination on the part of the county. It is ignorance on the applicants that these Negro [civil rights] organizations are finding scattered around to take tests. Many can't even read or write."

Such was the situation in the spring of 1963 when Bob Moses, James Forman and other SNCC activists were working out of the organization's ramshackle office across the railroad tracks from downtown Greenwood in the black section of the city known as Baptist Town.

Exacerbating the already dismal situation for blacks was the decision by the LeFlore County Board of Supervisors in October 1962 to cut off shipments of surplus food to county residents—a move that was clearly taken to intimidate the African American community since few whites in the county were receiving such food. "That winter," Forman wrote, "many blacks were going hungry. The situation for the poorest families was getting grim."

Forman said that, in response to what he called the "inhuman" decision by the county supervisors, SNCC organized the collection and shipment of food from around the country for distribution in Greenwood. But the people, he said, were told that they would only receive the food if they went to the courthouse to register to vote, "although adherence to this principle was not absolute." Registration lines at the courthouse, he said, grew longer every day.

Predictably, many whites reacted angrily to what they saw as a campaign driven by "professional agitators" to destroy their way of life. Some took the law into their own hands.

On March 6, 1963, two SNCC activists—Samuel Block and Willie Peacock—were sitting in a car in front of the

SNCC office when a shotgun blast shattered the car windows on the driver's side. No one was injured.

Then, on March 24, the SNCC office was set on fire and all of the organization's office equipment was destroyed. Several witnesses said that they had seen two white men running down an alley after smoke began pouring from the building.

Two days later, two shotgun blasts shattered the front door of the home of Dewey Greene, the father of two high school students—George and Freddie—who had been working on voter registration. Many local blacks considered Freddie to be the "nicest girl in Greenwood," as Forman put it, so they quickly stepped up the protests at the courthouse and elsewhere downtown.

Sara Criss recalled that tension at the time was beginning to build across the city, and on March 27, when she was at home preparing for her daughter Mary Carol's ninth birthday party, "things really started happening."

At about the same time, in Baptist Town, Forman and Moses were commiserating over what they believed was the increasing futility of attempting to register black people to vote under existing Mississippi state laws. Most blacks, they said, simply could not pass the test that was administered—assuming that it was even administered fairly, which it wasn't.

So, as a first step toward eventually changing the laws, Forman decided to begin mass protests in Greenwood aimed at attracting national media attention—part of Operation MOM, or "Move on Mississippi." He gathered together a hundred or so people and urged them to march to the county courthouse downtown to dramatize their right to vote and to protest the ongoing violence against African Americans in and around the city.

"The people cried 'Amen, Amen,' for they were ready to move," Forman recalled. "You could feel it. And they began moving."

When they reached the courthouse, after demanding to see the mayor at City Hall, they were met by a long line of police. Suddenly, one of them unleashed a German Shepard on the crowd, and a dozen of the protesters were immediately arrested and thrown in jail, including Forman and Moses, on charges of disorderly conduct.

The next day, about 50 reporters from around the country—representing The New York Times, Newsweek, TIME, The Wall Street Journal and other news outlets—arrived in Greenwood to cover the story.

"It was inconceivable to local people that one small march involving mostly outsiders could have invoked such a widespread response," Sara Criss wrote years later. "Perhaps it was the picture of the policeman and his dog which went out all over the country that helped to bring [the newsmen to Greenwood] or maybe it was just because the civil rights struggle was beginning to gather steam. Anyway, Greenwood was on the map, and it remained there throughout the coming years as one of the focal points of the civil rights movement."

On April 4, after their released from jail, Forman and Moses traveled to Atlanta to participate in SNCC's annual conference to discuss next steps. Attending the three-day session, held at Gammon Theological Seminary, were more than 350 students from across the South, plus the the entire SNCC staff, which had now grown to about 60 people.

Moses told the conference that what had been happening in Greenwood had made him wonder whether black people would ever turn out to register to vote in large numbers.

He said that, for most blacks, registering could mean losing their jobs, or worse.

More than 500 people in LeFlore County, he said, had registered to vote so far. "For us, that's a big number," he said. But about 13,000 blacks of voting age lived in the county, so "what you need is not 500 but 5,000. . . ." He also said that he doubted that people in the rest of the country would be able to do anything to help.

He said that they were, in effect, asking white people in the Delta to do something that they don't ask of white people elsewhere, "and that is to allow Negroes to vote in an area where they are educationally inferior but yet outnumber the white people and hence constitute a serious political threat."

"I don't for one minute think that the country is in a position or is willing to push this down the throats of white people in the Delta," Moses said. But he said that, in the end, it will have to be pushed down their throats "because they are determined not to have it done."

How determined the white people of the Delta were to oppose change would become increasingly clear over the next few months, as violence against blacks—individually and collectively—reached unprecedented proportions.

One of the individuals who was the target of that violence was a 15-year-old girl from Greenwood named June Johnson, who had befriended Moses and the other SNCC workers in Greenwood and had persuaded them to allow her to attend the SNCC conference in Atlanta, despite her age.

She had been told by her mother and other fearful blacks in the city that the SNCC activists were "troublemakers." But she was curious and wanted to know what they were up to. It was her first trip outside of Mississippi.

Her second trip was to Charleston, South Carolina, two months later, to attend a week-long voter registration workshop. On her return trip to Greenwood, on June 11, she and several other workshop attendees were arrested in Winona—thirty miles east of Greenwood—when they attempted to desegregate a rest-stop restaurant.

"I been hearing about you black sons of bitches over in Greenwood, raising all that hell," the county sheriff told them after they had been thrown in jail. "You come over here to Winona, you'll get the hell whipped out of you."

Johnson recalled that the sheriff then struck her on the cheek and the chin, then in the stomach. He was joined by three others—the chief of police, a state trooper and a white civilian—and she was then thrown to the floor and beaten. She said later that she was also hit in the back of the head by a white man wielding a club wrapped in black leather. Her fellow travelers—all women—were also beaten.

Stokely Carmichael, in his memoir Ready for Revolution, wrote that when those white men in Winona were in the process of beating three generations of black women, they had no idea how close they had come to triggering a race war.

"There were brothers in Greenwood," he wrote, "who had the means and certainly the intention [to retaliate]. That one was close, I mean narrowly averted, and I'm not talking hours. We're talking minutes. Brothers were about to roll on that two-bit jail. Maybe they should not have been dissuaded."

About 90 miles to the south, meanwhile, in the early morning hours of June 12, a 37-year-old field secretary for the NAACP named Medgar Evers was pulling into his driveway in Jackson when a shot suddenly rang out. He was struck in the back by a bullet fired from an Enfield rifle and died at a Jackson hospital later that day.

Arrested and charged with the crime, on June 21, was Byron De La Beckwith, a Greenwood native known locally as "Delay." Twice prosecuted for the murder, he was freed each time by an all-white, all-male jury. Later, he was convicted of first-degree murder by a jury composed of eight blacks and four whites and sentenced to life imprisonment. He died in 2001.

Residents of Greenwood knew De La Beckwith to be an odd and outspokenly racist member of the community. Some in the community, however, feinted disbelief when they heard that he had been arrested for murder. Mayor Charles E. Sampson, a member of the White Citizens' Council, said that "we are just stunned. I don't think he's the type. He would always greet you with a smile."

Other residents of the community, like Sara Criss, saw his arrest as yet another sign that their world was being turned upside down. "We knew [that the murder of Evers] would be trouble," she wrote, "but little [did we know] that Greenwood would be involved."

Criss was a year younger than De La Beckwith and had known him most of her life. "He hated Negroes and did not mind saying so," she wrote. She said that there was "no doubt" in her mind that he had killed Evers. She said that her husband Russell had once met De La Beckwith entering the police station in Greenwood with a wild look in his eyes and wearing yellow sun glasses. Her husband asked him about the glasses, and he replied, "These are my nigger-hunting glasses."

Not surprisingly, De La Beckwith was a member of the White Citizens' Council. But he was also a member of Greenwood's Episcopal Church of the Nativity, where he spoke up angrily when church leaders were thought to be too liberal on race-related issues. A fund was set up in

Greenwood to help with his defense. It was called the White Citizens' Legal Fund.

"We fussed at Mama for sending $5.00 to the fund," Criss wrote, "but she said she was remembering De La as that little boy whose mother died when he was very young and who played ball in the vacant lot across the street."

Criss said that, following De La Beckwith's arrest on June 21, the situation in Greenwood remained fairly quiet for the rest of the summer and into the fall. "The Negroes continued to come down to the courthouse to register but there were no more marches, and it was hoped that the worst was over."

Chapter 21: Good Relations Gone Bad

Early one morning in mid-July 1964, while her husband and two daughters were still asleep, Sara Criss sat down with a cup of coffee to write a letter to her former neighbor and good friend, Marge Doyle, who had recently moved to Ohio.

"Oh, Marge," she wrote, "you can't imagine how sad it is down here [in Greenwood], the terrible feeling of defeat and despair. We are so worried about what tomorrow will bring."

President Johnson had just signed the Civil Rights Act of 1964, and Criss, like most of her friends, were deeply worried about what it would mean for their city.

"The good relations with our Negroes are fast disappearing," she wrote, "and nobody trusts each other anymore. We are so sorry for the good Negroes (and we do have many). They are frightened and confused."

Criss said that many white civil rights workers from the North had begun to arrive in the city to participate in a

SNCC-initiated program known as Freedom Summer. She said that the northern whites "live with the Negroes and don't look like they've had a bath or a haircut in weeks." She said that she had recently been at a demonstration at the courthouse where a white boy and a Negro girl drank from the same water bottle.

"When they leave here, the damage they've done to our relations with the Negroes will be hard to repair," Criss, a reporter for the Memphis newspaper *The Commercial Appeal*, wrote to her friend. "We don't know what the future holds but it looks pretty gloomy. We still have twice as many Negroes as whites, so you know what a situation we'll have."

She said in the letter, which she never mailed, that white "roughnecks," as she called them, along with the KKK and the White Citizens' Council, were inflaming the situation by their hard-nosed response to the situation.

"Of course, we do have our roughneck whites who are just ready to get into something," Criss wrote to her friend. "We're really just wanting everything to be peaceful again, and someday maybe it will."

The plan by SNCC to flood the state with college students from the North had been in the works for several months. It had been carefully choreographed by, among others, Bob Moses, head of the SNCC office in Greenwood, who argued that it would provoke a crisis that would cause the Mississippi state law enforcement authorities to overreact, prompting federal intervention.

Bob Zellner, a white activist with SNCC, explained the situation by saying that neither the country nor the government would care if black people were brutalized and arrested. "But if the son of white lawyer so-and-so or the daughter of white senator such-and-such got beaten or arrested—or God forbid, killed—people would have to pay attention and demand that the [federal] government do something about it. . . . We would have to pull out all the stops. A thousand volunteers from middle-class families, black and white, from all over the United States would converge on Mississippi. That would get attention and possibly protection for people attempting to register to vote."

Entering the mix, as the situation in Greenwood grew more volatile, was Stokely Carmichael, who, in mid-June1964, was asked by Moses to come to Mississippi to work full-time. He had been involved with the movement as a student at Howard University in Washington, D.C. And now, at 22 years old, he was making his way to Greenwood and preparing to settle in for the summer at SNCC's headquarters in Baptist Town.

On June 21, however, his plans were changed with the news that three civil rights volunteers—Andrew Goodman, James Chaney and Michael Schwerner—had disappeared while investigating the burning of an African American church near Philadelphia, Mississippi.

Carmichael and his SNCC colleagues in Greenwood feared the worst. For several days, he and fellow activists Cleveland Sellers and Charles Cobb searched for the missing volunteers but without success. On August 4, their bullet-ridden bodies were found in an earthen dam south of Philadelphia. They had been killed by local white racists, with the assistance of the local police.

Back in Greenwood, Carmichael and his SNCC colleagues moved ahead with plans to establish dozens of Freedom Schools, Freedom Houses and community centers in small towns throughout Mississippi that would serve as hubs of progressive political and educational activity for the local black population.

Sara Criss was not impressed, writing that many of the Freedom Schools had been set up in black churches but that many black people did not want to have anything to do with them. She said that one day she and another reporter from *The Commercial Appeal* had visited some of the schools.

"Most of [the northern volunteers] looked as if they had not had a bath or washed their hair in a month," Criss wrote. "When we got back to the house for lunch, the first thing we did was give our hands a good scrubbing. It was quite an experience."

But most observers agreed that, from the perspective of the civil rights movement, Freedom Summer had been a success, noting, for instance, that about 17,000 African-Americans had been moved enough to fill out voter registration forms (although only about 1,600 were allowed by the local authorities to actually register to vote). Four civil rights workers had been killed. A total of 80 Freedom Summer workers had been beaten. Three African Americans from Mississippi who supported the project had been murdered. Thirty-seven churches were bombed or burned. And thirty African American homes or businesses were attacked.

Yet others argued that the ten weeks of Freedom Summer had generated widespread and generally positive coverage in the national press, which, for the movement, was unprecedented. Quite literally, according to one study, the summer's success could be measured in column inches of newsprint and running feet of video tape.

"Easily the most spectacular and sustained single event in recent civil rights history," the study said, "it provided summer-long, nationwide exposure of the inequities of white supremacy in the deepest of the Deep South states."

Stokely Carmichael said that Freedom Summer had been a turning point in the movement. "It was certainly the boldest, most dramatic and traumatic event of the entire movement," he wrote years later. "It certainly had the most far-reaching effect: for national party politics, for that activist college generation, for the state of Mississippi and the movement there, and especially for SNCC as an organization. After the summer, none of those would be the same."

But Bob Moses was less convinced that it had been worth it. Asked by one reporter if Freedom Summer had been a success, he replied, "Success? I have trouble with that word. When we started, we hoped no one would be killed."

Chapter 22: An End to Nonviolence?

SNCC militants like Willie Ricks, in the meantime, were becoming increasingly impatient with the lack of progress that they believed was being made through the nonviolent approach to civil rights being taken by Martin Luther King Jr. and his followers.

He and James Forman thought that King, in particular, had become too deferential to the federal government, which, after the events of "Bloody Sunday" in Selma on March 7, 1965, had supported a court injunction temporarily prohibiting the proposed voting rights march from Selma to Montgomery.

Ricks and the other militants began to view such protests as diversions from the more important task of addressing the real obstacles facing African-Americans, including poverty, discrimination in housing and a lack of educational opportunities.

Regarding the Selma-to-Montgomery march, the SNCC leadership agreed to allow individual members to participate in the march. But it refused to sign on as an organization.

"I knew that the ballot would never solve the basic problems of poor people," Forman later wrote. "For me, as for others, this period marked . . . an end to any belief in—or willingness to engage in—large, nonviolent demonstrations."

On the night of March 8—the day after "Bloody Sunday"—a marathon meeting was held in Selma between, on the one hand, King and members of his senior staff and, on the other, Forman, Lewis, Ricks and a few others, to plan future strategy.

But the meeting quickly deteriorated into an all-out verbal brawl between the representatives of SNCC and King's SCLC, with King arguing in favor of honoring the federal injunction against the march and Forman leading the charge on the other side, saying that "the people" were ready to march right now.

Cleveland Sellers, program director of SNCC, later wrote that King had argued during the meeting that the march should be postponed until a court order could be obtained authorizing it. "We told [him] that a court order just wasn't necessary," Sellers wrote. "The local people were ready to march on Montgomery and we saw no reason to ask them to wait."

Even Andrew Young, one of King's closest advisors, argued that postponing the march was risky because hundreds of people—prominent and otherwise—had begun to arrive in Selma to join street protests in response to the "Bloody Sunday" attack. "So we had to do something," Young wrote. "It was necessary to have some kind of march on Tuesday [March 9]."

It was decided, therefore, to lead a group of marchers across the Edmund Pettus Bridge to approximately where the "Bloody Sunday" assault by law enforcement officers had taken place, hold a brief prayer ceremony there and then turn around and return to Brown Chapel A.M.E. Church, where Ricks, coincidentally, was organizing a series of non-stop, unauthorized and impromptu marches.

Sellers wrote that Alabama state troopers had been stationed at each end of the block in front of Brown Chapel with orders to stop all marches. But Ricks had managed to assemble a large group of school children to march back and forth between the two lines of nervous troopers. Scuffles inevitably broke out between some of the students and the troopers.

When Ricks realized that the students would not be able to break through the lines, he jumped on to the front steps of Brown Chapel and urged them to disperse and reassemble in front of the courthouse downtown.

Sellers said that Ricks' behavior had infuriated King and his associates. "They were concerned that the impromptu marches would lead to additional violence. They attempted to talk to Ricks, to stop him from 'inciting the people.' But he wouldn't listen. When they tried to get us to stop him, we explained that we permitted SNCC's individual members to do whatever their consciences told them to do."

At the meeting between SNCC and SCLC on March 8, King was visibly angry, calling out to Ricks at one point saying, "Come here, son." Ricks came forward and stood in front of King, who told the 22-year-old that he had been fighting for a long time and that he knew what he was doing.

"I'm in charge here," Sellers quoted the 36-year-old leader of SCLC as saying, "and I intend to remain in charge. You can't hurt me. Remember that. You are not Martin Luther King! I'm Martin Luther King. No matter what you do, you'll never be a Martin Luther King."

Sellers said that Ricks did not reply. "There was no need," Sellers wrote. "For all practical purposes, the meeting was over. Nothing had been settled, but no one was surprised. We hadn't really expected to settle anything. We left [Brown Chapel] with the certain knowledge there was a wide breach between them and us."

That breach, according to Stokely Carmichael, who had arrived in Selma along with Ricks, Forman, Sellers and the other SNCC activists in early March, was caused by what Carmichael called a fundamental "strategic and philosophical" difference between SNCC and SCLC.

"The problem was in the SCLC approach of massive, temporary mobilization and press agentry," Carmichael later observed, "as opposed to creating powerfully organized communities capable of sustaining political struggle. . . . Here comes SCLC talking about mobilizing another two-week campaign, using our base [in Selma] and the magic of Dr. King's name. They going to bring in cameras, the media, prominent people, politicians, rat-tat-ta, turn the place upside down, and split." And they were at the mercy of the federal government once again, he said—"something we were over and done with."

On Tuesday, March 9, King led several hundred marchers from Brown Chapel toward the Edmund Pettus Bridge yet again.

"I would rather die on the highways of Alabama," King told the crowd, which now included many white activists, "than make a butchery of my conscience."

Just over the bridge, on U.S. Highway 80 leading to Montgomery, the demonstrators were again met by a contingent of state troopers—this time numbering about 500—who ordered them to halt. Sensing the possibility of yet another violent confrontation, and not wanting to alienate the federal authorities, particularly since assurances had not yet been received from President Johnson that federal troops would protect the demonstrators, King instructed the marchers to return to Brown Chapel.

Inside the church, King defended his decision to abandon the march. But Forman, backed by Ricks, angrily told the marchers that they should have challenged the state troopers and not turned back.

"I've paid my dues in Selma," Forman said from the pulpit of Brown Chapel. "I've been to jail here. I've been beaten here, so I have the right to ask this: why was there violence on [Bloody] Sunday and none on Tuesday? You know the answer. They don't beat white people. It's Negroes they beat and kill."

Outside, Ricks told the crowd that, with some preparation, the SNCC organizers could have easily bolted past King and stolen the march to Montgomery from him. "That is *your* bridge," Ricks shouted to the crowd. "If Sheriff Clark tries to stop you, what are you gonna to? If Martin Luther King says don't march, what are you gonna do?"

Ricks had worked up the crowd to such a frenzy—to the point that they were prepared to charge the bridge immediately—that Andrew Young worried that the young SNCC militant's actions could provoke another violent confrontation with the police. So, he quietly asked some of the SNCC leaders nearby to do what they could to tone him down. But they refused.

The next day, angry and frustrated, Ricks and several other SNCC activists, including Forman, headed for Montgomery to open a "second front," as Sellers put, at the state Capitol.

Earlier that day, a convoy of cars and chartered buses carrying some 700 students from Tuskegee Institute—about 35 miles west of Montgomery—had arrived in Montgomery. But Gov. Wallace had refused to see the delegation or to accept their petition calling for equal voting rights for African Americans.

Despite pleas from the institute's dean of students, who had accompanied the group to Montgomery, the SNCC activists who had come from Selma, including Ricks, persuaded about 200 of the students to stage a sit-down strike to attract the governor's attention.

Sellers wrote later that on Wednesday, March 10, the students sat down on the cold cement sidewalk outside the Capitol and began to sing freedom songs. But after sunset, they moved their vigil to the First Baptist Church, about a block away. Then, with Forman in the lead, they walked to Dexter Avenue Baptist Church nearby, where King and his father had been longtime pastors.

There, they were joined by students from Alabama State University, a local black institution, who had been recruited by Ricks, along with a group of students and clergy—mostly white—who had arrived at the Montgomery airport assuming they were on their way to Selma.

Police surrounded the church and refused to let anyone enter, except James Bevel, who arrived from Selma to argue on behalf of the SCLC that the students should halt their protests in Montgomery and move to Selma.

Ricks reported to SNCC headquarters in Atlanta on March 11 that Bevel and Forman had almost come to blows in the church. "Why are you *here* in Montgomery?" Bevel asked. "Why don't you go to Selma and find out what people see as the next logical stepping a nonviolent campaign to win the vote?" He said that their "foolishness" in Montgomery would only undermine the momentum that was building in Selma.

But Forman was unconvinced, announcing that he would resume the demonstrations at the Capitol by himself, if necessary. "Anyone who wants come with me can do so," he said.

Released from the church, Forman immediately issued a call for supporters nationwide to come to Montgomery to buttress SNCC's voter rights campaign. Over the next few days, hundreds of demonstrators peacefully picketed the Capitol.

Then, on March 15, President Johnson went before Congress to say in a nationally televised address that what was happening in Alabama was part of a larger movement "which reaches into every section and state of America. It is the effort of American Negroes to secure for themselves the full blessings of American life."

Listening to the speech on a radio in Montgomery, Forman was not impressed. He was no fan of Johnson to begin with, or of the voting rights legislation that he was about to send to Congress. He saw it primarily as a sophisticated means of coopting and dissipating the movement that he and his fellow SNCC leaders were pursuing.

Also unimpressed were several hundred students who had been trapped by the police on a dark street about a quarter-mile from the Capitol. That afternoon, they had attempted to march on the building but had been stopped.

The next day, Forman and Ricks led another march toward the Capitol—this one comprising about 1,000 people. As the marchers approached the building, Montgomery County sheriff's deputies led by Sheriff Mac Sim Butler on horseback cut the SNCC activists and a number of others off from the main group of protesters and began beating them with ropes and whips. A little later, the city police dispersed the main body of protesters with similar tactics.

Several people were injured in the melee. "We were fighting in the streets," Ricks later recalled.

A front-page story in *The Selma-Times Journal* on March 16 said that a demonstration the previous night near the Ben Moore Hotel had been broken up by "mounted deputies and patrolmen armed with shotguns" after the protesters had starting throwing "rocks, bricks and bottles." A report in the newspaper on March 17, also on the front page, said that deputies "astride quick-starting horses clubbed white and Negro civil rights demonstrators in a bloody melee Tuesday [March 16] that sent eight persons to hospitals."

The report said that many of the demonstrators were "white college students from other states," adding that the deputies on horseback had swung clubs, canes and doubled lengths of rope. "Some demonstrators ran. Others fell. A white coed was knocked down. . . . Another youth fell, blood pouring from a wound."

To help contain the situation, King hurried to Montgomery on March 17 and joined Forman and others from SNCC to lead a march of some 2,000 people to Sheriff Butler's office at the county courthouse. The crowd waited outside in a steady rain while King and Forman met with Butler inside to negotiate new protest procedures. Emerging from the meeting at around 5:15 p.m., King thanked the crowd and then announced—after hearing the news from Andrew Young—that U.S. District Judge Frank M. Johnson Jr. had just ruled that the Selma-to-Montgomery voting rights march could proceed.

Later, it was confirmed the march would begin on Sunday, March 21. It would take place, according to an agreement with the White House, under the protection of more than 1,800 armed members of the Alabama National Guard who would line the 54-mile route from Selma to

Montgomery, along with more than 1,000 U.S. Army troops, 100 FBI agents and another 100 U.S. marshals. Helicopters and light planes would patrol the skies watching for snipers. And federal demolition teams would inspect bridges and other potential targets for explosives.

Gov. Wallace, however, was not about to concede defeat, saying in a speech to a joint session of the Alabama legislature on Thursday, March 18, that a federal judge, "presiding over a mock court," had approved the march and that the marchers—nurtured by the "collectivist press"—aimed to "take all police powers unto the central government. "And sadly, the Negroes used as tools in this traditional type of Communist street warfare have no conception of the misery and slavery they are bringing to their children."

Wallace urged his fellow Alabamians, nevertheless, to obey Judge Johnson's order "though it be galling" and leave the march alone. "Please stay home. Let's have peace."

Chapter 23: Time to Come Together

After the the march, which began in Selma on March 21 and ended in Montgomery five days later, SNCC hardliners like Willie Ricks, Cleveland Sellers, James Forman and Stokely Carmichael said that the march had been, in the words of Sellers, "a gigantic waste: in terms of money, human resources and human lives." Carmichael called the march "nonsense."

But they decided, nevertheless, to attempt to use the march to their advantage, building on the publicity and momentum it had generated to seek to achieve greater black political power in the desperately poor, rural region that lay between Selma and Montgomery—Lowndes County.

At a meeting in Montgomery, according to Forman, the SNCC hardliners decided, in particular, to organize potential black voters in Lowndes County—"a notoriously racist, terrorized area with an 86 percent black population that was acutely poor and with not one black person registered to vote"—in part as a response to the KKK murder of the white civil rights volunteer from Detroit, Viola Liuzzo.

It was Carmichael who led the initial plunge into the county, arriving on Saturday, March 27, along with several other SNCC workers, including Bob Mants, Judy Richardson and Scott B. Smith. Three days later, he led two dozen SNCC workers on a solemn procession to the spot where Liuzzo had been shot along U.S. Highway 80.

Over the next few weeks, a series of mass meetings were held to fire up local residents about the importance of registering to vote, with Willie Ricks often as the principal speaker.

SNCC Chairman John Lewis said that Ricks was a "good agitator" who was "not interested at all in the philosophy of nonviolence or the concept of a biracial community." But he knew how to "stir up a crowd."

At one mass meeting in Lowndes County, on April 11, Ricks exhorted the crowd to go out and find "a thousand Negroes" and tell them to register to vote.

"You can get a thousand Negroes," he shouted. "All you got to do is go out and talk. . . . It's up to you. . . . It's time for Negroes in Lowndes County to come together."

"The white man asks what's wrong with Negroes," Ricks said. "There's nothing wrong with us. There's something wrong with the white folks. But we gotta move 'em. . . . I'm telling you it's time for us to come out of those kitchens, come out of that field, come out of the little two-cent job. And let's meet at the polls down there where you register. Let's get registered."

Sellers wrote years later that the plan for Lowndes County was simple: to register as many blacks as possible and to "take over the county." He said that Alabama law made it relatively easy to start a new political party, and "we believed that a complete victory was possible."

"After achieving success in Lowndes," he wrote, "we intended to widen our base by branching out and doing the same thing in surrounding counties. We were convinced that we had found The Lever we had been searching for."

For his part, Carmichael said that the plan also involved turning the Selma-to-Montgomery march from a "negative" into a "positive."

"Highway 80 traversed the length of the county," he wrote. "We knew that there was no way the march could go through without the aid of local people strong enough to let them pitch their tents on their land. People brave enough to come out, to cheer them on, offer a little food or some water, etc. etc. So what [Bob Mants] and I did, we trailed that march. Every time local folks came out, we'd sit and talk with them, get their names, find out where they lived, their addresses, what church, who their ministers were, like that. So all the information, everything, you'd need to organize, we got."

Carmichael said that he and Mants told the people that they would be back. "I promised them the movement was coming to Lowndes. Lowndes County was going to have its own movement."

A week or so later, when they returned to the county, the people remembered them. "We already had good contacts across the length and breadth of the county. You have any idea how long that would have taken as an organizer? Without the march? Dr. King handed all that to us on a platter, and we took it."

As spring turned to summer, teams of SNCC workers often led by Carmichael canvassed the county urging local residents to become more politically engaged—with only modest success. Many were scared.

Carmichael said that Lowndes County was one of the poorest counties in the nation. "It was feudal," he said, with about 80 families owning 90 percent of the land. Half of the black population of some 12,000—out of a total county population of about 15,000—lived below the poverty level, and the other half barely above it. Most of them were agricultural day laborers or sharecroppers. "It actually made the Mississippi Delta look advanced."

Few white activists were tempted to work in Lowndes County because, as Carmichael put it, it would be like "operating behind enemy lines."

"[It] was not because we had a formal policy of excluding them," Carmichael wrote years later. "We simply did not encourage them. . . . The general feeling [in SNCC] was that we couldn't, in principle, exclude anyone who genuinely wanted to struggle against racism. . . . But as a practical matter . . . we found it would have been foolhardy, even irresponsible, to bring in whites."

Even local African American activists, like R.L. Strickland, who, when told that Carmichael was planning to start a "movement" in his backyard, asked the 23-year-old SNCC leader, "Young fella, you one o' them nonviolence folks?" And without hesitating, he answered his own question by saying, "Wal, in this county, turn the other cheek and these here peckerwoods'll hand you back half of what you sitting on."

Carmichael said that, when he told Strickland straight out that, yes, he would be coming to the Lowndes County to start a movement, Strickland just looked at him and smiled.

Given that the white supremacists in Lowndes County were stepping up their campaign of intimidation through violent means, particularly in light of the newly enacted Voting Rights Act of 1965, Strickland's skepticism was understandable.

KKK nightriders, for instance, had fired repeatedly into the home of Pattie Mae McDonald, a 44-year-old homemaker, for allowing activists to use a vacant two-room house on her property near Hayneville as a "Freedom Library." Near White Hall, four men parked their pickup truck outside the home of Matthew Jackson, who had allowed SNCC workers to use his family's home as a safe haven, and opened fire with rifles and shotguns. He returned fire, and they fled.

Jackson's wife Emma later explained that her participation the civil rights movement was consistent with being a Christian. "Your duty is to serve people and I have always wanted to do that," she said. "I was taught that."

For many blacks, however, being a Christian did not mean giving up the right of self-defense. Gun ownership in Lowndes County among African Americans, who comprised roughly 80 percent of the county's population of around 15,000 were black, had been widespread for generations. Moreover, the concept of armed self-defense had existed among them since Reconstruction. Simply displaying a stockpile of weapons dissuaded many would-be white assailants. And when it did not, they often returned fire.

Many Lowndes County residents were opposed to nonviolent direct action because they thought it was dangerous to do so. One resident was quoted as saying, "You can't come here talking that nonviolence shit. You'll get yourself killed, and other people, too."

For their part, Carmichael and many of his SNCC colleagues, including Willie Ricks, understood the need for African Americans to arm themselves. "I have simply stopped telling people they should remain nonviolent," Carmichael said in January 1966. "This would be tantamount to suicide in the Black Belt countries were whites are shooting at Negroes and it would cost me the respect of the people."

At a SNCC executive committee meeting in Holly Springs, Mississippi, in mid-April 1965, several proponents of nonviolence, including SNCC Chairman John Lewis, chastised Roy Shields, the project director for southwest Georgia, for not dissuading his staff from carrying weapons. But several members of SNCC's Alabama staff, including Carmichael, defended Shields for not having done so.

"We are not King or SCLC," Carmichael said. "They don't do the kind of work we do nor do they live in the areas we live in. They don't ride the highways at night." He said that for King nonviolence was everything but for SNCC it was just a tactic.

Carmichael later recalled that the discussion ended when he asked those who were carrying weapons to place them on the table. Nearly all of the black SNCC organizers working in the deep South, he said, were well-armed.

At a rally in Tuskegee, Alabama, in early January 1966, Willie Ricks told a crowd of about 500 protesters that "the only way we can stop whites from killing us is to start buying rifles that they kill us with."

Meanwhile, Carmichael pressed ahead with setting up a grassroots organization in Lowndes County. He told reporters shortly after the murder of Jonathan Daniels that he and his fellow SNCC activists were determined to show the people of the county that "they can't run us out."

R.L. Strickland's close friend John Hulett, a 37-year-old father of seven, had already established the Lowndes County Christian Movement for Human Rights (LCCMHR). As its president, he had been encouraging blacks to register to vote and to fight for their rights through mass protests since the early spring of 1965.

According to Carmichael, Hulett was intelligent, committed and courageous. "He was familiar with organized protest," Carmichael said, "so he was ready to step out and provide serious leadership once we got there. In fact, he'd been agitating before we got there."

For Hulett and other rural blacks, "agitating" also meant carrying weapons. "Those of us who carried guns carried them for our own protection," Hulett said, "in case we were attacked by other peoples. That's what the purpose of that idea was. White peoples carried guns in this county and the law didn't do anything to them about it, so we started carrying guns, too. . . . We wasn't violent people. But we were just some people who was going to protect ourselves in case we were attacked by individuals."

But registering blacks to vote was different. Only about 250 African Americans had registered to vote in the first few months of Carmichael's time in the county. So he decided to contact SNCC's director of research, Jack Minnis, to see if it was possible under Alabama law to set up an independent political party. In less than a week, Minnis called Carmichael to say that it was allowed under state law. Under an obscure provision, he said, county residents could nominate independent candidates at a special nominating convention, and if those candidates received 20 percent or more of the votes cast in the county election, their party could obtain official state recognition.

One resident of Lowndes County reportedly said that it did not make sense to join the Alabama Democratic party, whose slogan was "White Supremacy/For the Right." Why would black voters align themselves with the very people "who had done the killing in the county and had beat our heads?" the resident asked.

Minnis later said that the people of Lowndes County soon realized that until they had real political power, all they could do was ask for their rights. "If they could take over the county government," he wrote, "they'd no longer have to ask for what they needed. They could take it."

SNCC's Cleveland Sellers, who worked with Carmichael and the others in Lowndes County, said that the plan was simple: to register as many blacks as they could, all of them if possible, and "take over the county."

"We believed that a complete victory was possible," Sellers wrote. "After achieving success in Lowndes, we intended to widen our base by branching out and doing the same thing in surrounding counties. We were convinced that we had found The Lever we had been searching for."

SNCC Executive Secretary James Forman said that the developments in Lowndes County during the summer and fall of 1965, which included plans for an independent political party, had injected new energy and optimism into the lives of the county's long-oppressed black population.

"A tremendous excitement and new hope began to flow as the black men and women of Lowndes County moved to shake off a hundred years of white supremacy," Forman wrote.

He said that against this background, SNCC held a staff meeting in Atlanta beginning on November 24. He said that most members were now "ready to think in long-range revolutionary terms."

At the meeting, the "turning point" for Forman came on Day Two when Courtland Cox, a SNCC field secretary who had been working with Carmichael in Lowndes County, began talking about the "Alabama Plan" and the need for black people to obtain power.

Forman quoted Cox as saying, "The people want power, power to control the courthouse, power to control their lives." As he listened, according to Forman, something "clicked" in him. "We were in a new day," he wrote.

Forman said that Cox then walked to the blackboard and wrote, "Power. Education. Organization." He said that Cox spoke of the need for movement organizers, like Ricks, to see their role as enabling the people to establish "basic organizations in order to achieve power."

It was the first time that the concept of power as such had been discussed at a meeting of the SNCC staff, Forman said. "From that time on," he said, "SNCC began to talk more and more about power for black people, organization and political education. . . . We were once again moving in harmony with the needs of the masses of black people."

Chapter 24: Black Panthers Don't Back Up

Deciding on a symbol to represent the new political party—the Lowndes County Freedom Organization (LCFO)—took some time. Several proposals were rejected early on: a cotton boll (too vague); a dove (too remote); clasped hands modeled on the SNCC logo (too passive).

John Hulett, who had resigned as president of the Lowndes County Christian Movement for Human Rights (LCCMHR) and became head the new Lowndes County Voters League, proposed using a cat because they "chase chickens." No one could argue with that, so Stokely Carmichael asked his staff at SNCC headquarters in Atlanta to begin sketching cats.

Eventually, it was Ruth Howard, a student activist at Howard University several years earlier, who came up with the winning drawing, which was based on the black panther mascot at Atlanta's Clark College.

Hulett, who, along with Carmichael, signed off on the idea, pointed out that the black panther was a vicious animal which, if attacked, "would not back up." He said that it sent a signal that "we would fight back if we had to do it." It was a political symbol, he said, that suggested that "we was here to stay and we were going to do whatever needed to be done to survive."

Carmichael explained to those who thought the black panther symbol might be seen too aggressive that the black panther was a powerful animal but also reclusive. "It avoided humans unless provoked," he wrote. "They liked that." And they said, according to Carmichael, alluding to the Alabama Democratic Party symbol—a rooster—that "it sure can eat up any ol' white fowl, too."

In early December 1965, a reporter for The New York Times—Gene Roberts, a 33-year-old North Carolinian who had been assigned to cover what was then called the "race beat"—visited SNCC headquarters in Atlanta. There, he learned that the LCFO would operate, in his words, as an "all-Negro 'third party' . . . and [would] use a black panther as its party symbol."

The first order of business for what would be dubbed the "Black Panther Party" was to organize a series of workshops on the fundamentals of county government for the black residents of Lowndes County, who had been conditioned to think that politics was, as Carmichael put it, the business of white people—a business "in which blacks were not allowed or competent."

"They assumed that the white folks who ran things had knowledge, experience and education that their leaders lacked," Carmichael later observed. "So how could we do the job?"

But the SNCC-sponsored political workshops that were first held in Atlanta and then in Lowndes County showed, according to Carmichael, "what a hoax that was, and with the workshops, their confidence grew." Attendees learned, for example, how individual county residents could become candidates for public office. They were also informed about the duties of the officials who were up for election in the fall of 1966: sheriff, tax assessor, tax collector, coroner and three members of the five-member school board.

Jack Minnis, SNCC's research director, said that the workshops also dealt with corruption in the political system—i.e., how people with money were able to pay off elected officials and get them to "sell out ordinary folks."

"The people in the workshops learned that rich people will invite the officials into their homes for dinner and parties, let them join their clubs and will almost treat them as equals," Minnis wrote. "There are many ways open to the rich person to gain favors from the elected official. Little by little, the official is made to feel better than the people who elected him, and he begins to see himself as the friend of the rich and powerful."

Along with the workshops came the arrival in Lowndes County of federal registrars charged with enforcing the Voting Rights Act of 1965, which had been signed into law by President Johnson in August. But that influx of the federal government officials—along with growing political activism among many African Americans—soon led to the eviction of thousands of sharecroppers from white-owned land.

Some of them moved in with relatives or friends, crowding dozens of already overcrowded living quarters. Others left the county. Others remained but were left homeless, which prompted Carmichael (who said that the evictions were "cruel to see") and his SNCC associates to set up a "tent city" on farmland owned by SNCC sympathizer Rosie Steele along U.S. Highway 80.

Carmichael later said that the 200 or so families that lived in the tents were changed for the better by the experience. "We set up freedom schools," he wrote. "We had literacy and political education classes. We played tapes of Malcolm [X]." The people, he said, "just blossomed" once they were out from under the oppressive plantation system.

"Every day you could see [their confidence] growing," Carmichael wrote. "When [KKK] nightriders started driving by firing guns, the men and boys posted sentries along the rode and returned fire. The night-riding stopped. The people organized themselves, worked communally and just ate up the education. It was beautiful to see."

Among those who helped set up the tents was a young U.S. Navy veteran named Samuel L. Younge Jr., a student at Tuskegee Institute. He had participated in the Selma-to-Montgomery march and the protests at the Capitol in Montgomery that were organized by James Forman and Willie Ricks.

Younge told Carmichael on December 30, 1965, that he was having difficulty sticking to his studies at Tuskegee because the civil rights movement was "in me." He said that he hoped to organize an independent Black Panther Party in his home county around Tuskegee.

Toward midnight on Monday, January 3, 1966, the staff at the SNCC-sponsored Freedom House in Tuskegee noticed that Younge had not yet returned from what should have been a short trip to buy cigarettes. Witnesses later reported that Younge had been involved in an argument with an elderly gas station attendant over his refusal to let him use a "Whites Only" restroom.

Following the argument, Younge drove off but then stopped when he saw the attendant, Marvin Segrest, waving a pistol at him. He jumped on a half-filled Greyhound bus and grabbed a golf club from luggage bound for Atlanta. Darting in and out of the bus while shouting at Segrest, Younge managed to dodge one shot that Segrest got off but was struck in the back of the head by a second bullet as he attempted to escape on foot. It killed him instantly.

The next day, more than two thousand Tuskegee students marched in downtown Tuskegee to protest the killing. But Carmichael was not there. Instead, he later told James Forman, "I just got me three bottles of wine and drank one for me and one for Sammy and one for Jonathan Daniels."

Later that day, an emergency meeting of SNCC staffers was held in Atlanta to come up with a response. Holding new marches or demonstrations was rejected as ineffective. A proposal was then made to denounce the killing of Younge in the context of the Vietnam War. Toward the end of a marathon discussion, Gloria Larry proposed drafting a statement that would be released to the press no later than Thursday, January 6. It would be the first statement by a civil rights organization linking the civil rights movement to the Vietnam conflict. The proposal was immediately adopted.

"The Student Nonviolent Coordinating Committee has a right and a responsibility to dissent with United States foreign policy on an issue when it sees fit," the statement began. "[It] now states its opposition to United States' involvement in Vietnam. . . ."

It said that the American government has never guaranteed the freedom of oppressed citizens "and is not yet truly determined to end the rule of terror and oppression within its own borders."

"The murder of Samuel Younge in Tuskegee, Alabama, is no different than the murder of peasants in Vietnam, for both Younge and the Vietnamese sought, and are seeking, to secure the rights guaranteed them by law. In each case, the United States government bears a great part of the responsibility for these deaths."

SNCC said that, therefore, "we are in sympathy with, and support, the men in this country who are unwilling to respond to a military draft which would compel them to contribute their lives to United States aggression in Vietnam in the name of the 'freedom' we find so false in this country." It said that 60 percent of the draftees were Negroes who were called on to "stifle the liberation of Vietnam, to preserve a 'democracy' which does not exist for them at home."

Not surprisingly, the SNCC statement provoked an uproar not only among those who supported the war. But it was also criticized by some liberals who argued that civil rights and the war were two separate issues and that SNCC, as a civil rights organization, had no business issuing a statement on the war.

Also caught up in the maelstrom was Julian Bond, a former SNCC staffer who had campaigned for a seat in the Georgia legislature and won. When he appeared at the Georgia statehouse on January 10, 1966, to take his oath of office, however, he was denied the opportunity. The reason: his opposition to the war in Vietnam.

Reflecting a vicious media blitz that was waged against Bond, a prominent southern white author, Lillian Smith, who had once supported SNCC, wrote a letter to the editor of the Atlanta Constitution implying that SNCC was now controlled by communists. She said that Bond "(whose parents are wonderful people, one of the finest Negro families in Georgia") was being "pulled this way and that," suggesting that he, too, could be harboring communist sympathies because of his association with SNCC.

Eventually, the U.S. Supreme Court ruled in Bond's favor. He was eventually seated as a member of the state legislature. But the damage to him personally and to SNCC as an organization had already been done.

Chapter 25: A Blueprint for Black Power

Some members of SNCC, like Bill Ware, reacted to the murder of Younge and the failure of the Georgia state legislature to seat Julian Bond by writing position papers. Others, like Willie Ricks, reacted by disturbing the peace.

Ware said he was shocked to learn that Bond had been denied his seat in the legislature because of his views on the war in Vietnam. Born and raised in rural Mississippi, he had worked for SNCC in Alabama and Mississippi promoting voter registration. But now he saw little point in continuing such work if a fairly elected black man like Bond could not express his opinions without being punished.

Like Ricks, Ware had sought to radicalize black students in Montgomery, Alabama, as part of SNCC, which included many white volunteers, particularly from the North. Now, he and several other SNCC militants sought to persuade the SNCC leadership to exclude whites from the organization, arguing that whites could never truly understand the plight of African Americans and that blacks needed to take control of their own destiny.

With the approval of Forman, Ware and several other members of SNCC set up what became known as the Atlanta Project and presented their relatively radical ideas in a paper that was submitted at a SNCC staff meeting in March 1966.

The major thesis of the paper was that the "form of white participation [in the struggle], as practiced in the past, is now obsolete." On a practical level, they wrote, "blacks were intimidated by the presence of whites [in SNCC] because of their knowledge of the power that whites have over their lives."

White activists, therefore, should be excluded from SNCC so that blacks could "determine their own destiny," the paper said. Some work could be contracted out to whites, "but in no way can they participate on a policy-making level." The organization must be "black-staffed, black-controlled and black-financed."

Willie Ricks, however, was not persuaded by the paper, arguing that it dealt exclusively with matters internal to SNCC and not with how to attract followers and build support in the black community. "We would always say," Ricks said, "'Mr. Say ain't the man, Mr. Do is the man.'" He said that Ware and his colleagues had addressed "nationalism and that kind of thing inside SNCC, but they do not have an organization in the community."

Ricks, therefore, decided that it was best to continue doing what he had repeatedly shown himself uniquely qualified to do: rallying crowds to action and building grassroots support for the fight for equal rights.

One week into the New Year, for example, Ricks was his own "Mr. Do" in Tuskegee, Alabama, leading some 500 other protesters who blocked the entrances to seven down-town businesses near the Macon County courthouse to express their outrage at the murder of Samuel Younge on January 3.

"The only way we can stop whites from killing us is to start buying rifles that kill us," Ricks screamed to the crowd from atop a parked car, according to an article in The New York Times. "This means that we are going to have to control our dollars. This means we are going to have to register to vote."

A week later, Ricks was in Atlanta with 1,000 or so pro-testers demonstrating at the Georgia State Capitol against the ouster of Rep.-elect Julian Bond from the state legislature.

An article in the January 15 edition of The New York Times said that, after the rally, Forman led a "singing, chant-ing line of young pickets" around the Capitol. Suddenly, according to the article, the demonstrators dashed for the steps leading to the main doors of the building.

"A barricade of state troopers stopped them," the Times reported. "The pickets then circled the building, shout-ing and singing. About 50 regrouped on the south side [of the building] where the door is only a few feet from the street. Willie Ricks, a militant member of [SNCC], started screaming and headed for the door. About 50 surged for-ward with him, shouting and swinging. A handful of troop-ers was overwhelmed [but reinforcements] pushed the dem-onstrators back to the sidewalk."

The protesters used umbrellas and protest signs as they engaged the troopers in a melee that left two law officers and one demonstrator injured. A female demonstrator used her purse to club two officers after they had jostled her. Following the confrontation, the protesters moved across the street to City Hall, where they sang "We Shall Overcome" and "You Can Do It, Julian Bond. You Can Do It" in the lobby of the building.

Stokely Carmichael said later that he agreed with many of the views expressed in the Ware-initiated "Atlanta Project" paper. But like the majority of the SNCC staff, he did not accept some of its more extreme formulations, such as the demand that whites be expelled from the organization—suggesting that it risked isolating blacks from the white community, particularly northern New Leftists. He was also acutely aware of SNCC's continuing reliance on northern white financial support.

Carmichael recalled that submitting the paper at the March staff meeting had been done "in the most divisive way." He said that, in his view, the Atlanta "separatists" were simply "opportunists" who were attempting to gain control of SNCC by appearing to be "blacker than thou."

Yet Carmichael was also influenced in a positive way by many of the basic tenets of the paper (which he opposed as official SNCC policy). It reflected the feelings of many of the more militant members of the SNCC staff, he conceded, and it was broadly in line with the underpinnings of the kind of mass organizing that he and others had been doing in Lowndes County.

His main interest overall, however, continued to be finding ways to transform society—or, as the put it, to build a true democracy. He argued in an article published in The New Republic in January 1966 that the political landscape in the United States had been impoverished by the naive belief that democracy's restorative powers were equally available to the rich and poor, black and white.

"The majority view is a lie," Carmichael wrote, "based on the premise of upward mobility which doesn't exist for most Americans."

Carmichael went on to criticize President Johnson's "Great Society" program as "preposterous," placing his hope instead in the disenfranchised African Americans, particularly sharecroppers, who, he said, had shown in Lowndes County that they could "articulate and be responsible and hold power."

In the winter and spring of 1966, in a series of interviews conducted by the staff of SNCC's monthly magazine, The Movement, Carmichael argued that organizing in Lowndes County had convinced him that political power, rather than moral persuasion, was the key to achieving economic and racial justice. Independent political power among blacks at the local level, he claimed, would ensure that blacks were in control of the law, taxes and other bread-and-butter issues. He said that he was making plans "to take over Lowndes County."

By the spring of 1966, Carmichael had begun to offer a blueprint for what he would later be called Black Power. He had spent nearly a year promoting a radical view of democracy at the local level. He had also begun to strike fear into the hearts and minds of many white Americans by espousing a philosophy that increasingly focused on separation rather than integration, arguing that integration was "irrelevant" and nothing more than an "insidious subterfuge for white supremacy."

He wrote in The New Republic that the people of Lowndes County wanted to form their own political party so that they could "redefine politics, make up new rules and play the game with some integrity. Out of a negative force, fear, grew the positive drive to think new."

Chapter 26: Brothers With Firepower

On the night of February 1, 1965, a few months before Stokely Carmichael entered Lowndes County to organize black sharecroppers, someone telephoned Robert Hicks, an African American factory worker in Bogalusa, Louisiana, to say that the Ku Klux Klan was coming to bomb his house. He called the police, but they said there was nothing they could do about it.

He surmised, correctly, that the KKK was furious that he was putting up two white civil rights workers from the North in his house. He was also right to take the call seriously because just six months earlier, three civil rights workers—James Chaney, Michael Schwerner and Andrew Goodman—had been murdered by the Klan near Philadelphia, Mississippi, some 200 miles to the north.

Hicks and his wife, Valeria, found neighbors who would take care of their children. They also called a few friends asking for protection, and within hours several armed black men showed up at their house. In the end, nothing happened: no Klan, no bombing.

Later that month, several leaders of a semi-secret paramilitary group known as the Deacons for Defense and Justice—an organization formed in Jonesboro, Louisiana, in 1964 to protect visiting civil rights workers—came to Bogalusa and met with Hicks. He listened to what they had to say and agreed to take the lead in forming a Bogalusa chapter of the Deacons, recruiting many of the men who had come to protect his family and their civil rights guests at his house a few weeks earlier.

The chapter that Hicks wound up establishing was one of some two dozen such chapters, in fact, that were eventually formed throughout the Deep South in the 1960s.

Their tactics, to be sure, were clearly inconsistent with the philosophy of nonviolence championed by Martin Luther King Jr. and other more moderate civil rights leaders.

A member of the Deacons, for instance, drew a pistol during a demonstration in Bogalusa on July 8, 1965, and shot a white man who had attacked him with his fists. The man narrowly survived. But as Roy Reed, a reporter for The New York Times, put it in an article on the Deacons that year, the word had gotten out that "Negroes armed with rifles, shotguns and pistols" were "willing, even eager, to shoot at white men. . . ." He said that, as a result, the Klan custom of burning crosses on lawns was "dying out" in Jonesboro. "Whatever their flaws," he wrote, "the Deacons have proved to be a natural instrument for building community feeling and nourishing the Negro identity."

Reed reported that some civil rights leaders, such as James Farmer, national director of CORE, supported what the Deacons were doing, and James Forman, of SNCC, said that they were a predictable phenomenon given that the federal government was tacitly permitting the perpetuation of violence against African Americans.

But King—the chief exponent of nonviolence in the civil rights movement—was unequivocally opposed to the organization. "The line between defensive violence and aggressive violence is very thin," King said, according to Reed. "You get people to thinking in terms of violence when you have a movement that is built around defensive violence."

For his part, Stokely Carmichael welcomed the Deacons to the county shortly after beginning his work in Lowndes County in the spring of 1965, calling them a necessary component of protecting a vulnerable rural people from "Klan violence."

"Our people were determined, brave, but they sure weren't soldiers," Carmichael later recalled. "Many were old, and the majority in most meetings were, as always, women. . . . Most young adults had been driven out [of the county] in search of work or less oppressive conditions. We were left with a lot of older folks—valiant old folks to be sure—but old nonetheless, young teenagers, kids, and some adult men. . . ."

Carmichael said that it was unconscionable to leave the people of Lowndes County exposed to the whims of the Klan. "If the government wouldn't enforce the laws to protect them," he argued, "we figured we had to." And he set out to find those individuals "who'd help us do that."

He said that he had heard about the Deacons through H. Rap Brown, who would later succeed Carmichael as chairman of SNCC and eventually become "minister of justice" of the Black Panther Party in California.

"Those brothers," Carmichael said, referring to the Deacons, "were organized, trained, and had some serious firepower. Their mission was defending black communities from the Louisiana Klan. We made contact. Once they heard what was going down in Lowndes, they said, 'Yeah, we coming.'"

But that was not the end of it. After discussing the issue with his colleagues in SNCC, Carmichael set off on a trip to several major northern cities "to talk with brothers and sisters willing to come down to [Lowndes County] to help defend the population." He said that the "militant, nationalist elements" in every city that he visited, including New York, Chicago, Detroit and Philadelphia—agreed to send a contingent, however small. "Paid for it. Brought their own arms too. Got quietly into the county."

All in all, he said, as many as 50 people came south to participate in the exercise. Most had had some military training. Some had served in Vietnam and had brought their weapons back with them. "We didn't parade them, of course," Carmichael said. "But we introduced them at the mass meetings, had them greet the community and say a few words of solidarity. . . . The people loved that. . . . And it was known to the whites that we'd brought in reinforcements. But they had no idea how many."

Carmichael said that he and the other SNCC workers in Lowndes County were aware of what he called white "terrorist strongholds." So they secretly posted the Deacons and other "fighters" close to those places and out of sight, with instructions not to act unless acted upon.

"We had a slogan among ourselves," Carmichael said. It was that "the white folks get the first shot and after that it's ours." Fortunately, he said, "the terrorists didn't take that first shot. It would have been grim, Jack."

Chapter 27: 'Nonviolence Is Irrelevant'

On Saturday, April 2, 1966, about 60 local activists gathered at Mt. Moriah Baptist Church in Hayneville, Alabama—the capital of Lowndes County. The purpose of the meeting was to discuss how to take advantage of the organizing campaign that Stokely Carmichael had spearheaded in the county and to take it to the next level.

John Hulett, president of the Lowndes County Christian Movement for Human Rights (LCCMHR), opened the meeting by explaining what he saw as the need to create an independent black political party. "We have to form our own power structure," he said. "If we stay within the Democratic Party, the same people will still be in control."

He reminded the audience that the leaders of the party had recently increased filing fees to deter African Americans from running in the primary, scheduled for May 3.

Hulett said that "power" was the key to effecting the change that everyone in the room had been working for over the past 12 months. "Once you get power, you don't have to beg," he said.

The political party that Hulett and the other local activists voted to create under Title 17, Section 337 of the Alabama Code that Saturday afternoon was called the Lowndes County Freedom Organization (LCFO), known as the Black Panther Party. Six officers were elected run the organization, and the rules that would govern the nominating convention were also discussed.

Before the meeting adjourned, Carmichael was asked to say a few words. "This meeting is very different from any other meeting taking place in the state," he said, "because the candidates are not important. It is the organization that is important."

The meeting ended, as it turned out, without the participants even discussing who would or should run for office even though the convention was only four weeks away.

Later, Carmichael would anger white power brokers and civil rights groups tied to the Democratic Party by urging blacks to boycott the party's primary on May 3 and to vote for independent candidates in the fall general election. "To ask Negroes to get in the Democratic Party is like asking Jews to join the Nazi Party," he told a reporter from The New York Times.

In its April 22 edition, the Times editorialized that SNCC's organizing efforts in Lowndes County were leading African Americans to political suicide. Extremist elements in Alabama's civil rights movement, it argued, had adopted a "rule-or-ruin" attitude toward the upcoming Democratic primary "that can only produce frustration and defeat for the state's Negroes." It said that SNCC's proposed boycott represented "destructive mischief-making" and revolutionary posturing "toward all of society and Government." It called on African Americans in Alabama to "fuse their strength with liberal white voters" in the Democratic primary.

Carmichael's venture into independent black politics also set him and SNCC on yet another collusion course with Martin Luther King Jr.'s SCLC, which was urging Alabama's African American community, for instance, to support the Democratic Party's candidate for governor, Richmond Flowers, the state attorney general who opposed Gov. Wallace's policy of racial segregation.

King spent six days in April traveling to 17 different towns in the state extolling blacks to participate in the political process. One of his senior aides—Hosea Williams, who was SCLC's director of voter registration and political education in Alabama—spent the weeks leading up to the May 3 primary arguing that since blacks knew little about politics and lacked the time to learn, they should support white candidates who offered them the best path to change.

"We must let the Negro vote hang there like ripe fruit," Williams told one crowd, "and whoever is willing to get the Negro the most freedom can pick it. We may not be able to elect a black man, but God knows we can say what white man."

Earlier, in fact, Williams had done little to hide his contempt for SNCC's separatist initiatives in Lowndes County, saying that it smelled of reverse racism. He wondered whether SNCC planned to "treat white folks like the white folks treated them."

In late April, in preparation for the LCFO nominating convention, Hulett asked Lowndes County Sheriff Frank Ryals for permission to use the lawn on the public square in front of the County Courthouse in Hayneville for the event. But Ryals refused, arguing that he could not protect African Americans from angry whites—to which Hulett responded by saying that the LCFO would proceed with plans to hold the convention at the courthouse and that "if the sheriff cannot protect us, then we are going to protect ourselves."

Seeking to avoid a major confrontation, Carmichael wrote to John Doar, chief lawyer at the civil rights division of the U.S. Justice Department, asking the federal government to agree to ensure the safety of the convention participants.

"If we do not hear from you, or if the U.S. government does not find itself able to protect the participants," Carmichael said in the letter, "we shall be forced to look to such resources as we can muster on our own."

He said that Alabama law required the founders of a local political party to convene their nominating convention "in or around a public polling place," and that the courthouse was the county's only site that qualified under the law.

Concerned about the potential for violence, Doar dispatched one of his assistants—a 27-year-old Harvard Law School graduate named Charles R. Nesson—to Hayneville to try to calm the situation.

On the Saturday before the convention, Nesson met with Hulett, who proceeded to tell him that if white vigilantes began shooting, "we are going to stay out there" and blacks and whites will die together. Nesson urged Hulett to call off the event, but Hulett refused. "We are going to have it," he said, "and we are going to protect ourselves."

For a second time, on Sunday afternoon, Nesson met with Hulett but again failed to convince him to cancel the convention. So Nesson went to State Attorney General Flowers and asked him to permit the LCFO to meet at an alternative site, which he did—the First Baptist Church, located a half mile from the courthouse.

After Nesson had relayed this information to Hulett, the LCFO official asked the Justice Department official whether he had received the permission in writing. And when Nesson said that he had not, Hulett told him to "got back and get it legalized," Hulett said later, and by 3 p.m. on Monday the necessary signed papers were waiting for Hulett at the county courthouse.

That account of the events leading up to the convention and to the eventual resolution of the standoff—taken from Hasan Kwame Jeffries' book, Bloody Lowndes: Civil Rights and Black Power in Alabama's Black Belt—differs markedly, however, from the more lively account given by Stokely Carmichael in his book, Ready for Revolution.

Carmichael wrote that Sheriff Frank Ryals had said that "no [expletive] nigger convention is going to happen in my courthouse."

Implicating Ryals in the murder of Episcopal seminarian and civil rights worker Jonathan Daniels in Hayneville eight months earlier, Carmichael wrote that a real crisis was looming. "Of course we were concerned. But the people would not back up an inch."

About a week before the primary, according to Carmichael, "one of those Justice Department men"—probably Nesson—came up to him and said that much violence was expected surrounding the convention. "Yeah," Carmichael replied. "Looks that way."

Carmichael said that the man from the Justice Department suggested that "you people ought to go slow." But Carmichael replied, "Tell the racists to go slow."

"The federal government just passed this voting rights act," Carmichael wrote, referring to the Voting Rights Act of 1965, signed into law by President Johnson on August 6, 1965. "Here I am organizing my people to exercise their democratic rights, and this representative of that same government comes to tell us, 'to go slow.' What's that 'go slow' mean, we shouldn't exercise our rights? I asked him that. Also I reminded him that we weren't the ones who started any violence. Not once. I told him, you should go tell the terrorists to go slow. You best cool out the whites, we ain't chilling nothing, Jack. Tell them, we going straight ahead."

Carmichael said that the official from the Justice Department looked at him like he was crazy. "But there's apt to be a lot of bloodshed," the Justice official said, according to Carmichael. "Yeah," Carmichael replied, "but this time it won't just be our blood," ending the conversation by walking away and saying, "Thank you very much for coming. But I have to go now. I've got to organize my people for war."

On Tuesday, May 3, about 900 registered black voters flocked to the First Baptist Church on the outskirts of Hayneville to cast their ballots , which were emblazoned with the black panther emblem. Jumping up on the church steps, as the voters stopped at seven separate voting stations on the lawn outside the church, Willie Ricks comically praised the "bad niggers" of Lowndes County for coming out.

Later, inside, volunteers counted the votes, and Hulett announced the winners: Sydney Logan Jr. won the nomination for sheriff; Frank Miles Jr. for tax collector; Alice Moore for tax assessor; Emory Ross for coroner; and Robert Logan, John Hinson and Willie Mae Strickland for the Lowndes County school board.

"We have our candidates," Carmichael told reporters that evening, obviously pleased with the turnout. "Their names will be on the ballot November 8 along with our symbol, the Black Panther. All the people have to do is pull the lever under the panther."

"November 8 we vote," Carmichael said. "November 9 we take over the courthouse."

Later, in an interview with the Socialist newsweekly The Militant, Carmichael said that the Lowndes County convention had opened a new political phase in the civil rights movement.

"Nonviolence is irrelevant," Carmichael said, alluding to the philosophy and tactics of Martin Luther King Jr. and his followers. "What King has working for him is a moral force, but we're building a force to take power. We're not a protest movement."

Chapter 28: A New Chairman of SNCC

Following the LFCO convention in Hayneville, the entire SNCC leadership team, including Carmichael, headed to a secluded church camp in Kingston Springs, Tennessee, near Nashville, for the organization's annual meeting.

It was bound to be a singularly important event—a "big 'un," as Carmichael put it—because James Forman had announced that he was stepping down as executive secretary. In addition, for almost two years, SNCC had been in a state of flux, and some serious internal issues needed to be resolved.

Forman wrote later that, as he looked toward the Kingston Springs gathering, "the black panther was growling with increasing vigor." He said that the weight of a century of fear among blacks in the Deep South seemed to be lifting. "Our sisters and brothers in one of the nation's most oppressed and terrorized areas"—Lowndes County—"were showing the way. . . . They were through with being intimidated and carried their guns to show it. They knew what they wanted [and] what they would do to get it. . . ."

But the same was not true, he said, of SNCC. "The basic question, 'What is SNCC?' had not yet been answered," he wrote, questioning whether SNCC could still be called a "nonviolent" organization while it remained in the vanguard of black militancy. "If we were revolutionaries, what was it that we sought to overthrow? Was racism the only problem of black people, or was racism part of a larger system of oppression? Was our struggle simply one of black against white, or also a class struggle of the exploited against those who exploited them?"

Forman said that the Kingston Springs meeting, not unexpectedly, was "very intense," with the 200-plus participants spending a day discussing the assumptions on which SNCC's work had proceeded to date. He said that the discussion was the necessary prelude to changing the nature and direction of SNCC's work—"a prelude to Black Power and more intensive work in the black community. We were shedding the mantle of nonviolence as a tactic."

The discussion also centered around the role of whites in the organization (there were about 40 at the time), and whether they had any role to play. Some participants argued that whites should be expelled from SNCC. A resolution (drafted by Forman) was adopted saying that whites should work in the white community and blacks in the black community "if we were serious," as Forman put it, "about revolutionary change." But the adoption of the resolution did not put an end to the discussion within SNCC over the role of whites.

Also central to defining the future shape and direction of SNCC was whether John Lewis should remain as chairman given that many members were growing increasingly unhappy with his leadership.

Carmichael wrote that everyone in the organization liked Lewis personally. "Personally," he said, "what was there not to like? John was a regular guy, uncomplicated, friendly, brave, always willing to put his body on the line." He recalled a remark made by one of his fellow Freedom Riders—Paul Dietrich, a white seminary student—after the March on Washington in 1963. "Wow," Carmichael recalled Dietrich saying, "this is the first time I've seen John without a bandage on his head."

But politically, according to Carmichael, Lewis no longer represented the majority of SNCC members, particularly those on the Alabama staff. He had participated in the planning of the White House Conference on Civil Rights, scheduled for June 1–2, even though SNCC had decided to boycott the event because, as Carmichael put it, it was nothing more than a "totally cosmetic, public relations" exercise by the Johnson administration.

More importantly, however, Lewis had campaigned actively for several Democratic Party candidates in Alabama despite the fact that Carmichael and the other members of the Alabama SNCC staff had worked to create an independent black political party.

"I had to question whether John had fully understood the implications of that act," Carmichael wrote. "For the staff. For our program. I still wonder. 'Cause it was hard to believe that he, knowingly and deliberately, would publicly undercut our work so blatantly. But what does it say if the chairman is that far out of touch with his organization?"

Carmichael said that it was only after he had arrived in Kingston Springs that he realized that the dissatisfaction with Lewis' leadership was far stronger and more widespread than he had thought.

Toward midnight on May 13, after many of the participants had left the meeting and returned to their cabins for some sleep, a vote was taken on whether to reelect Lewis as chairman of SNCC. He prevailed easily, winning election to a fourth term by 60–22.

But shortly after the vote, Worth Long, who had worked for SNCC, most notably in Arkansas, for many years, showed up at the meeting late and asked what had happened. "John Lewis?" he frowned. "How'd y'all do that? You can't do that. . . . I challenge this election."

Lewis, however, refused to step down, and at around 2 a.m. on the morning of May 14, after those who had left the meeting earlier had returned, a new debate over the chairmanship began.

According to Lewis, the earlier discussion over his role as chairman of the organization—a position he had held since 1963—had become "very low and nasty, very bitter and mean." He said that he had supported keeping whites in the organization but that there was some "backlash" from some of the more strident voices in the room. He was also criticized for spending so much time visiting college campuses around the country—"white" college campuses, he said. He was attacked, he said, for his allegiance to Martin Luther King Jr. Even his strong religious orientation, he said, was attacked.

"People stood up and said we needed someone who could grab Lyndon Johnson by his balls [for not being supportive enough of the civil rights movement] and tell him to kiss our ass," Lewis recalled. "We needed someone who would stand up to Dr. King and tell him the same thing."

Lewis said that he was not about to turn his back on King—"my friend, my hero"—or on whites or any segment of society, including the federal government. "No matter how many times our hopes and dreams seemed dashed," he wrote, "I continued to believe that the American government, along with American society at large, would ultimately respond and open itself up and embrace all of its people."

Willie Ricks, who was chairing the post-midnight meeting, said that when Worth Long and others started talking about a "re-vote," Lewis came up to him and whispered, "Save me. You gotta save me, Willie." But Ricks said that there was no way he could do that, especially after Fay Bellamy, who headed the SNCC office in Selma, rose to criticize Lewis' leadership. "Bro, that sister lit into John like a duck on a June bug," Ricks later recalled. "Man, she turned him every which way but loose. It was after that they decided to vote everything over again."

This time, Lewis was soundly defeated as chairman of SNCC and replaced by Stokely Carmichael, whose star within the organization had been rising measurably in large part because of his success in organizing African Americans in Lowndes County.

For his part, Worth Long, who had initiated the "re-vote," said later that, like most SNCC members, he admired and respected Lewis, who, he said, was "the most courageous person that I have ever worked with in the movement. John would not just follow you into the lion's den, he would lead you into it."

Long said that his motive in challenging Lewis' reelection had been to ensure that SNCC remained on the "cutting edge" of the civil rights movement by putting someone in charge who reflected the increasingly militant mood of the staff.

As for Lewis, he said that he had been ousted as chairman in part because of Forman. "He wanted me out," Lewis wrote in his book Walking With the Wind. "He'd wanted me out for a long time. He was in sympathy with this new wave of militance and separatism [within SNCC]. He had never accepted the philosophy of nonviolence. He'd never accepted the concept of interracial democracy, of a truly biracial society." It had always irked Forman, according to Lewis, to hear him preaching about love and tolerance and nonviolence.

"And that was it," Lewis later recalled. "Stokely Carmichael was the new chairman of SNCC."

Chapter 29: Talk of Retaliation and Violence

A week after Stokely Carmichael was elected chairman of SNCC, replacing John Lewis, the organization issued a statement rejecting as "absolutely unnecessary" President Johnson's proposed White House Conference on Civil Rights. It called the event a "useless endeavor."

The statement reflected a shift to the left within the organization that had been gaining traction since the Selma-to-Montgomery voting rights march a year earlier.

Ruby Doris Robinson, who had replaced James Forman as executive secretary, was asked by a reporter whether snubbing the Johnson administration meant that SNCC no longer considered desegregation to be its primary objective.

"We've been head-lifted and upstarted into white societies all our lives, and we're tired of that," Robinson replied. "What we need is black power."

The aim of the Washington, D.C., conference—scheduled for June 1–2—was to build on the momentum gained with the enactment of the Civil Rights Act of 1964 and the Voting Rights Act of 1965, which legislatively at least addressed certain forms of discrimination against African Americans. Planners of the conference, including Lewis, had organized the agenda around four areas of discussion: housing, economic security, education, and the administration of justice.

But SNCC—the only major civil rights organization to boycott the high-profile conference, which was attended by more than 2,400 participants—said that regardless of what proposals might emerge from the conference, "we know that [the federal government is] not serious about insuring constitutional rights to black Americans." Murderers of civil right workers and black citizens roam free throughout the country, the statement said, while the government claims it is impotent in many situations to bring about justice.

"In the process of exploiting black Americans," the statement said, "white America had tried to shift the responsibility for the degrading position in which blacks now find themselves away from the oppressors to the oppressed. The White House Conference, especially with its original focus on the Negro family as the main problem with which America must deal, accentuates this process of shifting the burden of the problem"—a reference to a speech by President Johnson in which he suggested that many of the problems that blacks had stemmed from the disintegration of the black family.

The SNCC statement concluded by saying that the "people who suffer" must make their own decisions about how to change and direct their lives. "We therefore call upon all black Americans to begin building political, economic and cultural institutions that they will control and use as instruments of social change in this country."

Several days later, in an interview on "Face the Nation," Martin Luther King Jr. was peppered with questions from reporters on whether he agreed with, as one newsman put it, "the most militant of the civil rights organizations" that "integration is irrelevant." Did he feel that his message was being overshadowed by SNCC's intention to "take the battle for civil rights into the streets"?

King was not about to be drawn into a long conversation about militancy. Instead, he responded to a question about whether "militancy" may be more appealing to blacks than "nonviolence" by saying, "Well, I hate to put it like that. . . . We must be militantly nonviolent."

Outside the hotel where the White House conference was being held, several SNCC supporters demonstrated against King and other black leaders who spoke at the conference with signs saying, "Save Us from Our Negro Leaders" and "Uncle Toms!" White students who attempted to join the all-black protest were turned away.

Across the country, in California, Stokely Carmichael was in the process of presenting a surprise guest speaker at the rallies that he had attended in Berkeley on May 24 and Los Angeles the next day: John Hulett.

Hulett, on his first trip west, told the crowd that "there was something in Alabama a few months ago they called fear." But now, he said, blacks were going to "start moving."

Responding to questions about using the black panther as a symbol of the new political party, he said that it is a creature that retreats "backwards, backwards and backwards into his corner, and then he comes out to destroy everything that's before him. Negroes in Lowndes County have been pushed back through the years. We have been deprived of our rights to speak, to move and to do whatever we want to do at all times. And now we are going to start to move."

John Lewis, however, who had joined SNCC in 1961 following its founding a year earlier, decided that he would not be part of whatever the new SNCC planned to do. He served for a brief period as director of its newly formed Committee for International Affairs and resigned from SNCC in mid-July 1966.

"I still had faith in the principles we had applied to the formation of SNCC," Lewis later recalled. "But SNCC itself had now abandoned them. The organization was riddled with bitterness and talk of retaliation and violence, actions that might deliver some quick comfort but that in the long run were debasing. I felt I owed an allegiance to a higher principle than SNCC, and so it was time for me to leave."

At only 26 years ago, he had no idea what to do. "My feelings were hurt. I felt abandoned, cast out. . . . The pain of that experience is something I will never be able to forget."

Luckily, he was offered a job with the Field Foundation, a New York City-based group that supported civil rights and child welfare programs around the country, and he took it.

"I didn't exactly have a lot of options," Lewis recalled. "Leaving the South would be difficult, no question, but maybe it would be good for me to put some space between what was behind me and what lay ahead. Besides, I needed a job. And so, on the first day of August 1966, I went to work as the associate director of the Field Foundation in New York City."

He said that, as he rode the train north from Atlanta, he felt more lonesome than he had ever felt before. "I had lived a lifetime in the past six years, and now the rest of my life lay ahead of me, without a map, without a blueprint. All I kept thinking was, Where am I going? And why? Why?"

Chapter 30:
Self-Defeating
Extremism?

Defenders of the new SNCC, led by Stokely Carmichael, sought to downplay the significance of the leadership change for several weeks following his election. Even John Lewis, speaking just before he resigned from SNCC, said that the organization would remain committed to ridding society of racism and building a world community "at peace with itself."

But the white-controlled mainstream media saw only gloom and doom in the new SNCC.

Jack Nelson, of the Los Angeles Times, said in an article published on the day after Carmichael's election that Carmichael, in his view, was "one of the more radical leaders of SNCC," pointing to his role in forming an all-black political party in Lowndes County, Alabama.

Conservative columnists such as the widely syndicated team of Roland Evans and Robert Novak were particularly incensed—albeit gleeful—saying that SNCC had now completely "disengaged" itself from the civil rights movement. "For responsible Negro leaders who long have viewed [SNCC's] extremism as self-defeating," they wrote, "such disengagement would be too good to be true."

The editors of TIME magazine wrote that Carmichael's emphasis on creating an all-black political party was an "emotional and possibly persuasive argument to many Negroes." But the editors concluded that "it could only lead to even greater isolation and bitterness for the Negro in the South."

For his part, Carmichael attempted to reassure his white allies in the weeks following his election that SNCC had no plans to instigate a policy of "racism in reverse." Or to promote violence for its own sake. He told a reporter for the radical weekly National Guardian that whites could play an important role in the black struggle by fighting racism in white communities.

Carmichael said that white liberals needed to understand that African Americans wanted to build something of their own. "And that is not anti-white. When you build your own house, it doesn't mean you tear down the house across the street."

He said that columnists like Evans and Novak, who had once "red-baited" SNCC, were now beginning to "black-bait" the organization by criticizing its focus on black independence.

A year earlier, Evans and Novak had blamed Carmichael for making it impossible for Lowndes County Sheriff Frank Ryals to abandon his "hereditary segregationism," arguing that Ryals had become alienated from the African American community because of their push for voting rights. The columnists had also written that John Lewis and James Forman were "hot-headed extremists" and that SNCC was "substantially infiltrated by "beatnik left-wing revolutionaries and—worst of all—by Communists."

The New York office of SNCC echoed Carmichael's attempts to ease the concerns of the organization's white allies by issuing a statement, "What's Happening in SNCC?", which sought to correct what it called the "vastly distorted reports and outright lies" concerning SNCC that had appeared in the press. It said that SNCC indeed had changed course but that the election of Carmichael as chairman did not represent a "take-over" by "anti-white extremists."

The statement compared raising black consciousness to what other ethnic groups had done in the past by developing "cultural awareness" and "pride," particularly in times of struggle. Its supporters were assured that SNCC's "emphasis on the need for power" existed alongside the "basic, humanistic spirit for which SNCC has long been known."

At a press conference in Atlanta, Carmichael and the new leadership team also stressed continuity. But the press, according to Carmichael, did not understand what they were saying. It was, he wrote, "as if they were stuck in 1960 with the student sit-ins and we were speaking in unknown tongues. . . . And they missed that the new direction was simply a necessary response to current political realities."

"It was as though the unity and progress of the civil rights movement was under threat from 'young, black militants' who had suddenly materialized inside SNCC—apparently from outer space and speaking . . . no language known to the American media," Carmichael wrote. "And the efforts at clarification made by Julian Bond and SNCC's small, hardworking publicity staff seemed to fall on deaf ears. . . . I saw then that the major part of my job—projecting publicly a new role and identify for SNCC—was not going to be so easy."

SNCC's New York office also announced that Carmichael would be devoting the bulk of his time to "traveling around our southern projects, strengthening the staff."

Carmichael said that he was looking forward to it, to evaluating conditions on the ground, the morale of the staff, their needs and, most importantly, finding out how they wanted to be represented.

But even before he began that task, he and the other leaders of SNCC were drawn into a series of events in Mississippi that would—as the African American scholar Clayborne Carson put it—"profoundly affect the future of SNCC and of the black struggle."

Chapter 31:
Negroes With Guns

One of the first trips that Stokely Carmichael took after assuming the SNCC chairmanship was to Little Rock, Arkansas. On the first day he was there, someone rushed into a meeting and said that James Meredith had been killed on a highway in Mississippi just south of Memphis.

Carmichael's first reaction was that Meredith had been murdered. "I felt cold, suddenly numb from the top of my head to the soles of my feet," he wrote. "Weary to the bone."

Four years earlier, Meredith had become the first African American student to be admitted to the University of Mississippi. And with it, he had gained a degree of notoriety which he now hoped to exploit by showing that a black man could walk alone through Mississippi without fear.

At a press conference in late May, Meredith said that his so-called March Against Fear—some 220 miles along U.S. Highway 51 from Memphis to Jackson—would challenge "that all-pervasive fear that dominates the day-to-day life of the Negro in the United States, especially in the South, and particularly in Mississippi." Along the route of the march, he said, he would also encourage the 450,000 or so unregistered African Americans in Mississippi to register to vote.

He said that others might want to join him but that they only be allowed to participate if they were independent men. "Absolutely no women or children should be allowed," he said. "I am sick and tired of Negro men hiding behind their women and children."

Carmichael wrote later that Meredith had always been, in his view, "a strange, almost eccentric brother." Now he had embarked almost single-handily on a protest that, Carmichael said, was a noble but bad idea. "With predictable results."

"Now the brother was dead, uselessly and senselessly," Carmichael remembered thinking at the time. "Worse than useless, because the only message our people would get would be the one the assassin wanted them to get."

It wasn't until several hours later that Carmichael and his traveling staff, including SNCC Program Secretary Cleveland Sellers and SNCC Executive Secretary Stanley Wise, learned that Meredith, in fact, had not been killed but only slightly injured in the attack.

They had learned that a white man named Aubrey James Norvell—on the second day of the march, Monday, June 6—had jumped out of the woods just south of Hernando, Mississippi, and opened fire on Meredith with a shotgun. He fell to the ground bleeding from his right shoulder, head, neck, right leg and right arm. Laying on the shoulder of U.S. Highway 51, as he recalled later, he lamented having taken only his Bible along. He should have taken a gun.

The 32-year-old Meredith was rushed to John Gaston Hospital in Memphis, where an emergency room doctor pronounced him in satisfactory condition with only superficial wounds. He was later transferred to a better-equipped medical facility nearby, Bowld Hospital, where FBI agents and Memphis police officers occupied three adjacent rooms.

In Little Rock, after a brief discussion, Carmichael, Sellers and Wise decided to make the relatively short drive to Memphis to pay their respects.

"Our mood during the drive was grim, bordering on desperation," Carmichael recalled. "We were angry and tired, tired, tired. Tired of folks being brutalized or killed with impunity. Tired of the indifference and complicity of the nation. Tired of mealymouthed politicians. Tired, too, especially of half-baked, knee-jerk ideas from our side. Particularly of those wretched, pointless marches, appealing to whom? Accomplishing what? What we felt in that car was an all-encompassing anger and frustration, as much with movement futility as with the racist violence."

Other movement leaders were equally outraged. The NAACP in New York wrote a threatening letter to "The People of Mississippi"—care of the office of Gov. Paul Johnson—saying that the days of peaceful protest were over. And J. Franklyn Bourne, of the Prince George's County, Maryland, chapter of the NAACP said that, from now on, he would be armed. "I've been leaning over backward," Bourne told a reporter from The Washington Star. "But this is ridiculous. Anybody who comes my way had better be armed because I'm going to be ready."

In Atlanta, Martin Luther King Jr. was attending a staff meeting at SCLC headquarters when they heard the news. The room went silent, then erupted in rage. After some discussion, and after learning that Meredith had survived, they decided to fly to Memphis immediately.

The next morning, at Bowld Hospital, the leaders of several major civil rights organizations, including King,

Carmichael and McKissick (of CORE), met for about an hour with Meredith in his hospital room and asked him if they could continue the march that he had begun. He was initially wary, but he finally agreed.

Andrew Young, one of King's principal assistants, opposed the march. He said that it was not something that SCLC, SNCC, CORE or any other national organization had initiated but simply an "ego trip by one man." He wrote later that he thought it was wrong to set aside SCLC's priorities at the time, which focused on Chicago, to pursue Meredith's dream. "There were times to go with the spirit. This was not one of them."

But in the end, King prevailed by arguing that SCLC had a moral obligation to continue the march. "Wouldn't failure to continue only intensify fears of the oppressed and deprived Negroes of Mississippi?" he wrote. "Would this not be a setback for the whole civil rights movement and a blow to nonviolent discipline?"

While still not convinced of the effectiveness of mass marches, Carmichael thought that this one might make sense. It would be proceeding through the heart of the Mississippi Delta, where SNCC had been engaged with the local population since the early 1960s. It was "our turf," he later wrote. "How could SNCC let other organizations march through and we be absent? No way we could explain that to the local people, especially the youth."

The Mississippi Delta was also where Carmichael—along with Sellers, Wise and others—had spent the summer of 1964 organizing "Freedom Summer." So there was an emotional component to the march for him as well.

Carmichael also began to see the march as an opportunity to showcase the new SNCC approach to the movement for justice.

"[We could be] doing voter registration at every court-house we passed," he reasoned. "Have a rally every night. We could involve the local communities. Address their needs." He contrasted it with previous mass protests, such as the voting rights march from Selma-to-Montgomery, which he called "promenades of the prominent."

But the final decision on whether to continue the march on Meredith's behalf could only be taken in concert with the other civil rights leaders.

On Tuesday, June 7, Roy Wilkins, of the NAACP, and the Urban League's Whitney Young flew to Memphis for a late-night strategy session with the leaders of the other "big five" civil rights organizations: King, Carmichael and McKissick.

The leaders, along with several aides, met at the Lorraine Motel (where King would be killed by an assassin's bullet in April 1968). Accounts of the meeting vary. But broadly speaking, it pitted Wilkins and Young, on the one hand, against Carmichael and McKissick, on the other, with King playing the role of mediator.

Two demands that Carmichael put forward at the meeting, which were supported by McKissick, were particularly offensive to Wilkins and Young: that whites should be excluded from the march and that the Deacons for Defense and Justice should be invited to provide armed security for the marchers.

An original co-founder of the Deacons, Earnest "Chilly Willy" Thomas, had already arrived in Memphis, having driven down from Chicago, where he had formed a West Side chapter of the Deacons. With him was a contingent of heavily armed men. As they pulled into the Lorraine Motel parking lot and piled out of their van with M-1 rifles and bandoliers, they were questioned by the police. Asked by one officer why they were so heavily armed, Thomas reportedly replied, "That's the only way we're going to Mississippi." They were not detained because guns were legal as long as they were not concealed.

Carmichael later recalled that, prior to the meeting of the "big five" leaders that night, he had run into a "brother" from the Deacons—probably Thomas—who formally offered to provide security for the march.

"We knew the Deacons from over in Lowndes," Carmichael wrote. "We owed them. Besides, they were as brave, well-trained and as disciplined a group of brothers you could hope to find. . . . Businesslike, no posturing, no rhetoric. Plus, we needed them. . . ." He became convinced, therefore, that there would be at least one tough issue to be resolved at the "big five" meeting that night: "Negroes with guns."

At the meeting, Carmichael made it clear from the outset that SNCC supported having Deacons provide protection for the march. But when Thomas entered the room uninvited—on a tip from the comedian and activist, Dick Gregory, that the meeting was being held—not only did Wilkins and Young object to Carmichael's proposal but so did Hosea Williams, one of King's senior aides. "Well, I'm going to tell you right now," Williams said, "there ain't going to be no Deacons on the march."

But Thomas cautioned Williams and the others in the room that they risked losing the support of local blacks by allowing people to get hurt. "Then you get back on them god-damn airplanes and you fly off and forget about them." This was going to be a "different" march, he said.

As for King, he looked surprised and asked Thomas whether he was saying that the Deacons were planning to march.

"I have no intention of marching one block in Mississippi," Thomas replied. "But we're going to be up and down the highways and the byways. And if someone gets shot again, they going to have somebody to give account to for that."

As the meeting progress, King sought to maintain a semblance of unity among the leaders. But that proved to be virtually impossible.

Wilkins and Young proposed issuing a nationwide call for whites to join the march; insisted that the Deacons be excluded; and demanded that the leaders issue a statement proclaiming adherence to nonviolence.

Toward morning, McKissick announced his support for whatever Carmichael proposed, which was exactly the opposite of what Wilkins and Young wanted. So McKissick said that he was tired of arguing and went to bed.

Furious that King had refused to repudiate Carmichael, Wilkins and Young packed up their briefcases, saying that they would have nothing to do with the march.

The next day, the three leaders who had remained at the meeting—King, Carmichael and McKissick—issued a "manifesto" pledging to continue the march that Meredith had begun, explaining that it would be a "massive public indictment and protest of the failure of American society, the Government of the United States and the State of Mississippi" to ensure the rights of African Americans.

"We are all aware that Mississippi is symbolic of every evil that American Negroes have long endured," the statement said. "James Meredith returned to Mississippi to confront the problems of fear and political disenfranchisement that have plagued black Americans of this state. Mississippi's reply to Meredith's witness was a blast from a 16-gauge shotgun. Decent Americans will not allow this march for freedom and justice to end here. We are determined that

James Meredith's pilgrimage and wounds will not have been in vain."

In the end, after Wilkins and Young had left the meeting, Carmichael and McKissick prevailed, convincing King that the Deacons would be allowed to protect the marchers. But Carmichael and McKissick had to drop their demand that whites be excluded.

"All night Dr. King had played a patient, conciliatory role, seeking, if at all possible, unity," Carmichael wrote of the meeting years later. "He tried to steer a middle course, to reconcile differences and find common ground. Seeking at all times to be fair and practical."

Chapter 32: 'We Have Another Weapon'

The spot where James Meredith had been shot on the afternoon of June 6 was near the town of Hernando, Mississippi, about 25 miles south of Memphis. It was there, the next day, that King, Carmichael and McKissick decided to resume the March Against Fear that Meredith had started earlier in the week.

From Memphis, after visiting Meredith at the hospital, the three civil rights leaders, along with several staff members, drove to the site of the shooting, and there King led the protesters in prayer before locking arms with other protesters beginning to walk slowly while singing "We Shall Overcome."

They had only moved about 200 yards along the highway, however, when three highway patrolmen began bellowing orders, telling them to move off the highway and on to the shoulder of the road.

One officer, Fred Ogg, shoved King in the chest. SNCC's Cleveland Sellers fell backward into the mud, and King half-tripped over him, throwing Carmichael into a rage. But before Carmichael could attack the officer, King pulled him back.

"I yanked free to go after [the officer]," Carmichael later wrote, "got one arm free, but Dr. King had my right hand and was not letting go. I was fighting to get to that cracker. . . . A bunch of folks piled on top of me. After they cooled me out, we continued the march. We walked on the highway."

King later joked that he had restrained Carmichael—"nonviolently."

At a meeting in Memphis that night, King gently lectured Carmichael over the way he had reacted during the incident earlier in the day, telling him that he now had a special responsibility as the leader of SNCC. But Carmichael, while appreciating what King said, told King that if "those good white folk" want nonviolence to stay alive, "they had better not touch you. . . . Because, Dr. King, the moment they touch you is the moment that nonviolence is finished, done."

Coincidentally, as Carmichael was addressing the issue of nonviolence with the SCLC leader in Memphis, SNCC's office in San Francisco was publishing an interview with him in its monthly newsletter in which he did not mince words.

"[Y]ou don't work for integration in this country—what you've got to work for is power," Carmichael said in the interview, published in the June 1966 issue of The Movement. "[And when] you talk about going for power, moral force and nonviolence become completely irrelevant. When you go for power, you go for it the way everyone in the country goes for it."

Carmichael also had some harsh words to say about what he said was King's notion that "anything all black," as Carmichael put it, "is as bad as anything all white." But that, according to Carmichael, is not true because "anything all white" is only bad if you use force to keep it that way. Similarly, he said, the same holds true for something all black.

On the night of June 7, after returning to Memphis after walking several miles along U.S. Highway 51 from just south of Hernando to just north of Coldwater, the three civil rights leaders—King, Carmichael and McKissick—held a mass meeting at Centenary Methodist Church, the official headquarters of the march, which was attended by more than 600 people.

Also attending the meeting were Roy Wilkins, of the NAACP, and Whitney Young, of the Urban League, who had reconsidered their earlier decision to boycott the march and flown back to Memphis from New York.

Wilkins spoke first, urging the crowd to reject the message that he said was being conveyed implicitly by Carmichael and McKissick. "If you start hating all white men," he said, "you're going to be wasting your energies." Young echoed the NAACP executive director's comments, saying that he would "disassociate" himself from anyone calling for a "segregated black nationalist society." Both men received loud applause.

But the loudest cheers were reserved for McKissick and Carmichael, who challenged the crowd to act. McKissick said that the Statue of Liberty was a hypocrite and that it ought to be thrown into Mississippi River. And Carmichael said that if the people wanted justice, they would have to take control of the levers of power. "We need power!" he said.

Again King, who spoke last, was forced to play the role of mediator. "We have power," he said, seeking to appease those like Carmichael who were now focusing their message on control, "and it isn't in bricks and guns. We have another weapon: nonviolence."

Throughout the march, however, Carmichael was not about to rely on nonviolence to protect the marchers. The job of protecting the marchers, he said, would fall to Earnest "Chilly Willy" Thomas and his fellow Deacons for Defense and Justice.

He wrote later that he met with the Deacons before the march "to clarify their responsibilities." Their role would be to patrol the perimeters of the march and to guard the campsites at night. During the day, he said, they would walk along the small ridges paralleling the highway and look for possible ambush sites and "very politely check out anyone found loitering there."

Some Deacons would also be positioned in cars in front of and behind the marchers; others would guard King. Another co-founder of the Deacons, Charles R. Sims, later recalled that he was armed with two snub-nosed .38 revolvers and two boxes of shells, and three of his men had driven up and down the highway with semi-automatic rifles and thirty rounds of ammunition apiece. "See," he was quoted as saying, "I didn't believe in that naked shit, no way."

The first week of the march went relatively smoothly. More than 20 state highway patrol cars were onsite allegedly to protect the marchers during the day—although Carmichael would later call the state troopers a joke. At night, the Deacons stood guard at the campsites with rifles, shotguns and pistols. The number of marchers varied from about 30 to some 250 each day, with many local blacks joining in briefly as the parade passed through town.

Voter registration remained a principal focus of the march in large part because Mississippi had the lowest percentage of registered black voters in the South. In 1964, only 6.7 percent of the state's voting-age African American population were registered, compared with 38.3 percent of all southern blacks and 69.9 percent of whites.

A high point of the march came in the town of Batesville on June 11 when a black farmer named El Fondren, whose age was variously reported by friends and family as somewhere between 104 and 106, registered to vote for the first time in his life. Several young men hoisted him on their shoulders as he emerged from the courthouse and carried him through a cheering crowd.

Teams of organizers, including Willie Ricks, who had been asked by Carmichael to come to Mississippi for the march, went ahead of the marchers to encourage local sharecroppers and others to join in. Other organizers fanned out across neighboring counties and pressed blacks to make sure they registered to vote.

Carmichael later wrote that the voter registration teams were often harassed by local whites throwing rocks and bottles. They would be followed by groups with guns and clubs swearing to kill them. "Those teams went through hell, man," he wrote, "yet they registered a lot of folk. But it was nerve-wracking and you'd have folks saying the teams should be allowed to carry weapons. Before someone got killed. But the leadership counseled restraint, nonviolent discipline. But the debate [over whether the civil rights workers should carry weapons] went on inside the tents every night."

On June 13, at a campsite near the Enid Reservoir, the debate spilled out into the open when the Rev. Theodore Seamans, a white Methodist pastor from New Jersey, saw a .45-caliber pistol lying on the seat of a car belonging to Deacons co-founder Earnest Thomas. He confronted

Thomas, saying that this was no place for guns. He also said that many more people would have participated in the march if it hadn't been for the unsettling presence of armed Deacons.

A reporter for The New York Times—Gene Roberts— filed a story on the incident later in the day, quoting Thomas saying that it was wrong to tell blacks that they could not fight back when their lives were at stake.

From there, according to Roberts, the discussion spread throughout the campsite to the other marchers. It only ended, he wrote, when Bruce Baines, a field worker for CORE, called the marchers together, telling them, "If you want to discuss violence and nonviolence, don't talk around the press. This march is too important."

McKissick later told reporters that he was not aware of any weapons at the campsite. He said that he had met with the Deacons and the marchers well into the night and insisted that the march must remain nonviolent. "I don't believe in no damn war," he said.

Chapter 33: Keeping Willie in Check

By the time the March Against Fear had reached Grenada—"one of those horrible, bigoted little Mississippi towns," as Andrew Young put it—several members of Martin Luther King Jr.'s inner circle, including Young, were becoming increasingly concerned with Stokely Carmichael's rejection of nonviolence as a tool for fighting injustice.

Young feared that Carmichael's growing militancy threatened to disrupt the cohesion of the civil rights movement and, therefore, its effectiveness in pursuing the struggle.

As executive director of King's SCLC, Young felt a special responsibility for keeping Carmichael and his associates, like Willie Ricks, in line. He was particularly concerned with the tendency of the 24-year-old Carmichael to break with what he called the "shared discipline" of the march in order to advance some personal agenda.

"We were in the midst of a march involving a group of people, including women and children," Young later wrote, "and if someone broke discipline and caused the march to be attacked, then everyone was endangered."

Young said he understood the frustration that Carmichael felt when a Mississippi state trooper had charged at him just after the march had begun. But he said that, in his view, it was the "height of stupidity" for Carmichael to have threatened the law officer.

"What was he going to do?" Young asked. "Beat up an armed state trooper single-handedly?" He said that, during the incident, Carmichael became enraged over the officer's behavior and shouted, "To hell with nonviolence. If someone shoves me, I'm going to shove him back." But the problem was, according to Young, that Carmichael was not responsible for himself alone but for the other marchers as well.

Young saw Carmichael's "stunt" as a bad omen—but not the only one. A good friend of his, Robert L. Green, who had taken a leave of absence from his professorship at Michigan State University to join the civil rights movement, had also shown a lack of discipline when the march reached Grenada, about half way between Memphis and Jackson. He said that Green had acted like a "frustrated classroom intellectual" trying to prove his "movement credentials."

In the town square of Grenada, according to Young, Green had climbed onto the statue of Jefferson Davis and draped an American flag over it, yelling, " . . . we want brother Jeff Davis to know the South he represented will never rise again!" He had performed this act as state troopers stood by trying to control their anger and as white townspeople nearby were seething.

Then, a few miles away, as a train was approaching a crossing and threatening to split the march in two, Green ran after the train and jumped aboard, telling the engineer to stop the train. "Stop this train now!" he shouted.

Young called Green's behavior "grandstanding," saying that his friend was obviously caught up in the "freedom high" of the moment. "He had lost all sense of reason," Young wrote later. "Maybe this is what Meredith meant by a 'march against fear'."

But the stop in Grenada also had resulted in some substantial accomplishments. Nearly 200 local residents had registered to vote prior to a celebration at New Hope Missionary Baptist Church, where King announced that Grenada County officials had agreed to deputize six Negro teachers as registrars. "This, my friends," he said, "is our great opportunity. Now is the time to make real the promises of democracy."

In all, about a thousand African Americans had registered to vote since earlier in the week, when the marchers had entered Grenada County, bringing the total to about 1,700 out of about 4,300 in the county who were eligible to cast ballots.

Mississippi Gov. Paul Johnson, for his part, was so upset that the march appeared to be turning into what he called a "voter registration campaign" that he announced a reduction in the number of highway patrol vehicles assigned to protect the marchers from 20 to four.

"We aren't going to wet-nurse a bunch of showmen all over the country," Johnson said at a news conference. He said that local police would now take over the responsibility for protecting the marchers.

From Grenada, on the morning of June 15, the marchers turned west from U.S. Highway 51 into the Mississippi Delta toward Greenwood. As they were leaving Grenada, City Manager John McEachin that all that the city wanted was "to get these people through town and out of here. Good niggers don't want anything to do with this march. And there are more good niggers than sorry niggers."

CHAPTER 34: GOING WILD FOR BLACK POWER

Ahead of the march, Willie Ricks moved through the cotton fields and past the small churches of the Mississippi Delta encouraging sharecroppers and others to join the procession that was heading their way to register to vote. He also used the occasion to test their response to the notion of Black Power, urging local blacks not to respond to his chant of "What do we want?" with "Freedom Now!" but with "Black Power!

Ricks later told Carmichael, "They're going wild for it."

On June 10, Carmichael returned to Atlanta for a meeting of SNCC's Central Committee and used Ricks' assessment to persuade the initially reluctant members of the committee to back the March Against Fear as a way to organize poor black enclaves in the Mississippi Delta along the lines of the Lowndes County model. He called the process "people relating to the concept of Black Power."

Earlier, en route to Mississippi from southwest Georgia, Ricks had stopped in Atlanta to meet with James Forman at SNCC headquarters to raise the idea of using the phrase "Black Power" to rally support among blacks.

Forman said he was receptive to listening to any idea that Ricks might have because he had acquired a reputation as being one of the most effective organizers that SNCC had. He called Ricks "brilliant."

"Suppose I get over there to Mississippi and I'm speaking, I start hollering for 'Black Power'?" Forman said that Ricks asked him. "What do you think of that? Would you back me up? You think it would scare people in SNCC?"

Forman said he urged Ricks to try it. "After all, you'd only be shortening the phrase we are always using—power for poor black people. 'Black Power' is shorter and means the same thing. Go on, try it."

In his memoir The Making of Black Revolutionaries, Forman wrote that Ricks was "one of those unknown heroes who captured the mood of history." In calling for Black Power, he wrote, Ricks caught the essence of "the spirit moving black people in the United States and around the world who were poor, black and without power."

The African American scholar Clayborne Carson, in his book, In Struggle: SNCC and the Black Awakening of the 1960s, wrote that Ricks was the first person to sense the impact that could be achieved by "publicly combining a racial term that previously held negative connotations with a goal that always had been beyond the reach of black people as a group."

Ricks later recalled that Carmichael at first did not believe him when he said that the response to Black Power among local Delta sharecroppers and other field workers had been overwhelming.

"Stokely tried to get me thrown off the march for exaggerating," Ricks said, adding, however, that Carmichael soon became convinced after seeing and hearing Ricks "preach" at a local church.

After five days at SNCC headquarters in Atlanta, while Ricks was spreading the Black Power message and mantra in towns and cotton fields throughout the Delta, Carmichael returned to Mississippi on the evening of Wednesday, June 15, arriving at Mt. Zion Missionary Baptist Church in Batesville to meet with other leaders from SNCC, along with CORE and the Deacons for Defense and Justice.

An informant for the Mississippi State Sovereignty Commission—the state-sponsored internal spy agency charged with working to maintain racial segregation—was present when Carmichael spoke and reported that he had talked about "a new SNCC."

According to the informant, Carmichael said that justice would not arrive until "every black man in the South gets a gun and fights fire with fire." He said, according to the informant, that SNCC would bring thousands of blacks to courthouses across Mississippi in cooperation with the Deacons. If white racists stood in their way, he was quoted as saying, "my men will mow them down like dogs."

On the morning of Thursday, June 16, Carmichael led the marchers out of Holcomb, where they had spent the night, down Route 7 toward Greenwood, some 20 miles away. Several young white men harassed the marchers, driving back and forth in two cars and yelling racial insults.

That afternoon, an advance team was searching for a place for the marchers to rest near Avalon, about 10 northeast of Greenwood, when a white man, Eugene H. Neill, came out of his house and demanded that they get off of his property.

R. B. Cottonreader, a veteran SCLC "foot soldier," jumped off a truck and approached Neill, saying, "We are both adults. You don't have to shout." But Neill pulled out a revolver and threatened Cottonreader, prompting the police to intervene before the conflict had escalated.

Born in Texas, Cottonreader spent several years in San Francisco working with CORE before moving South, where he devoted nearly four decades of his life to the movement. He eventually joined King's SCLC, working primarily in Georgia, Alabama and Mississippi.

Another SCLC "foot soldier," Willie Bolden, said after Cottonreader's death in 2013, at the age of 81, that he loved working with Cottonreader "because you knew something was going to happen, you just didn't know what it was."

"There was going to be a riot, someone was going to jail, something was going to happen," Bolden said, "Cottonreader was going to see to it that something changed."

Crossing into LeFlore County, the marchers entered a part of the South known for its blues music and cotton—but also for its uniquely vicious brand of racial oppression.

It was in LeFlore County that the first chapter of the White Citizens' Councils was formed. Lynchings were commonplace. Intimidation, beatings and cold-blooded killings were regularly used as tools to keep blacks "in their place."

It was the very viciousness of racism in LeFlore County, in fact, that drove some of the early SNCC activists like Bob Moses to establish a beachhead in the county seat of Greenwood, which, according to one writer, "sheltered some of the nastiest segregationists in the entire South."

For Stokely Carmichael, entering the city of Greenwood on the afternoon of June 16 as part of the March Against Fear was like a "homecoming." He had worked there as the head of the SNCC office during the the summer of 1964. "Everyone in the community knew me," he recalled. "Even the whites. I'd been in jail so much even the police chief knew me."

By the spring of 1966, however, the SNCC presence in the city had become a shadow of what it had once been. So when the route of the March Against Fear was redirected from the north-south highway running from Memphis to Jackson—U.S. Highway 51—to Greenwood, Carmichael saw it as an opportunity to reignite some of the lost spirit of the old movement. But this time, something new would be added to the mix: a call for Black Power.

Chapter 35: Let's Put Up This Tent

The white power structure of Greenwood, for their part, looked forward to the arrival of Stokely Carmichael and the March Against Fear in their city with a sense of heightened apprehension, if not downright fear.

As a precaution, Mayor Charles E. Sampson cancelled the leave of the city's entire police force and put all 33 officers on 12-hour shifts. He also sent a telegram to Mississippi Gov. Paul Johnson seeking additional state law enforcement support, saying that Greenwood had been a favorite target of "racial agitators" for years—aided and encouraged by the U.S. Department of Justice, "which is actively seeking and sponsoring this present unrest in our state."

A front-page editorial in The Greenwood Commonwealth on June 16—the day that Carmichael arrived in the city— urged residents to ignore the marchers. It compared Martin Luther King Jr., who was expected to join the marchers in Greenwood, to Joseph Stalin and Mao Tse-tung.

"This man has created more violence and left more hatred in his path than any other civil rights leader in the country's history," the newspaper's editors wrote. They called on residents to "let King walk his merry way down the highway."

Local residents like Sara Criss, a reporter for The Commercial Appeal in Memphis, recalled that Carmichael had spent time in Greenwood before. "He always spelled trouble," she said. Racial tension was high, she said, noting that the Ku Klux Klan was active and even threatening to increase its presence in the city.

A few weeks earlier, Criss and Carol Franklin, a reporter for The Greenwood Commonwealth, had covered a meeting of the KKK on a hot Sunday afternoon, attended by about 200 people. "Many of those attending wore white robes," Criss wrote. "'Dixie' and 'The Star-Spangled Banner' were being played on record players."

She said that Byron De La Beckwith, who was later convicted of murdering Mississippi civil rights leader Medgar Evers, was introduced to loud applause. The featured speaker at the event, she said, was E.L. McDaniel, the Mississippi Grand Dragon of the United Klans of America (UKA), who told the crowd that the KKK was "coming back from every hill and hollow. It is the only thing left." He referred to Martin Luther King Jr. as a "dirty rotten filthy skunk nigger."

McDaniel had been recruited to the Louisiana-based Original Knights of the Ku Klux Klan in 1962. Two years later he helped form the White Knights of Mississippi— an extremely militant organization later implicated in the murders of civil rights workers Andrew Goodman, James Chaney and Michael Schwerner. He became Mississippi Grand Dragon of the UKA in August 1964.

The House Un-American Activities Committee (HUAC), which conducted an investigation into the Klan in 1966, concluded that membership in the UKA had surged because it had done a better job than other Klans of exploiting the Civil Rights Act of 1964, portraying the legislation "as the beginning of the extinction of the white race and the start of Negro domination of the South. . . ."

Covering the March Against Fear were reporters from the major national news outlets, including Charles Murphy, of NBC News. On the day before the march was due to arrive in Greenwood, Murphy asked Sara Criss if she wanted to join him and the other newsman on the flatbed truck that the reporters had rented to cover the march.

"I would have loved to have been able to," Criss wrote, "but would not have dared." Such a move, she said, would not have been popular with her friends and neighbors, many of whom distrusted the media.

She said that, in the end, it was a good thing that she had let her better judgement rule because after the truck loaded with the news crews left Greenwood on the day the march-ers were to arrive, someone opened an ice chest on the truck and found a rattlesnake inside. The rumor around town, she said, was that the man who had been hired to drive the truck was a member of the KKK.

On the morning of June 16, as tension in the city remained elevated, an advance team of marchers attempted to erect a tent on the grounds of the Stone Street Negro Elementary School but were told that they did not be have permission to do so. When they returned to the march on Route 7, however, they were told to go back and set up the tent anyway.

At around 1 p.m., as crews were unloading the tent at the Stone Street school, several city officials arrived on the scene, including William "W.G." Mize, the city commis-sioner and Curtis Lary, the police chief, who read a letter from the Board of Education denying them the use of school property.

When Carmichael arrived, he asked, "What's the problem? Let's put this tent up." But Police Commissioner B.A. "Buff" Hammond, who had also come to the school, he told Carmichael that "you are not putting those tents here." To which Carmichael responded, "We are raising these tents up here."

Hammond then ordered his officers to arrest Carmichael if he "put a hand on that tent," and when Carmichael and two other march leaders—Bob Smith, of SNCC, and Bruce Baines, of CORE—grabbed the canvas, they were handcuffed, charged with trespassing and hauled off to jail.

Afterword, Hammond appeared to regret the incident, saying that there had been no problem except for "Stokely's mouth." The police commissioner said that he had wanted to avoid a confrontation but that Carmichael had provoked him. "What's a man going to do? There are times when you have to hold your head up. Stokely said he was going to turn this town upside down."

Chapter 36: Lashing Out at Whites

As Carmichael was being arrested in Greenwood on June 16, his friend and SNCC colleague Willie Ricks, who was a also on the scene, told him not to resist arrest and to let the police take him to jail. "We'll get you out," Ricks said, "and you come out and make the speech tonight."

The speech that Ricks wanted Carmichael to deliver would deal in large part with the need for black people to gain power—Black Power. Ricks had spent the day prepping the black residents of the city for that message.

That evening, after his release from jail on $100 bond, Carmichael went to Broad Street Park in the African American neighborhood of Greenwood known as Baptist Town, where Ricks and other activists were already conducting a rally attended by as many as 3,000 people. When Carmichael arrived, Ricks told him, "We have everything prepared. We're ready for Black Power."

David Dawley, a graduate student at the University of Michigan who had come to Mississippi to join the march after Meredith had been shot, said that earlier in the day he had heard Ricks speaking to a crowd in Baptist Town and was shocked.

"He was angry," Dawley recalled, "and he was lashing out at whites like a cracking whip. And as he talked, there was a chill, there was a feeling of a rising storm." He said that Ricks exhorted the crowd not to demand "Freedom Now"—the slogan used by Martin Luther King Jr.'s SCLC—but "Black Power."

Dawley said that Ricks' message was "frightening" to hear. "Suddenly, the happy feeling of the march was threatened," he later recalled. "Suddenly I felt threatened. It seemed like a division between black and white. It seemed like a hit on well-intentioned northern whites like me, that the message from Willie Ricks was 'Go home, white boy, we don't need you.'"

That evening, Carmichael addressed the crowd at Broad Street Park in a fiery speech from a makeshift stage on the back of truck—with Ricks urging him over and over again to "hit them now" with the "Black Power" chant.

Cleveland Sellers, who was also there, said that when Carmichael moved forward to speak, the crowd greeted him with a huge roar, and he acknowledged the reception with a raised arm and a clenched first.

"This is the twenty-seventh time I've been arrested," Carmichael shouted. "I ain't going to jail no more." He said that black people had done nothing but beg. "We begged the federal government. We begged and begged. . . . We've got to stop begging and take power."

"The only way we gonna stop them white men from whuppin' us is to take over," Carmichael yelled. "We been saying freedom for six years and we ain't got nothin'. What we got to start saying now is Black Power! We want Black Power! We want Black Power!"

Then, according to Sellers, Willie Ricks sprang into action, demonstrating that he was, as Sellers put it, "as good at orchestrating the emotions of a crowd as anyone I have ever seen."

According to Sellers, Ricks jumped up on the stage next to Carmichael and asked the crowd, "What do you want?" The reply from the crowd came back as expected. "BLACK POWER!" "What do you want? "BLACK POWER!" "What do you want?" "BLACK POWER!" "What do you want?" "BLACK POWER!" "What do you want?" "BLACK POWER! BLACK POWER! BLACK POWER!"

Even John Lewis, who had just been unseated as the chairman of SNCC by Carmichael, had to admire him and Ricks for so effectively introducing a phrase that reflected what Lewis called "the shift of the entire civil rights movement."

"It was . . . Willie Ricks who brought this about," Lewis wrote. "Ricks was twenty-three, three years younger than I. He had come out of Chattanooga, Tennessee, as a high school student in the early '60s. He was brash, aggressive and understandably angry—early on, a close friend of his was killed during a demonstration."

On the night of June 16 in Greenwood, according to Lewis, people were clearly ready for a concept like Black Power, "and they really responded." He said that Ricks's timing was perfect. "A nerve was struck."

According to Carmichael, that night in Greenwood "belonged to us," noting that King was away in Memphis taping a television interview.

The next day, King returned to Greenwood and privately urged Carmichael not to use the phrase "Black Power," calling it "an unfortunate choice of words." But Carmichael told him that he could not decide on his own not to use the phrase—"this was an organizational decision, not mine. . . ."

After Greenwood, Carmichael used every opportunity he had—rallies, interviews and press conferences—to promote the phrase. At gatherings in small towns, he would mount a platform and ask, "What do you want?" And the answer was always the same, "BLACK POWER! BLACK POWER!"

Sellers said that, at those rallies, he and Ricks would move through the crowd distributing Black Power leaflets and placards that had been printed at SNCC headquarters in Atlanta.

In Greenwood on Friday, June 17—the day after Carmichael's "Black Power" speech in Broad Street Park—King led about 600 people from the park, where the marchers had camped that night, to the LeFlore County Courthouse.

As they passed a local gas station, the attendant, Booker Riley, turned a garden hose on them, and Carmichael quickly bolted toward him before several highway patrolmen responded by blocking his path. Retreating to the station, Riley soon emerged wielding a billy club, with a pistol also stuffed in his back pocket. Six policemen quickly brought the situation under control.

Sara Criss, a Greenwood native and a reporter for The Commercial Appeal, said that the marchers would have loved to have provoked "an incident," but the townspeople "just went on about their business and tried to ignore them."

She recalled that at one point she and her husband looked down from the courthouse steps on hundreds of black people raising their fists and shouting, "Black Power!"

"It became a chant," she said, "and I was really getting nervous." She began to wonder what she was doing there when she had two young children at home. "The rally did not last too long," she said, "and there was no trouble when it broke up. But we felt better when they had moved on toward Jackson."

At the courthouse rally, Carmichael told the crowd that black nationalism did not mean being anti-white. "That's the trick bag the press is trying to get me into. But I'm not anti-white."

Not surprisingly, King did not use the phrase "Black Power" but did try to explain what was meant by power for black people. "You can always tell where the Negro community begins because that is where the pavement ends," he said. "We're going to change that when we get the ballot. That's what we mean when we say power." Then, implicitly rejecting black nationalism, King added that "when we get this power, we will try to achieve a society of brotherhood."

SCLC Executive Director Andrew Young said that the Black Power chant, which he called a "militant expression," was born out of the "bitterness and disillusionment" of SNCC activists who were "optimistic and naive." He said that King and his associates at SCLC were "more cautious in our struggle and moderate in our expectations."

But Young wrote in his memoir An Easy Burden, published in 1996, that SCLC at the same time had no quarrel with the concept of Black Power. On the contrary, its campaigns—selective boycotts, voter registration initiatives etc.—were very much aimed at empowering black people. But King, he wrote, was uncomfortable with the "rhetoric and tone" of the slogan and with its lack of substance. It was just a chant, he wrote, with no program.

Young said that King had told him, "Listen, Andy, if Stokely is saying the same thing I'm saying, he becomes my assistant. Stokely and the students are struggling to develop their own identify. We just have to accept that." In fact, Young said, King and Carmichael were saying essentially the same thing. "Their styles were different, and Stokely's style was new, startling and attention-getting."

His dispute with the phrase "Black Power," Young wrote, was less about what those espousing it might do than about how the words might be misinterpreted, adding that some members of the media, for example, were already associating violence with the phrase.

Three decades later, Young wrote, "I now realize that if we [in SCLC] were older, more settled and more conventional in our thinking, we needed the energy and daring of younger people [in SNCC], though we may not have liked to admit it."

Chapter 37: The Murderers Around Him

From Greenwood, the main contingent of marchers, led by SCLC's Robert L. Green and SNCC's Willie Ricks, made their way slowly south through the heart of the Mississippi Delta to the small town of Belzoni.

It was here—the so-called Farm-Raised Catfish Capital of the World—where George W. Lee, a black entrepreneur, pastor and president of the local chapter of the NAACP, was shot to death for organizing African Americans to vote in 1955.

On the morning of Monday, June 20, Green told a crowd outside the Green Grove Baptist Church to make sure that they cooperated with the white police officers, while Ricks interrupted him with his now-familiar chants of "Black Power!"

Later, after a rally at the Humphreys County courthouse, Green led a small group into the building and refused to leave until the sheriff unlocked the doors to the "Whites Only" restrooms. "This toilet is symbolic of all the things the Negro has been locked out of in Mississippi," Green said.

From Belzoni, where Green and Ricks had only managed to register about 40 black voters, the marchers continued south along Highway 49 to Silver City, where they turned off onto Highway 149 toward Midnight. There, whites locked up the town's two stores and one outdoor water spigot.

Disappointed at the poor turnout along the sparsely populated route, Ricks headed east alone about 35 miles to a rally in Lexington, the county seat of Holmes County, where black landowners had already led a voter registration drive in cooperation with SNCC and had even dared to shoot back at white terrorists. It was fertile soil for Ricks and his fiery message of "Black Power."

Ricks gently urged the crowd to move closer to him, saying that they were black "and the sun can't hurt you." He blasted the whites who exploited them, and he struck out against Uncle Toms and "nigger preachers."

"We have black power and we intend to use it," Ricks said. "We are going to make them pay for every black person they've beaten, murdered and killed."

That evening, of the 247 people who had begun the march from Belzoni earlier in the day, only about 90 had had the strength to reach the day's stated objective—a 250-acre farm near Louise owned by H.L. Montgomery, the son of a former slave who had purchased the land after the Civil War.

At a closed-door meeting of march leaders on Montgomery's property, according to an informant for the Mississippi State Sovereignty Commission, Ricks spoke "along the revolutionary line," saying that blacks wanted guns and other means of protection "so they could create a black power structure."

The informant wrote in a memo to the Commission that Green, of SCLC, had said that Dr. Martin Luther King Jr. was "very displeased" at the tactics being used by some of the more militant participants in the march—an obvious reference to Carmichael and Ricks. He noted that two white activists who had been participating in the march had packed up and left because of the disturbing cries for Black Power.

Reflecting what he called a "heated argument" at the meeting, the informant concluded that "if it were not for all of the nationwide publicity and financial support, a large percentage of [the civil rights groups] participating in this march would like to call a halt to it. However, they are committed and cannot do anything about it."

The previous day—Sunday, June 19—Ricks had antagonized King and his followers further with cries for Black Power. They were especially upset with his talk of "white blood" flowing in the streets.

Standing on top of a car, leading a rally that blocked off Route 7 just north of Belzoni, Ricks shouted that "from now on, it's not gonna be all black blood. We're gonna get some of that white blood."

King responded by saying that such talk was not only "unfortunate" but that it could incite unrest in such tension-filled cities as Chicago, where his civil rights campaign was now in full swing, as well as in Los Angeles, particularly the predominantly black district known as Watts.

"It is absolutely necessary for the Negro to gain power," King said in an interview with United Press International at SCLC's headquarters in Atlanta, "but the term 'Black Power' is unfortunate because it tends to give the impression of black nationalism."

King said that civil rights activists should never seek power exclusively for the Negro but instead work toward sharing power with white people. Any other course is exchanging one form of tyranny for another, he said. Black supremacy would be equally as evil as white supremacy.

Without naming Carmichael or Ricks, King said that a "very small segment" of the civil rights movement had been speaking of the need for black power. "I see no significant trend in the country toward black nationalism," he said. "The civil rights movement is generally strongly opposed to this philosophy." He said that Negroes have made "their greatest strides" through adherence to nonviolence.

On the morning of Tuesday, June 21, King and his SCLC associates flew to Philadelphia, Mississippi, to lead a march and memorial service in honor of the three civil rights workers—Andrew Goodman, James Chaney and Michael Schwerner—who had been killed by the KKK two years earlier.

But the event quickly turned chaotic as marauding whites struck out against the King-led contingent and local blacks.

The plan was to hold the memorial service at the Neshoba County courthouse after walking from the black section of the city known as Independence Quarters. As soon the group set out, however, they were attacked by cursing mobs of whites.

"Every block there would be an attack," recalled Carmichael. "First came the rocks, bottles and firecrackers. Followed by small gangs with fists and clubs. Cars swerving into the marchers."

At the courthouse, where hundreds of whites awaited the marchers, King addressed lines of blacks kneeling along the pavement. "In this county," he said, "Andrew Goodman, James Chaney and Michael Schwerner were brutally murdered. I believe in my heart that the murderers are somewhere around me at this moment." Reporters heard calls of "right behind you" and "you're damned right."

Deputy Sheriff Cecil Price, in fact, who was at the courthouse with other law officers, had just been charged, along with Sheriff Lawrence Rainey and 16 other white men, with taking part in a conspiracy that ended in the deaths of the three civil rights workers.

"They ought to search their hearts," King said. "I want them to know that we are not afraid. If they kill three of us, they will have to kill all of us." The brief memorial service in front of the courthouse ended with the singing of "We Shall Overcome."

On the return march to the black section of town, according to Roy Reed, a reporter for The New York Times, about 25 white men pushed aside two television reporters and swinging and flailing surged into the line of marchers, "their eyes wild with anger."

"One white man brandished a five-foot wooden club," Reed wrote. "Another held a hoe. Negroes separated him from his companions and mauled him. Several young Negro men struck back with their fists. . . . Bottles and stones flew from the yelling, cursing whites."

That evening, after King and his aides had left Philadelphia for Yazoo City, groups of roving whites launched attacks in the black section of the city beginning at about 8:10 p.m. Several whites in a car drove up to street corner and and exchanged insults with a group of blacks. One of the passengers fired a gun, and the car drove off.

At about 8:25 p.m., another car drove past Freedom House, the headquarters of local black activists, and four shots were fired. This time, the activists returned fire—from the street and the rooftop. About 20 minutes later, whites in another car fired eight to ten shots into Freedom House. Return fire struck the driver of the car, Stanley Stewart, wounding him superficially.

Reed, of The New York Times, reported that, in the final attack by whites, four shots were fired at an FBI agent standing in front of Freedom House.

At a rally that night in Yazoo City attended by nearly a thousand people, King again made the case for nonviolence—despite what had happened in Philadelphia earlier in the day, which he later conceded was the most violent display of anger that he had ever witnessed.

"We can't win violently," King said. "We have neither the instruments nor the techniques at our disposal,and it would be totally absurd for us to believe we could do it. . . . But we have another method, and I've seen it, and they can't stop it."

King said that the reason that no one was killed in Philadelphia earlier in the day was because the march had gained order and discipline.

But earlier at the rally, Willie Ricks, standing on the back of a flat-bed truck, told the crowd that the reason that nobody had been killed was because blacks had shown that they could and would defend themselves if attacked.

"Negroes in Mississippi will never have anything until they show black power," Ricks roared. "When a white man attacks us, attack him back!"

Chapter 38: A Scene from Hell

Again, Willie Ricks was standing on top of a car rallying his troops—this time in Canton, Mississippi, at the end of a day-long march through rain storms from Benton, some 20 miles away—telling the crowd to set several highway patrol cruisers nearby on fire. But this time, many of his fellow activists were thinking that he had gone too far.

The crowd on this evening of Thursday, June 23, which numbered about 2,000, had just been attacked and tear-gassed by several dozen state troopers on the grounds of McNeal Elementary School for Negroes, where they were planning to spend the night.

Now, Ricks was shouting from the top of the automobile, challenging the state troopers to a fight. "We ain' gon' take this shit," he yelled. "We gon' get these mothers."

Furious, SCLC's Andrew Young jumped up and grabbed Ricks by the collar and said, "Look, those motha fuckahs out there got machine guns. And they're crazy. And you got nothing but your mouth and some bricks and bottles."

Young told Ricks that if he wanted to get himself killed, that was fine. "But you are not sending women and children over there to get killed. If you want to fight somebody, fight me." He said that Ricks, thankfully, shut up and climbed down.

The attack by the Mississippi state troopers, in full riot gear, had come after the march's marshals had driven up to the grounds of McNeal Elementary School in a U-Haul truck and dropped off tents that would be used by the marchers that night.

As the state troopers approached, Stokely Carmichael and the other march leaders climbed up on the truck to address the crowd. "The time for anybody running has come to an end!" Carmichael said. "You tell them white folk in Mississippi that all the scared niggers are dead!"

Martin Luther King Jr. told the crowd, "We're gonna stick together. If necessary, we are willing to fill up all the jails in Mississippi. And I don't believe they have enough jails to hold all the people!" He pleaded for calm and said that confronting the troopers would only make a potentially bad situation worse.

But Canton City Attorney Robert Goza said that they would not be allowed to erect the tents on the school grounds. "If you continue doing so, you will be placed under arrest."

The chaos that ensued was described by Arlie Schardt, a reporter for TIME magazine, as being the most awful moment he had experienced in his seven or eight years covering the civil rights movement.

"It was without any warning," he said, "and suddenly the troopers donned their gas masks and started lobbing tear gas into this crowd of women, children, elderly people. . . . It was a scene of hell, with the smoke rising and people vomiting and crawling around and choking and crying, and then there was a kind of eerie silence and one thing you could hear over and over again was the thud, thud, thud sound of the Mississippi troopers kicking people on the ground or hitting them with their rifle butts. . . . It was just horrible. It was just unbelievable."

In the melee, Stokely Carmichael had taken a direct hit in the chest from a tear-gas canister and was knocked to the ground, semiconscious and unable to breathe. "Choking for breath, I could hear screams, shouts, and Dr. King calling on people to remain calm amid the sickening thud of blows. . . . Obviously, it had simply been a demonstration of naked force for its own sake."

By 8 p.m., the state troopers had gathered up the tents at McNeal Elementary School and impounded the U-Haul truck. Some marchers spent the night in a local gymnasium.

Later that night, in an act of defiance, Rev. James McRee, head of the Madison County civil rights movement, led some 500–600 demonstrators through the streets of Canton and called for a general strike and boycott by the city's African American community the next day.

An investigator for the Mississippi State Sovereignty Commission, A.L. Hopkins, reported on June 25 that King and Carmichael were "mainly responsible" for the violence that had occurred in Canton. He said that they had provoked the police "by not pitching their tents in one of the three locations where they had been told they could erect them. But, instead, they seemed determined to erect them on school property which was forbidden and resulted in the officials have to use tear-gas and some force to remove these people from the restricted area. . . . The tolerance of all officials and citizens concerned is the only thing that kept down serious trouble in Canton yesterday."

Mississippi Gov. Paul Johnson sought to downplay situation, saying that in the end no one got hurt, which was not true. He even said that using tear gas was "the humane thing to do."

The next day, speaking to reporters in Washington, D.C., U.S. Attorney General Nicholas Katzenbach said that he regretted the use of tear gas by the law enforcement officers, adding that "it always makes the situation more difficult." But he did not condemn the state troopers or pledge to send more federal officials to Mississippi to deal with the situation.

Robert H. Fleming, deputy White House press secretary, said that Katzenbach had assured the president that order was being maintained by the Mississippi state troopers. He said that the president had "no specific reaction" to the tear gas incident.

"The president knows it is going to take time to produce understanding down there," Fleming added, "but he thinks the effort should be made."

In Canton, following the attack, Martin Luther King Jr. was told of the Johnson administration's tepid response. He also learned that the Deacons for Defense were planning to buy gas masks and would consider firing warning shots over the heads of the troopers in the event of another attack.

The next day, Friday, June 24, King told Paul Good, a freelance reporter, that he was beginning to despair. He said that he had heard "that terrible statement" by Attorney General Katzenbach and nothing from the president.

"I don't know what I'm going to do," King said. "The government has got to give me some victories if I'm gonna to keep people nonviolent. I know I'm gonna stay nonviolent no matter what happens. But a lot of people are getting hurt and bitter, and they can't see it that way any more."

Chapter 39: 'This Will Be a New Day'

Thousands of protesters were beginning to arrive at Tougaloo College—about 10 miles north of Jackson, where the two-week, 225-mile March Against Fear was scheduled to end on Sunday, June 26—when a chartered airliner filled with famous faces was taking off from Los Angeles International Airport, heading east.

On board the aircraft were several movie stars and other entertainers, including Sammy Davis Jr., Marlon Brando, James Brown and Burt Lancaster, who were on their way to Tougaloo to appear at an end-of-march rally scheduled to be held on Saturday night.

On Saturday afternoon, Martin Luther King Jr. led about 600 marchers from Tougaloo to catch up with James Meredith, who had begun the march alone in Memphis on June 6—only to be shot by a white supremacist the next day. Nearly recovered, he was now rejoining what he called "my march."

King had spent the previous day in Philadelphia, Mississippi—the scene of widespread mob violence during his visit to the city earlier in the week—to show that he and his fellow civil rights activists would not be intimidated.

On Thursday, Hosea Williams, a member of King's inner circle, had led an advance team to Philadelphia to drum up support for King's return visit. He also wanted to make sure that local blacks remained nonviolent. "If you can't come without a knife or gun in your pocket," Williams told a mass meeting at Mount Nebo Baptist Church, "don't come at all."

At a mid-day rally at the Neshoba County Courthouse on Saturday, Philadelphia Mayor Clayton Lewis urged his fellow city residents to remain calm. King referenced the Bible, and Stokely Carmichael pushed his Black Power agenda. No incidents were reported.

On Saturday night, at a mass rally at Tougaloo College, about 9,000 people, including Willie Ricks and James Forman, who sat together alongside the makeshift stage, listened enthusiastically to Carmichael as he again spoke of the need for Black Power.

King also spoke, as did Marlon Brando, who was at the height of his film career. As he came to the microphone, someone handed him one of the fliers that Ricks had been distributing, which showed a lunging black panther with the words "We're the Greatest."

Brando tried playfully but unsuccessfully to affix the flyer to his forehead and then, smiling broadly, said he was happy to be at Tougaloo.

"You can't imagine how I feel because I haven't really participated in this movement, not in the way my conscience gnaws at me that I should," Brando said. "You are the heroes of America. You know what suffering is. You really know it."

James Forman wrote later that he and several other SNCC activists, including Ricks, joined together in shouting "Black Power!"

"Over and over, the chant resounded [from the crowd]," Forman wrote. "We wanted black people in all parts of the United States to hear the slogan, to be stirred by it, to adopt. It was a spontaneous move on our part, with nothing false about it. We felt, we knew, we could see that 'Black Power' was a slogan of the masses."

Later that night, several leaders of the march, including King, Carmichael and McKissick, met to finalize plans for the trek into Jackson the next day, which would culminate in a mass rally at the Capitol.

King had told reporters earlier in the month that he expected the March Against Fear to rival the Selma-to-Montgomery march, which had been staged in March 1965. Some 25,000 people had attended a rally in Montgomery at the end of the Selma-to-Montgomery march. He said that the Mississippi march could attract the same number on the final day of the march into downtown Jackson, although privately he hoped for somewhere between 45,000 and 75,000.

Just after dawn on Sunday, June 26, Marlon Brando and Burt Lancaster moved through the crowd—some had still not slept—encouraging them to stay strong for the 10-mile hike to downtown Jackson.

At the same time, thousands of local and out-of-state supporters began streaming into Jackson, preparing for what would become the largest civil rights demonstration in the history of Mississippi.

It was hot and humid, with the temperature expected to climb into the mid-90s by mid-day. At around 11 a.m., some 2,000 marchers left the Tougaloo College campus for Jackson, picking up another 1,000 or so people along the way. At the head of the column were Meredith, King (accompanied by his wife Coretta and three of their four children, ages five to ten), Carmichael, McKissick and several other civil rights leaders.

As the marchers approached the tracks of the Illinois Central Railroad, Ricks and SCLC's Robert L. Green suddenly saw a white engineer beginning to roll his train toward the crossing. Quickly, Green ran and stood squarely on the tracks, demanding that the engineer stop. Then, Ricks and several teenagers jumped onto the locomotive, banging on the window and yelling, "Black Power! Black Power! Black Power!" Luckily, the engine ground to a halt just short of the column of marchers.

Ricks was also involved in another incident along the route of the march into Jackson when he saw several black people waving American flags and demanded, "Give me those flags! Those flags don't represent you!"

An Episcopal priest—the Rev. John B. Morris, executive director of the Episcopal Society of Cultural and Racial Unity (ESCRU)—tried to intervene, urging Ricks to stop, and another activist grabbed the flags from Ricks and returned them to the marchers.

The incident was an example of what the African American scholar Peniel E. Joseph has called Ricks' "unpredictable energy," which, Joseph said, could make him appear to be "unhinged." But just as quickly, Joseph wrote, Ricks' behavior could "reveal itself as the peculiar method of a brilliant, if unconventional, organizer."

Passing through the predominantly black neighborhoods of North Jackson, the marchers arrived at the Mississippi state Capitol only to be met by about 1,500 whites waving Confederate flags and jeering. Hundreds of state police kept the two groups apart. The marchers were confined to an area some 75 yards from the building itself. Later, Ricks and several other SNCC militants pulled down a large Confederate flag from a flagpole and set it on fire.

By mid-afternoon, a crowd estimated to be between 12,000 and 15,000 had settled in on the north side of the Capitol. A flatbed truck served as a stage.

Speaker after speaker lamented the plight of race relations in the United States. Some were hopeful, some were not. Some were militant.

Lawrence Guyot, a veteran SNCC activist and chairman of the Mississippi Freedom Democratic Party, was cheered when he said that there were three things that African Americans should learn from birth: white supremacy, neocolonialism and Black Power.

Another spokesman for the movement—Floyd McKissick, the head of CORE—said that there is nothing wrong with Black Power. "It's just an adjective inserted before a noun. . . . You can call it orange power, green power or whatever you want. But we want power."

Predictably, Stokely Carmichael used his five minutes of speaking time to bang home the message of black pride and the need for unity among African Americans. He also threatened action if their demands were not met. Surprisingly, however, he did not use the phrase "Black Power" to reinforce his message.

Instead, he noted several things that needed to be done. "Number one, we have to stop being ashamed of being black [and] we have to move to a position where we can feel strength and unity amongst each other from Watts to Harlem, where we won't ever be afraid. And . . . we have to build a power base so strong in this country that it will bring [whites] to their knees every time they mess with us."

The message that Martin Luther King Jr. chose to convey was different. It built on the themes established in his "I Have a Dream" speech in Washington, D.C., nearly three years earlier. But this time, his speech had a sharper edge, and at times it even bordered on mournful.

"I have watched my dreams turn into a nightmare," he said, adding that during the March Against Fear he had met people who were barely able to survive and worked in fields for two or three dollars a day. He said that he had seen too many African Americans perish "in a vast ocean of prosperity" and too much injustice in the way laws were enforced.

But he said that he still had a dream in which "justice will come to all of God's children" and poverty will become a national priority that needs to be addressed.

"This will be a new day," King said. "This will be the day of all men living together as brothers. It will not be the day of the white man. It will not be the day of the black man. It will be the day of man, *as* man!"

The March Against Fear, from the perspective of SNCC, had been a huge success. It registered thousands of new black voters. It transformed Stokely Carmichael—with his call for Black Power in Greenwood and beyond—into a national leader and even into a hero for some. It focused national attention on Mississippi for the first time since the Freedom Summer of 1964. It injected new energy into the Mississippi movement. And it generated widespread interest in creating independent black political organizations across the country.

Yet the outrageous but predictable behavior of white mobs and law enforcement officers along the route of the march also reminded the nation that white supremacy remained a central fact of life the Deep South.

Importantly, the March Against Fear prompted the national media to shift its attention away from the indignities associated with racial injustice in Mississippi to the stark ideological differences between SNCC and Martin Luther King Jr.'s Southern Christian Leadership Conference (SCLC)—and to obsess over what it saw as the threat of Black Power to the nation's stability.

The historian Clayborne Carson, founding director of the Martin Luther King Jr. Research and Education Institute, has said that Carmichael's popularization of the concept of Black Power opened a new chapter in the transformation of the political consciousness of African Americans, particularly among those—mainly in the urban centers of the North—whose hopes had been raised by the nonviolent civil rights struggle but had not been fulfilled.

"It was during the year of Carmichael's chairmanship that SNCC acquired unprecedented importance as a source of new political ideas," Carson wrote. "SNCC did not itself change the direction of black politics, but it did reflect a shift in the focus of black struggles from the rural South to the urban North and from civil rights reforms to complex, interrelated problems of poverty, powerlessness and cultural subordination. . . . Millions of black people were prepared to adopt the rhetoric of black power in order to express their accumulated anger and to assume new, more satisfying racial identities."

For the rest of this life, Carmichael would argue that seizing political power—and not simply relying on legal remedies or moral suasion—was the only realistic path to racial justice in the United States.

Yet internal divisions within SNCC and the rise in racial violence hampered the ability of the organization, according to Carson, to transform black discontent into programs for achieving black power.

"[A]s it became more isolated from former white allies and more openly identified with uncontrollable urban black militancy," Carson wrote, "[SNCC] encountered ruthless government repression [and] their message would reach an ever-decreasing number of blacks."

After the March Against Fear, Carmichael exploited his newfound celebrity by embarking on extensive speaking tour that included large cities in the North such as New York, Philadelphia, Chicago, Los Angeles and Detroit.

A profile of Carmichael by the historian Lerone Bennett Jr., published in the July 1966 issue of *Ebony* magazine, said that no other young man, with the possible exception of King, had risen so far so fast.

Yet, not surprisingly, Carmichael's advocacy of Black Power also made him a target of the establishment. His movements were closely monitored by the White House, the FBI and other intelligence agencies, which increasingly feared the outbreak of a Carmichael-inspired race war.

President Johnson is said to have predicted privately that Carmichael would be killed within three months, and Sen. Robert F. Kennedy (D-N.Y.), the former attorney general, publicly labeled the term Black Power "very damaging" to race relations.

After only a year as chairman of SNCC, Carmichael willingly relinquished the post to H. Rap Brown in June 1967. He had a brief association with the Black Panther Party for Self Defense, co-founded by Huey P. Newton and Bobby Seale in Oakland, California, in October 1966. But he severed his ties with the organization (whose name and symbol were appropriated from the political party established by Carmichael and others in Lowndes County, Alabama, in 1965) after Newton accused him of being a CIA agent.

Carmichael moved to Guinea in 1969, where he became an aide to then-President Ahmed Sékou Touré and a student of the exiled Ghanaian president Kwame Nkrumah. He continued to travel, write and speak in support of leftist causes and to devote himself to the All-African People's Revolutionary Party (A-APRP). He died in Guinea in 1998 following a long battle with prostate cancer. He was 57 years old.

For his part, James Forman left Jackson, Mississippi, following the March Against Fear with the feeling that Black Power had now become "a slogan of the masses," as he put it.

"This initial articulation meant that another stage of the struggle had been reached," he wrote. "It was a higher one than 'One Man, One Vote' or 'Freedom Now'. We had moved to verbalizing our drive for power—not merely for the vote, not for some vague kind of freedom, not for legal rights, but the basic force in any society—power. Power for black people, black power."

Having been replaced as executive secretary of SNCC by Ruby Doris Robinson, Forman nevertheless stayed close to the SNCC leadership and even helped negotiate SNCC's ill-fated merger with the Black Panther Party in California.

In 1969, after the merger had been dissolved, he began to associate himself increasingly with radical black political organizations. He earned a master's degree at Cornell University and a doctorate at Union Institute and spent the rest of his life organizing disenfranchised people around issues related to progressive economic and social development and equality.

He also taught at American University in Washington, D.C., and wrote several books, including *The Making of Black Revolutionaries*, which Julian Bond called a "classic" written by one of the "under-appreciated figures" of the modern civil rights movement. He died of colon cancer in 2005. He was 76 years old.

Like Forman and Carmichael, Cleveland Sellers concluded that the March Against Fear had been a success. He said that, on a personal level, one of the most important accomplishments of the march was the deep personal friendship that had developed between Martin Luther King Jr. and the SNCC members who participated in the march.

"I have nothing but fond memories of the long, hot hours we spent trudging along the highway," Sellers wrote in 1973, five years after King had been assassinated in Memphis, "discussing strategy, tactics and our dreams."

Sellers said that he will never forget King's magnificent speeches at the nightly rallies along the route of the march. "Though [King] was forced by political circumstance to disavow Black Power for himself and for his organization, there has never been any question in my mind since our March Against Fear that Dr. King was a staunch ally and a true brother."

Yet the affection that Sellers felt for King was tempered in the short run by what Sellers called the "hysteria-ridden" responses to the call for Black Power. It was impossible, Sellers wrote, to pick up a newspaper or magazine or listen to the radio without encountering some warning about the dangers of Black Power.

"No matter how many speeches we gave in order to set the record straight," Sellers wrote, "we were unable to convince most Americans that we weren't interested in sacking cities or dragging white women off to the Black Belt to be gang-raped by black fiends."

In 1968, Sellers returned to his native South Carolina and began organizing black students at South Carolina State University in Orangeburg. "By working with students," he later wrote, "I believed I could develop a movement focusing attention on the problems of poor blacks in South Carolina."

But his noble ambition quickly turned ugly in early February 1968 when about 200 protesters from South Carolina State University attempted to integrate a local bowling alley owned by a white man.

On the night of February 8, the protesters lit a bonfire on the university campus, and as the police and firefighters attempted to put out the fire, one officer was injured by an object thrown from the crowd. Shortly thereafter, at around 10:30 p.m., the South Carolina Patrol Officers panicked and began firing into the crowd. Three young men were killed in what became known as the Orangeburg Massacre, and twenty-eight people were injured, including Sellers, who was shot in the arm.

Then-Gov. Robert Evander McNair blamed the incident on "outside Black Power agitators." In a subsequent trial, nine police officers were acquitted of using excessive force. Sellers, however, was convicted of inciting a riot and wound up spending seven months in prison. Twenty-five years later, he received a full pardon but decided against having his record cleared, arguing that he wanted to keep it as a "badge of honor."

After his release from prison, Sellers earned a master's degree in education from Harvard University. In 1984, he worked on the presidential election campaign of Jesse Jackson, and in 1987 he went on to earn his Ed.D at the University of North Carolina at Greensboro.

Later, he served as director of the African American Studies Program at the University of South Carolina, and in 2008 he was named president of Voorhees College in Denmark, South Carolina. He retired in the spring of 2016.

Chapter 40: White Men on Their Knees

Following the March Against Fear, in the spring of 1966, even as its organizers were calling it a success, the backlash against Black Power and those who championed it, like Willie Ricks, continued to grow.

The Wall Street Journal, for instance, said in an editorial published on February 1, 1967, that Ricks exemplified the dangers of Black Power, and that he was too radical even for SNCC. It even suggested that Ricks was to blame for the "Atlanta riots" in the fall of 1966 by noting that he had taken the microphone at a demonstration and, screaming for Black Power, urged the crowd "into the streets to get theirs, and they went."

Yet Ricks did not back down. He could be found wherever mass protests were occurring—organizing and agitating. He could also be spotted performing lone acts of civil disobedience, like ripping the "Whites Only" and "Colored Only" signs off the walls of a courthouse restroom.

In May of 1966, Ricks traveled to Jackson, Mississippi, to participate in demonstrations against the police shooting death of 21-year-old civil rights activist named Benjamin Brown. He was reported to have said at mass meeting that "the honky that comes to kill me better be ready to meet his Jesus. I'm not going to march to any Capitol building. I'm going for power. You need to get your stuff and get ready!"

That summer, Ricks turned up in cities where public protests often turned violent. By mid-June, according to *U.S. News & World Report*, outbreaks of "racial violence" had occurred in no fewer than 27 cities.

The magazine reported in an article in its June 26 issue— "Riot Season: How Hot Will It Get?"—that Ricks and H. Rap Brown, who by then had replaced Stokely Carmichael as chairman of SNCC, had arrived in Dayton, Ohio, "just before Negro violence erupted there on June 14." It said that Brown had called Ricks his "minister of defense."

Brown told protesters in Dayton that it was impossible to be nonviolent in the United States—"the most violent country in the world." He said that "you better shoot that man to death," according to the *U.S. News & World Report* article. "That's what he's doing to you."

After Brown spoke, Ricks told reporters that he and Brown had come to Dayton "to make white men get on their knees," the magazine said.

Throughout the 1960s, the Mississippi state-sponsored spy agency, the Mississippi State Sovereignty Commission (MSSC) did its best to keep track of Ricks as he moved about the state looking "to start riots," as the commission's informants put it.

Erle E. Johnston Jr., the director of the Commission, said in a memo dated August 21, 1967, for example, that an informant had found out that Ricks was either in Jackson or on his way. "Our informant states he hopes this does not happen as he feels there will be trouble if Ricks comes here."

Johnston said that the reason for Ricks' likely appearance in Jackson was connected to the students who had recently been arrested in downtown Jackson. "He is coming to start riots and organize marches as they did in Baton Rouge," Johnston wrote. "There are still rumors about burning down Jackson. . . . Our source will keep us informed about Ricks."

On August 29, an MSSC informant said in a report filed by telephone that Ricks had attended a meeting of the Community Service Association in Jackson the previous day and that he would remain in Jackson to "organize riots, picketing, etc., as well as other activities."

"As far as riots being planned," the informant said, however, "no information was obtained about this, but close watch will be kept on the situation."

The FBI was also keeping a close watch on Ricks. Charles E. Snodgrass, an assistant to Mississippi Commissioner of Public Safety, for example, said in a memo to his boss, T.B. Birdsong, on August 22, 1967, that an FBI informant had talked to Ricks at Stevens Kitchen in downtown Jackson.

"Informant states that Ricks had no contacts which would result in any type of demonstration," the memo said, "but rather Ricks' purpose in being in Jackson was to look over Jackson with an eye toward future SNCC activity. Informant believes nothing is planned for the near future. . . . FBI believes Ricks has left Jackson; however, they are attempting to verify this and will attempt to interview some of the group who was with Ricks."

Even some members of Congress were interested in Ricks' whereabouts and activities.

A Washington, D.C., police officer named John E. Drass, who was on loan to Sen. John L. McClellan's Permanent Subcommittee on Investigations for the purpose of investigating the Black Panthers, reported on August 19, 1968, that Ricks had visited Cuba, along with many other members of SNCC, to study guerrilla warfare.

"It is a well-established theory (although not confirmed) that a great deal of SNCC finances come from Red Cuba," Drass wrote, adding that SNCC had been "directly involved" in inciting riots "all over the United States."

Later, Ricks traveled with Carmichael to college campuses and elsewhere around the country to spread the Black Power message.

At San Francisco State University in November 1968, for example, Carmichael addressed black students on the eve of a planned strike aimed at persuading the university to start a Black Studies program. "Our fight is a fight of this entire generation," he said. The next day, the students launched what would become a 134-day strike that ended with the creation of a Black Studies program at the school.

Accompanied by Ricks and Cleveland Sellers, Carmichael next traveled to North Carolina where he warned black students at St. Augustine's College (now St. Augustine's University) in Raleigh that there was a national conspiracy to commit anti-black genocide. He urged the students at the all-black school to "be prepared" like "good boy scouts" for violent confrontation.

Ricks also accompanied Carmichael on a speaking tour to Mississippi, appearing in Greenwood, for example, in March 1971, where Carmichael, at Ricks' urging, he had launched the Black Power slogan for the first time publicly in a speech on June 16, 1966.

From Mississippi, the pair traveled to Lowndes County in Alabama, where six years earlier they had worked to create the Lowndes County Freedom Organization (LCFO), considered to be the original Black Panther Party. At Mount

Moriah Baptist Church in Hayneville, Carmichael spoke about Pan-Africanism and shared stories with old friends, while Ricks spoke of the need to create new political institutions.

The African American scholar Peniel E. Joseph, who has written several books on Black Power, has said that Ricks has worked tirelessly over the years, particularly following Carmichael's death in 1998, to keep the flame of what he called the "Black Power heyday" alive.

Joseph wrote in his book, *Stokely: A Life*, published in 2014, that Ricks, from his "political base" in Atlanta, has continued to chide black students to fight for racial justice. "In this he remained consistent."

"As a young SNCC organizer dressed in blue overalls," Joseph wrote, "Ricks chastised potential recruits about how and his colleagues were making history instead of merely studying it." New generations of students have been introduced to the legacy of Black Power and Carmichael's work, Joseph wrote, "through Ricks' tireless activism."

Ricks' longtime friend and former SNCC colleague, Cleveland Sellers, recalled that in the late 1960s, after SNCC effectively had collapsed as an organization, he and Ricks shared a "small roach-filled apartment" in Atlanta.

"We really didn't have any furniture," Sellers wrote, "just a few threadbare items we'd managed to scrounge from friends and acquaintances. The electricity was never on because we couldn't afford to pay the bill. On those rare occasions when we wanted to hear a little music from Ricks's radio, we would jimmy the fuse box with wires and bypass the cutoff switch."

Sellers said that it was always difficult, if not impossible, to come up with $70 a month for rent. "We were always two and three months behind. And more times than I care to recall we had to hide behind the curtain so that the land-lord wouldn't know we were home."

"I am an early riser," Sellers wrote, "and my first stop after getting out of bed each morning was the refrigera-tor . . . to see if Ricks had managed to procure any food the night before. Usually he hadn't."

Although separated by ideology, Ricks and Martin Luther King Jr., as it turned out, were actually fond of each other on a personal level.

Bernard Lee, who was King's personal assistant for many years, told the historian and author Taylor Branch that Ricks and Carmichael never saw what they were doing as hurting King, but instead thought that they were "enhanc-ing the movement, they were enhancing the cause of black people."

Branch wrote in his book *At Canaan's Edge* that King often teased Ricks over his nickname, "the Reverend," say-ing that the only thing he lacked to be a good preacher were the right clothes. To his surprise, when Ricks asked to bor-row some of King's clothes, the real Reverend invited him to his house and told him to select what he wanted from his closet.

In the end, Ricks never became a preacher—at least in the traditional sense of the word. And he has consistently questioned the usefulness of nonviolent protests like the Selma-to-Montgomery march.

Today, in the spring of 2021, Ricks lives in Atlanta—the father of three adult children, all college graduates. He can still be found upholding his reputation as a "fiery orator," firing up crowds with various versions of revolutionary rhet-oric, just as he did at an event I attended in Greenwood, Mississippi, in June 2016 marking the 50th anniversary of Carmichael's Black Power speech. But always, wherever he is, he will be seen raising his fist and shouting, "Black Power!" "Black Power!" "Black Power!"

Bibliography

Bass, S. Jonathan. *Blessed Are the Peacemakers: Martin Luther King, Jr., Eight White Religious Leaders and the "Letter from Birmingham Jail."* Baton Rouge: Louisiana State University Press, 2001.

Belafonte, Harry. *My Song: A Memoir.* New York: Alfred A. Knopf, 2011.

Belfrage, Sally. *Freedom Summer.* New York: The Viking Press, 1965.

Boyd, Malcolm. *As I Live and Breathe: Stages of an Autobiography.* New York: Random House, Inc. 1965.

Branch, Taylor. *At Canaan's Edge: America in the King Years 1965–68.* New York: Simon & Schuster, 2006.

——*Parting the Waters: American in the King Years 1954–1963.* New York: Simon & Schuster, 1988.

—*Pillar of Fire: America in the King Years 1963–65.* New York: Simon & Schuster, 1998.

Bruns, Roger. *Jesse Jackson: A Biography.* Westport, CT: Greenwood Press, 2005.

Carmichael, Stokely (with Ekwueme Michael Thelwell). *Ready for Revolution: The Life and Struggles of Stokely Carmichael.* New York: Scribner, 2003.

Carpenter, Douglas M. *A Powerful Blessing: The Life of Charles Colcock Jones Carpenter, Sr.* Birmingham, AL: TransAmerica Printing, 2012.

Carson, Clayborne. *In Struggle: SNCC and the Black Awakening of the 1960s.* Cambridge, MA: Harvard University Press, 1981.

Carter, Dan T. *The Politics of Rage: George Wallace, the Origins of the New Conservatism, and the Transformation of American Politics.* New York: Simon & Schuster, 1995.

Curry, Constance. *Deep in Our Hearts: Nine White Women in the Freedom Movement.* Athens, GA: University of Georgia Press, 2000.

Dittmer, John. *Local People: The Struggle for Civil Rights in Mississippi.* Urbana and Chicago: University of Illinois Press, 1994.

Eagles, Charles W. *Outside Agitator: Jon Daniels and the Civil Rights Movement in Alabama.* Tuscaloosa, AL: University of Alabama Press, 2000.

Edelman, Marian Wright. *Lanterns: A Memoir of Mentors.* Boston: Beacon Press, 1999.

Fager, Charles E. *Selma, 1965.* New York: Charles Scribner's Sons, 1974.

Forman, James. *The Making of Black Revolutionaries.* New York: The Macmillan Company, 1972.

Friedland, Michael B. *Lift Up Your Voice Like a Trumpet: White Clergy and the Civil Rights and Antiwar Movements, 1954–1973*. Chapel Hill, NC: University of North Carolina Press, 1998.

Garrow, David J. *Protest at Selma: Martin Luther King, Jr., and the Voting Rights Act of 1965*. New Haven, CT: Yale University Press, 1978.

Goudsouzian, Aram. *Down at the Crossroads: Civil Rights, Black Power, and the Meredith March Against Fear*. New York: Farrar, Straus and Giroux, 2014.

Hampton, Henry, and Fayer, Steve. *Voices of Freedom: An Oral History of the Civil Rights Movement From the 1950s through the 1980s*. New York: Bantam Books, 1990.

Hill, Lance. *The Deacons for Defense: Armed Resistance and the Civil Rights Movement*. Chapel Hill, NC: University of North Carolina Press, 2004.

Holsaert, Faith S.; Noonan, Martha Prescod Norman; Richardson, Judy; Robinson, Betty Garman; Young, Jean Smith; Zellner, Dorothy M, eds. *Hands on the Freedom Plow: Personal Accounts by Women in SNCC*. Urbana, Illinois: University of Illinois Press, 2010.

Howlett, Duncan. *No Greater Love: The James Reeb Story*. Boston: Skinner House Books, 1993.

Jackson, Richie Jean Sherrod. *The House by the Side of the Road: The Selma Civil Rights Movement*. Tuscaloosa, Alabama: The University of Alabama Press, 2011.

Jeffries, Hasan Kwame. *Bloody Lowndes: Civil Rights and Black Power in Alabama's Black Belt*. New York: New York University Press, 2009.

Jenkins, Carol, and Hines, Elizabeth Gardiner. *Black Titan: A. G. Gaston and the Making of a Black American Millionaire.* New York: Random House Publishing Group, 2004.

Joseph, Peniel E. *Dark Days, Bright Nights: From Black Power to Barack Obama.* Philadelphia: Basic Civitas Books, 2010.
  —*Stokely: A Life.* Philadelphia: Basic Civitas Books, 2014.

Katagiri, Yasuhiro. *The Mississippi State Sovereignty Commission: Civil Rights and States' Rights.* Jackson, MS: University Press of Mississippi, 2001.

Kennan, George F. *Sketches from a Life.* New York: Pantheon Books, 1989.

King, Coretta Scott. *My Life with Martin Luther King, Jr.* New York: Holt, Rinehart and Winston, 1969.

King, Martin Luther, Jr. *Where Do We Go from Here: Chaos or Community?* Boston: Beacon Press, 1968.

Lewis, John. *Walking with the Wind: A Memoir of the Movement.* New York: Harcourt Brace & Company, 1998.

Longenecker, Stephen L. *Selma's Peacemaker: Ralph Smeltzer and Civil Rights Mediation.* Philadelphia: Temple University Press, 1987.

May, Gary. *The Informant: The FBI, the Ku Klux Klan and the Murder of Viola Liuzzo.* New Haven, CT: Yale University Press, 2005.

McGuire, Danielle L. *At the Dark End of the Street: Black Women, Rape, and Resistance—a New History of the Civil Rights Movement from Rosa Parks to the Rise of Black Power.* New York: Alfred A. Knopf, 2010.

Mendelsohn, Jack. *The Martyrs: 16 Who Gave Their Lives for Racial Justice.* New York: Harper & Row, 1966.

Moore, Paul. *Presences: A Bishop's Life in the City.* New York: Farrar, Straus and Giroux, 1997.

Nelson, Jack. *Scoop: The Evolution of a Southern Reporter.* Jackson, MS: University of Mississippi Press, 2013.

Olson, Lynn. *Freedom's Daughters: The Unsung Heroines of the Civil Rights Movement from 1830 to 1970.* Simon & Schuster: New York, 2001.

Patterson, James T. *The Eve of Destruction: How 1965 Transformed America.* New York: Basic Books, 2012.

Payne, Charles M. *I've Got the Light of Freedom: The Organizing Tradition and the Mississippi Freedom Struggle.* Berkeley, CA: University of California Press, 1995.

Priestley, Justine. *By Gertrude Wilson: Dispatches of the 1960s, From a White Writer in a Black World.* Edgartown, MA: Vineyard Stories, 2005.

Raines, Howell. *My Soul Is Rested.* New York: G. P. Putnam's Sons, 1977.

Reed, Roy. *Beware of Limbo Dancers: A Correspondent's Adventures with the New York Times.* Fayetteville, AR: University of Arkansas Press, 2012.

Rice, Condoleezza. *Extraordinary, Ordinary People: A Memoir of Family.* New York: Crown Archetype, 2010.

Roberts, Gene, and Klibanoff, Hank. *The Race Beat: The Press, the Civil Rights Struggle, and the Awakening of a Nation.* New York: Alfred A. Knopf, 2006.

Sellers, Cleveland. *The River of No Return: The Autobiography of a Black Militant and the Life and Death of SNCC.* New York: William Morrow & Company, Inc., 1973.

Shattuck, Gardiner H., Jr. *Episcopalians and Race: Civil War to Civil Rights.* Lexington, KY: University Press of Kentucky, 2000.

Washington, James Melvin, ed. *A Testament of Hope: The Essential Writings of Martin Luther King, Jr.* San Francisco: Harper and Row, 1986.

Watson, Bruce. *Freedom Summer: The Savage Season That Made Mississippi Burn and Made America a Democracy.* New York: Viking Penguin, 2010.

Williams, Juan. *Eyes on the Prize: America's Civil Rights Years, 1954–1965.* New York: Viking Penguin Inc., 1987.

Wilford, Hugh. *The Mighty Wurlitzer: How the CIA Played America.* Cambridge, MA: Harvard University Press, 2008.

Young, Andrew. *An Easy Burden: The Civil Rights Movement and the Transformation of America.* New York: HarperCollins Publishers, Inc., 1996.

Zellner, Bob. *The Wrong Side of Murder Creek: A White Southerner in the Freedom Movement.* Montgomery, AL: NewSouth Books, 2008.

INDEX